LABYRINTHS
OF IRON

LABYRINTHS OF IRON

Subways in History, Myth, Art, Technology, and War

BENSON BOBRICK

QUILL
WILLIAM MORROW
New York

Library of Congress Cataloging-in-Publication Data

Bobrick, Benson, 1947–
Labyrinths of iron.

Rev. pbk. ed.
Bibliography: p.
Includes index.
1. Subways—History. I. Title.
TF845.B6   1986   388.4'28   86-8099
ISBN 0-688-06517-1 (pbk.)

Printed in the United States of America

First Quill Edition

1 2 3 4 5 6 7 8 9 10

BOOK DESIGN BY MARY ANN JOULWAN—BENSON BOBRICK

FOR THE MEMBERS OF MY FAMILY, EACH ONE

CONTENTS

Dark accurate plunger down the successive knell
Of arch on arch, where ogives burst a red
Reverberance of hail upon the dead
Thunder like an exploding crucible!
Harshly articulate, musical steel shell
Of angry worship, hurled religiously
Upon your business of humility
Into the iron forestries of hell . . .

ALLEN TATE, *The Subway*

PREFACE

When I began to look into the history of subways, I had no idea where my curiosity would lead. Certainly I did not expect it to lead me to the writing of a book. What started me off was the remarkable fact that a large and increasing proportion of the world's population had come to travel every day in tunnels underground. The degree to which this development was regarded as normal I found surprising. Quite simply, I wanted to know how it all had come about.

The answer proved difficult to find, which made my curiosity keener. Subway literature, as a whole, glossed over certain questions or found them inconvenient to raise. With a sort of biblical confidence, book after book explained that subways were built in response to traffic congestion and, in the light of scientific advance, were inevitable and good. Early resistance to subway construction was written off as "resistance to progress," an atavistic voice raised against an inexorably emerging new world. The nonchalance of this view was not reassuring: first, because the "doctrine" of progress is largely a habit of mind, a theory that is constantly bumping its head against the uncongenial surprises of time; second, because though it was obvious that traffic congestion had played a critical role, it was equally obvious that such a radical sociological and engineering development could not have come about as a direct result. It had to have a unique history and, as I guessed, a complicated one at that. I set out to discover what it was.

What is important to the engineering part of the story, certainly what was of particular interest to me, is easily understood by the layman. Because I am not an engineer, I tried to find interesting ways to clarify complex technical matters and to present the information in a clear and simple way.

Claims to originality do not enhance a book, though I'd like to think I have broken new ground—especially in uncovering certain connections that make up the broad historical context out of which subways came. Some of the factual information is new and, I think, indispensable to understanding the story.

On the other hand, I am much indebted to those who have written about subways before. By and large their accounts include information of another kind, and succeed in their own way, either as nostalgic evocations of "the way things were"—with a special fondness for the period charms of early subway systems—or as technical treatises written by and for train buffs or other engineering initiates. I have made use of material from both sources. My book has a bias of its own, of course—roughly speaking, the history of ideas.

The whole subject, however, is a vast one, with so many compelling aspects that I could have easily chosen to write a sociological study, a monograph on engineering history, or a meditation on the meaning of the "underground." In the end I felt most at home with a weave of things, cast in narrative form.

It gives me great pleasure to have an opportunity to thank

publicly everyone who has helped along the way. I am particularly grateful to my wife, Danielle, who, from the very beginning, through the long hours of research and writing, gave me encouragement and assistance in a thousand and one ways.

The staffs of the Museum of the City of New York, the Barnard College Library, the Library of Congress, the Cooper-Hewitt Museum, the Musée Carnavalet in Paris, Keystone Press Photos, the Newsweek Library, the German Information Office, and the New York Public Library (surely one of our national treasures) courteously cooperated with my every request. My brother, James, went over the penultimate draft of the manuscript and made several shrewd and valuable suggestions; Patricia and Mary Ellen King, Wallace Kunukau, and Roger Lugsdin prepared successive typescripts of the manuscript, with admirable speed. Others who at one time or another gave help or advice are Elizabeth Most Bobrick, John Callender, Catherine Dreyfus, Susan Duncan, Uta Hoffmann, James LeMoyne, R. J. Melvin, and Charles Woerner.

Alvin Garfin, my original publisher, showed gratifying interest in the project early on, and patience and understanding as it evolved. John Hawkins, Alice Martell, and Alison Brown Cerier ensured my labor was not lost. Mary Ann Joulwan was splendid in her collaboration with me on the book design. Eva Galan edited the text with sympathy and tact.

Whatever errors remain are my own.

CHAPTER 1

The
Phlegraean
Fields

One afternoon in the fall of 1816, a French emigré engineer, Marc Isambard Brunel, was at work installing a sawmill at Chatham dockyard in England when he came upon a fragment of keel timber deeply pierced with holes. Worm-eaten timber was a common dockyard sight, and there was nothing odd or unusual about the specimen at his feet. Nevertheless, he paused and picked it up. Within he could see the notorious shipworm, *teredo navalis—calamitas patrium*, Linnaeus had called it, because of all the vessels it had sunk—still indefatigably at work. Admiringly, he noted the shell-shielded structure of the head, with its two serrated edges like files, grinding casually through the hard oak, while the soft transparent body smoothly lined the surrounding passageway with a shell-like secretion of lime. For a moment he stood as if transfixed, as an idea began to take shape in his mind that would revolutionize the history of tunneling and prepare the way for the subways of the modern world.

If the idea of underground travel has a beginning, it is in the timeless present of the mythological past. Fables of indeterminate antiquity tell of it; the names of the heroes whose adventures make it real seem almost to encompass mythology itself— Orpheus, Hercules, Theseus, Odysseus, Aeneas (and Christ, in the apocryphal Gospel of Nicodemus). These, among others, are known to almost everyone, for their adventures form part of our lasting heritage.

Yet, like the gigantic figures of the *Pentateuch*, who lived to an extraordinary age and wrestled with angels, the heroic dimensions of their deeds are apt to seem remote to us and to our lives. "Mythology," Robert Graves once observed, "is the study of whatever religious or heroic legends are so foreign to a student's experience that he cannot believe them to be true"—though they may be true and even present, right before his very eyes. The Golden Bough is, we may guess, not only to be found in a particular forest in southern Europe close by a particular cave, nor, speaking in an ironic way, composed of a rust-resistant yellow metallic element with an atomic number of 79.

Wherever the bough may be found, the Underworld to which it vouchsafed entrance was once upon a time a fearful place, inhabited by demons, lost souls, and the Dead. To journey into this realm required extraordinary daring; it was a treacherous ordeal which only a godlike few might undertake.

Today, through an engineering marvel, it has become commonplace. Millions of ordinary mortals throughout the world descend into the Underworld, pass through it at a superhuman speed, and come up again as part of their everyday routine.

In the period since World War II, and especially in the last twenty years, subways have proliferated in what seems an unstoppable boom. Their number has more than doubled from twenty-four to sixty, with several more under construction. New lines are opening at the rate of fifty miles per year. Stockholm, Brussels, Montreal, Santiago, San Francisco, Washington, Atlanta, Pittsburgh, Buffalo, Caracas, Venezuela, and Mexico City are just some of the latest cities to join this trend. There is even a line under construction in Calcutta, another planned for Istanbul. According to a recent estimate, over twelve and a half billion people ride the subways every year.

Yet there was a time, hardly more than a century ago, when the idea of underground transit was caught up in a controversy that provoked more heated debate than almost any other issue in the cities of the West. From their pulpits clergymen denounced the idea as satanic; civic groups petitioned and marched for and against it; engineers took to pamphleteering in some-times-libelous exchanges with their colleagues; politicians made it the focus of partisan campaigns. The factionalism it stimulated was analogous to the political splinter-grouping that usually afflicts nations only in times of great trial.

Why should feelings have run so high?

In the middle of the nineteenth century urban planning was still largely archaic. The organization of traffic had hardly advanced since the last years of the Roman empire—in fact, was less organized than when Julius Caesar had banned all daytime commercial traffic from the streets of Rome. In most of the cities of Europe and America, streets followed the same narrow, meandering routes as the old dirt paths they covered over. This was not in itself an evil, since their organic ramification had served to bind neighborhoods together in a natural way. But under the impact of the Industrial Revolution the social habits of communities disintegrated. As the cities grew at a phenomenal rate, their new ways and by-ways evolved into a kind of maze, with no overall plan. Traffic, instead of flowing directly along connecting routes, was chronically caught up in bottlenecks and dead-end lanes. An endless carousel of vehicles—sedan chairs, pony chaises, cabriolets, costers, gigs, barrows, wagonettes, phaetons, hackney coaches, and omnibuses—perpetually jammed the streets, while the racket of their iron wheels on the cobblestones may have exceeded that of our own worst traffic snarls, with all our sirens and horns.

Two urban ages met but were not bridged, and they met with calamitous force. Traffic became an obsession, the overwhelming civic issue. Engraving after engraving in the illustrated periodicals portrayed this urban chaos in terms borrowed from the Apocalypse. In the daily newspapers the phrase "traffic congestion" recurred like a tic. "Next to the air we breathe, or the food we eat," declared Simeon E. Church, a typical speaker at a typical town meeting on the subject in New York in 1873, "no one thing in city life touches so vitally the comfort and interest of every citizen, of every condition, in every calling, every day, as this question of city transit."

Turmoil in the streets, however, was but one manifestation of the general upheaval across the new industrial landscape. Henry Booth, treasurer of the Liverpool & Manchester Railway, summed up the situation frankly in 1830, almost as soon as it appeared:

> We must determine ... whether it is desirable that a nation should continue in the quiet enjoyment of pastoral or agricultural life, or that it should be launched into the bustle and excitement of commerce and manufacture. [But] it must be admitted that the golden age is past, and it is to be feared that the iron age has succeeded. The locomotive engine and railway were reserved for the present day. From west to east, and from north to south, the mechanical principle, the philosophy of the nineteenth century, will spread and extend itself. The world has received a new impulse. The genius of the age, like a mighty river of a new world, flows onward, full, rapid, and irresistible.

It was this impulse that would bring the subject of subways to the fore, more or less simultaneously, in London, Paris, and New York, the first cities to build major systems. And it was in response to the early stages of the full, rapid, and irresistibly developing morass it spread that Marc Isambard Brunel, inspired by a lowly mollusk, came forth with his historic invention of the tunneling shield.

But subways would not be realized without trial. Irresistible, they met resistance. One reason was psychological, and is rooted in the mythology of the Underworld. Our nineteenth-century forebears, in ways not wholly strange to ourselves, instinctively recoiled from trespassing into a traditionally forbidden zone. Another reason was technological. What, after all, were the precedents for such an undertaking? Few engineering accomplishments of the past stood as a guide.

According to medieval legend, the first great road tunnel in history was the work of a Roman sorcerer. One midnight, under a moonless sky, sometime between the assassination of Julius Caesar and the coronation of Augustus, the poet Vergil was said to have assembled eighty thousand devils before a mountain in

Campania in southern Italy, and by means of incantations, spells, and other devices of supernatural power set the horde to tunneling through the mountain's base. The following day, when the sun rose, the devils were nowhere to be seen, but from one end of the mountain to the other was a chasm as broad as a road.

This story reflects more than mere medieval wonder at the spectacular engineering feats of antiquity. As it happens, the tunnel exists, it can be dated to 36 B.C., and its association with Vergil, demons, and the Underworld is both profound and right. For our purposes, at least, any history of tunneling ought to begin there, for the underground and the Underworld can never be very far apart.

East of Lake Avernus, not far from the grotto of the Cumaean Sibyl who foretold the future to Aeneas and guided his descent into the Underworld, stands a monumental headland off the Bay of Naples which almost impassably separates Naples and its environs from a region known to antiquity as the Phlegraean Fields, once the scene of battle between the gods and the subterranean giants of water and fire. To this day the charred volcanic soil yields up the sulphurous traces of that mythological war.

The headland is called the Pausilypon, or Posilipo, which means "pain-stopping" or "a stay to grief." On its extreme southwestern edge, on the long, green promontory that extends far out into the bay, once stood the Villa of Augustus, the axis of imperial power outside the city of Rome. Southwestward across the bay, where the peninsular hook forms a double basin, lies the harbor of Misenum, the chief naval base of the empire under Augustus and headquarters for defense of the Mediterranean. North of Misenum is Baia, the favorite spa and playground retreat of the Roman aristocracy, to which "all the gay, gallant and polite world used to resort in autumn." Following the coast in a semicircular arc northeastward from Baia, one comes to Pozzuoli, which by the time of Augustus had superseded Naples as the major commercial port of Rome. A few miles to the west stands Cumae, a cultural center, and fortified city whose steep western escarpments thwarted seaborne assault.

It was in order to unite all these sites with Naples—and thus the whole Campanian coast with Rome by a direct route—that the greatest road tunnels of antiquity were built.

At the time of the assassination of Julius Caesar in 44 B.C., which plunged the Roman world into a series of civil wars, the only road that roughly traversed the area was the Via Antiniana, a twisting, mountainous path that rose over the northern shoulder of the Pausilypon at its lowest point. As Octavian (later Augustus) maneuvered for control of the empire, he undertook a vast engineering program as part of a strategic plan for coordinating his forces in southern Italy. A system of canals was made to join Avernus with the sea, transforming the lake into a large inland naval base and shipyard. Three road tunnels were also cut: two through the Pausilypon, and one through a hill that stood between Avernus and Cumae. Marcus Agrippa, Augustus' most capable advisor, supervised these projects; the engineer directly in charge was L. Cocceius Auctus, a native of Campania with a deep affinity for the mysterious and perhaps inimitable traditions of the region.

As far back as history can reveal, and farther still, into mythology, Campania and the Underworld have been identified as one. From Naples to Cumae, especially along the coast, the region is honeycombed with quarries, grottoes, caverns, and galleries—some the work of natural volcanic and hydrological forces, some the work of man. Here the ancient Cimmerians, a fabulous race of miners whom Odysseus encountered on his way to Hades, were reputed to have lived in caverns under ground, communicating by means of tunnels and emerging only at night. Here lies the Mare Morto, Stygian Lake of the Dead, and round about a scattering of numerous hot springs and fountains believed to be fed by infernal rivers—by Styx itself and by Pyriphlegethon ("flaming with fire"), a tributary of the Acheron. Here lies Avernus, the traditional entrance to the Underworld, whose immobile leaden waters, at once both unreflecting and impenetrable, exhaled vapors so noxious as to drive the birds above it from the sky. Beyond its shores once lay the fearsome wild forest, Silva Gallinaria, which wrapped the lake in shadows like a shroud. Indeed, the Greek geographer Strabo writes that nearly every feature of the landscape seemed to the inhabitants fraught with Plutonian significance.

Even as late as 1740, when a learned traveler of the Enlightenment, Charles Burney, visited the *solfatara* plain, heart of the Phlegraean Fields, the region irresistibly suggested hell itself.

'Tis still burning, [he reported], so furiously hot as to hiss and make a violent noise like that of a great fire when water is poured on it. At its mouth there is genuine salammoniac, cinaber and sulphur—a piece of iron sweats in it immediately in large drops of water. Here are alum pits—and much genuine flower of brimstone is found about the mountain—some places are so hot as to burn one's feet. There is likewise here a boiling spring. It seems hollow underneath, by the noise it makes when a heavy stone is thrown on it with violence.

The Sibyl who guided Aeneas beneath this chthonic crust had her grotto in Cumae—nor was this legend only. In 1932, a tunnel more ancient than any other of its kind in the region was discovered just below the gate of the Acropolis, cut deep into the western flank of the hill: exactly where Aeneas had found it. In form and workmanship more akin to archaic Etruscan and Mycenaean tombs than to anything Roman, the long aisle down which, perhaps, the petitioner was conducted to the prophetess is perfectly cut, in cross-section like a trapezoid, with six lateral galleries at right angles. Where the galleries meet the aisle there once hung shutters or doors, an acoustic device which sent the Sibyl's voice echoing and reechoing through the cavern—the awesome hundred voices which Aeneas heard. At the end of this aisle lies a niche-like chamber, more like a chapel than a tomb, where the virgin Sibyl, inspired by the god Apollo, gathered about her the prophetic leaves.

The road tunnels built by Agrippa and Cocceius were at once assimilated into the folklore of the region. The tunnel linking Avernus with Cumae seems to have served as Vergil's model in the *Aeneid* for the passage down to Hades. A century later Petronius in the *Satyricon* poetically evoked one of the Pausilypon tunnels in a similar spirit:

Twixt Naples and Dicarchian* Fields extends
A horrid gulf, immensely deep and wide,
Through which Cocytus† rolls his lazy streams,
And poisons all the air with sulphurous fogs.
No autumn here e'er clothes himself with green,
No joyful spring, the languid herbage cheers:
No feathered warblers chant their mirthless strains
In vernal comfort to the rustling boughs
But Chaos reigns, and ragged rocks around
With naught but baleful cypress are adorned.

We will meet this profile of symbolic attributes again—the sulphurous fogs, the banishment of life and vegetation, especially of birds, for Avernus itself means "birdless"—the sign of the Underworld.

After Augustus became emperor in 27 B.C., one of the Pausilypon tunnels was used as a highway for the common man, the other as a private road for the upper classes. The first, known as the Grotto di Posilipo, was by all accounts dark, unventilated, cramped, and low. Seneca called it dismal and complained of the choking dust. "There is no prison," he wrote, "longer than that *crypta*, no torch dimmer than those they shielded before us, which served not to lighten the darkness but only to look upon one another. And, in any case, even if there had been a glimmer of light, the dust would have robbed us of it: it was dense enough to darken an out-of-doors spot. What then must be said of it in that place where it turns upon itself and, unstirred by any breath of wind, falls back upon those who raise it?" Petronius claimed he had to stoop when going through.

Like its successors in a later age, the tunnel was peculiarly vulnerable to crime. As a deterrent there stood for centuries at its center, carved out of the rock, a small shrine to Mithras, Persian god of light. It bore the Latin inscription OMNI POTENTI DEO

*Dicarchia = *Pozzuoli*.
†*Cocytus = "river of wailing," a tributary of the Acheron.*

MITHRAE ("To the all-powerful god Mithras"), and comforted wayfarers as they passed through the gloom. The manly attributes of the god, exemplified by his martial appearance, together with the virtues ascribed to him of obedience and humility, made him equally appealing to Roman legionnaires and to the downtrodden and poor. In 1546 the shrine was replaced by a Christian chapel dedicated to Santa Maria della Grotta, and "images and pictures of saints were hung on the sides of the cavern with small votive lamps burning dimly before them."

The Grotto di Posilipo stood more or less unchanged for about fifteen hundred years. In the fifteenth and sixteenth centuries Campania came under Aragonese and then Spanish domination, and a succession of viceroys and princes improved the tunnel in various ways. In 1442 Alphonso of Aragon enlarged it overall and pierced it centrally with circular shafts for ventilation and light. In 1546 Pietro di Toledo paved and leveled it in such a way "that the light at one end could be seen from the other as a star, and for a few days about the equinox the sun actually shone through." In 1754 the Bourbon King Charles III reinforced the ceiling with supporting arches. Although enlarged to more than twice its original size, the tunnel continued to be regarded with misgiving by the local inhabitants. When the Duke of Buckingham visited the site in April 1828, he found it "desolate except for a single begging friar."

The second tunnel—known as the Grotto di Seiano through some obscure connection with Sejanus, captain of the guard under the Emperor Tiberius—was, in contrast, spacious, well-lighted, and -ventilated. It was enjoyed by officials on errands to the Villa of Augustus (onto which its western portal opened) and by holiday crowds that surged through every autumn on their way to the coastal resorts. In the fifth century earthfalls closed the western entrance and stopped up segments of its length; over the centuries wild vegetation kept it partially concealed. The eastern entrance was known only as a large cave, believed by some to be the Cyclops' lair. In 1840, when a new road was surveyed from Coroglio to Bagnoli under King Ferdinand, it was rediscovered and cleared.

During the Middle Ages the Grotto di Posilipo passed into folklore. Cocceius and Agrippa were forgotten; in their place emerged Vergil, not as a poet, but in his powerful rebirth as a sorcerer. Stories told of his magical deeds, his superhuman feats and conquests of nature, many of a spectacular engineering kind. With a wave of his hand he could fling bridges over rivers, build aqueducts for a city in a single day, and tunnel through mountains in a single night. As an adept of white magic he could, by mechanical, astrological, or mathematical means, create talismanic objects endowed with occult properties. He was said to have rid Naples of all her flies by means of a magical fly fashioned out of bronze, which he placed on a city gate. He subdued the fires of Vesuvius with a bronze archer, whose arrow was made to point at the volcano's crest. These stories arose out of the adoration of Vergil as a sort of Neapolitan patron saint.

Another folklore tradition transmogrified Vergil into a "child of Hell." In the *Aeneid* he had revealed himself as an intimate of the Underworld. Once the ardent religious feeling of the poem was obscured, the volume became the fabled "Magick Book" from which he drew his satanic power. Legend supplied him with a disciple, Milino (every sorcerer must have an apprentice), who reappeared later as the Merlin of Arthurian romance.

The Posilipo legend survived at least until the latter part of the sixteenth century. In Christopher Marlowe's tragic drama *Doctor Faustus* Mephistopheles shows Faustus the tunnel as a reward for forfeiting his soul:

> *There saw we learned Maro's* golden tombe,*
> *The way he cut an English mile in length,*
> *Through a rocke of stone, in one nyghte's space.*
> *(Act III, Scene I, 13–15)*

Vergil's tomb stands on a ridge overlooking the tunnel's eastern approach.

Restored to its original identity as the Latin epic, Vergil's "Magick Book" retained its mystical character well into the seventeenth century, when it was still consulted frequently as a prophetic text—much as the *I Ching,* or Chinese "Book of Changes," is today. Charles I is said to have consulted it (by

---

*Maro = Vergil (Publius Virgilius Maro).

opening it at random) for his own fate in the outcome of the English Civil War. His eyes fell on the terrible words of Dido's curse for Aeneas:

> . . . *May he have to*
> *Sue for aid, and see his friends squalidly dying,*
> *Yes, and when he's accepted the terms of a harsh peace,*
> *Let him never enjoy his realm or the allotted span,*
> *But fall before his time and lie on the sands, unburied.*
> *(Book IV, 616–620)*

So it was. Charles, who eventually had to settle on Oliver Cromwell's harsh terms, lost his realm and was beheaded. Across the block the executioner scattered sand to blot up the blood.

One could do worse in this world of mysterious history, of Newtonian laws and the riddles of Providence than pay heed to a poet's voice or play the *sortes Virgilianae*, the game of Vergilian fates. The poet's searching portrait of the Underworld, rooted in Campanian fact, may prove useful as an intuitive historical guide, not at all at variance with the revelations of conventional research. Prophecy is another face of destiny; and as Jorge Luis Borges has observed, "destiny takes pleasure in repetition, variants and symmetries."

The Roman road tunnels in southern Italy marked a rather late and exceptional development in the history of tunnel engineering; nothing quite like them had been built before; and nothing quite like them would be built again for almost two thousand years. In their function as highways or roads they were unique.

Technologically, however, they were neither unique nor exceptional; tunnels, even on the grand scale, had played a role in antiquity for centuries, encompassing a variety of ends—from supplying water and disposing of sewage to honoring royalty with monumental tombs, from mining metals to facilitating assaults on citadels and towns. The great Egyptian temple tombs of Abu Simbel, for example, built by Ramses II (the Pharaoh of the Bible) in 1250 B.C., penetrated a sandstone cliff to a depth of several hundred feet, with corridors, stairways, and an ever-deepening succession of rooms terminating in a chamber where the king's sarcophagus reposed. Some of the rooms (there were fourteen in all) were 55 feet square and 30 feet high. The tomb of Mineptah at Thebes has a similar grandeur, as do some of the magnificent hillside temples of the Nubians on the Upper Nile.

Considerably older was the Egyptian Labyrinth, "a little above Lake Moeris, near the place called the City of the Crocodiles." Erected during the reign of Amenemhet III of the Twelfth Dynasty, around 1850 B.C., as a reminder of the bond between the twelve kings who had divided the realm between them, the Labyrinth was visited by the Greek historian Herodotus in the mid-fifth century B.C. "I have seen this building," he marveled,

> and it is beyond my power to describe; it must have cost more in labor and money than all the walls and public works of the Greeks put together—though no one would deny that the temples at Ephesus and Samos are remarkable buildings. The pyramids, too, are astonishing structures, each one of them equal to many of the most ambitious works of Greece, but the labyrinth surpasses them. It has twelve covered courts—six in a row facing north, six south—the gates of the one range exactly fronting the gates of the other, with a continuous wall around the outside of the whole. Inside, the building is of two storeys and contains three thousand rooms, of which half are underground and the other half directly above them. I was taken through the rooms in the upper storey, so what I shall say of them is from my own observation, but the underground ones I can speak of only from report, because the Egyptians in charge refused to let me see them, as they contain the tombs of the kings who built the labyrinth, and also the tombs of the sacred crocodiles. The upper rooms, on the contrary, I did actually see, and it is hard to believe that they are the work of men; the baffling and intricate passages from room to room and from court to court were an endless wonder to me, as we passed from a courtyard into rooms, from rooms into galleries, from galleries into more rooms, and thence into yet more courtyards.

Four hundred years later Strabo corroborated this account, as did the Roman historian Pliny in the first century A.D. In the nineteenth century, the archaeologist Flinders Petrie identified the actual site and its scanty remains.

The Cretan Labyrinth at Knossos, devised by Daedalus for the captivity of the Minotaur, may well have been modeled on the Egyptian. Pliny reported that it contained "intricate windings and turnings ... with frequent doors to baulk advance and cause a return into the same strayings." The twentieth-century excavations of Sir Arthur Evans disclosed "a bewildering complex of walls, chambers, courts and corridors, well-deserving the name of Labyrinth." According to Homer, the shield of Achilles—wrought by Hephaestus, the fiery god of metals and the mine—bore a design "like unto the Cretan Labyrinth." And when Vergil's Aeneas pauses at the shrine of Apollo at Cumae, on his way to consult the Sibyl, he finds an image of the Labyrinth sculpted on the wall. It is the image he carries with him into the Underworld, whose eternally binding corridors are the ultimate model for the maze. The Sibyl tells him:

> ... *The way to Avernus is easy;*
> *Night and day lie open the gates of death's dark kingdom:*
> *But to retrace your steps, to find the way back to daylight—*
> *That is the task, the hard thing.*

The labyrinthine catacombs of Rome, begun and ramified during the first Christian centuries, are perhaps the most remarkable historical reminiscence of the pattern. Their seemingly infinite meanderings and many-storied depths, sudden corridors and turns, almost make them a historical archetype.

Tunneling has always had a military aspect. Although the Marquis de Vauban, the great French specialist in fortifications, may have been the first to work out precise formulae in the 1700's, tunneling was certainly common military practice by the time Joshua sounded his clarion blasts and the wall of Jericho came tumbling down.

So the people shouted when the priests blew with the trumpets; and it came to pass, when the people heard the sound of the

trumpet, and the people shouted with a great shout, that the wall
fell down flat, so that the people went up into the city, every man
straight before him, and they took the city.

(Joshua 6:20)

The power of the people's faith notwithstanding, the technique
used in the siege was already time-honored: a series of tunnels
was dug beneath the ramparts and reinforced with timber
frames; then, at a signal (such as a shout or the blast of a horn)
the wood was set on fire, causing the tunnels and therefore the
ramparts above them to collapse.

Tunnels might also be driven under the walls of a city in order
to invade it. Such assaults sometimes fostered ingenious coun-
termeasures. In his classic work *On Architecture*, Vitruvius de-
scribes how enemy sappers were outwitted in the battle for
Appolonia in 214 B.C.:

> The Appolonians entrusted the defense of their city to the archi-
> tect Typho of Alexandria. He instructed the defenders to dig a
> deep trench parallel to and within bow shot of the walls. Along
> this trench he hung a number of bronze vessels. When the vessels
> reverberated to the sound of the sappers' tools, he knew the lo-
> cation and direction of the tunnel they were boring. From the
> sound of the vibrating he calculated where the sappers would
> break through and at these points he hung large vessels filled
> with boiling water and pitch, and for good measure human dung
> and sand roasted to a fiery heat. In the night he sank holes over
> the headings and dropped the contents of the vessels on the en-
> emy.

This must have been discouraging; not surprisingly, tunnel
builders preferred to use their talents in other ways. Indeed, it
was in the field of hydraulic engineering that they achieved
their most notable results.

In the Indus Valley, sewage tunnels served the city of Mohen-
jo-daro as early as 2500 B.C. Babylonian irrigation tunnels
branched through the plain that separates the Euphrates from
the Tigris River, while throughout ancient Etruria rock-cut water channels, hewn by the Etruscans from a series of vertical

shafts, drew upon the water-bearing veins of the earth. Some of these channels, including the great Cloaca Maxima which drains the valley around Rome into the Tiber, were later rebuilt and enlarged by the Romans.

In 700 B.C. King Hezekiah of Judah, anticipating the onslaught of the Assyrians under Sennacherib, cut a channel 1,750 feet long from within the walls of Jerusalem outside to the concealed Spring of Gihon, the perennial spring of Israel. Though the tunnel varied in height from 5 to 18 feet and followed a meandering course, the gradient was so precise that water flowed smoothly along its whole length into the Pool of Siloam, the reservoir within the outer defense lines of the city walls. Jerusalem, reported Strabo seven hundred years later, though "wholly dry without," is yet a "rocky fortress well-watered within." Similar engineering has been revealed at Tiryns, Hazor, Roshenra, Megiddo, and other early Middle Eastern strongholds.

A century after Hezekiah, on the island of Samos in the Aegean, a water tunnel over $\frac{1}{2}$ mile long was driven through a solid limestone mountain 900 feet high. The tunnel had an overall diameter of 6 feet and was furnished with clay pipes. Herodotus called it "one of the greatest building and engineering feats in the Greek world." Roughly two centuries later, in the fourth century B.C., the Romans excavated a 6,000-foot *emissarium* or drainage conduit for Lake Albano, a small but extremely deep volcanic lake. During the siege of the Veii, according to the historian Livy, the waters "had suddenly risen up without apparent cause. The Romans, taking this as an ill-omen, dug the subterranean channel to let the waters out, and their luck turned immediately."

The most stupendous feat of this kind, however, came under the Emperor Claudius in the mid-first century A.D. Claudius, normally shy of public works on the grand scale, was persuaded by a group of businessmen to revive the project of an *emissarium* for Lake Fucinus, in central Italy. The lake was large, some 30 miles around, and many streams of the Apennines poured into it. Every spring it tended to overflow, turning the surrounding terrain into a swamp. The idea was to extend the tunnel for $3\frac{1}{2}$ miles to the River Liris, a proverbially sluggish stream to the west. Along the way, part of a mountain would have to be leveled before tunneling through the base. Years before, Augustus had dismissed the scheme as impractical. But the businessmen won Claudius over by agreeing to shoulder the expense if he would award them the reclaimed land. As Suetonius points out, the work had very little to do with imperial glory—it was simply a real estate deal. Begun in 41 A.D., it took eleven years to complete, with thirty thousand slaves working at depths of up to 400 feet, night and day. Forty shafts as well as "a number of *cuniculi* or inclined galleries were sunk and the excavated material was raised in ten gallon capacity pails by windlasses."

To celebrate the achievement, Claudius staged a gigantic naval battle on the lake, using nineteen thousand gladiators in twenty-four warships—twelve Rhodian and twelve Sicilian triremes. Large rafts manned by double companies of the guard behind ramparts encircled the vessels to prevent escape. Thousands of spectators turned the surrounding hills and slopes into an amphitheater. The emperor himself presided, resplendent in a military cloak.

But from the first things did not go well. The gladiators shouted the customary "Hail, Caesar, we salute you, we who are about to die!" to which Claudius replied: "Or not, as the case may be." The gladiators took this as a pardon and refused to fight. An argument ensued, with Claudius storming at them from the shore and threatening to have them burned in their ships. At length he won them over. A "mechanical silver Triton emerged from the lake bottom and blew on a conch," signaling the battle to begin. "Though the fighters were criminals," wrote Tacitus, "they fought like brave men and after much bloodletting they were spared extermination." The crowd then waited in disorderly excitement for the sluice-gates to open and the debouchment to begin. Claudius gave the signal—and nothing happened. Not a single drop of water entered the tunnel. Investigation revealed that the grade was way off. The emperor hurried back to Rome in humiliation, while another year was spent correcting the work.

A second crowd was then assembled, even larger than the first, "this time to witness an infantry battle fought by gladiators on pontoons." Claudius held a banquet near the lake's outlet so he could witness the drainage up close. This time when the gates opened, "the water came rushing out in a deluge and almost drowned him." Everything in the vicinity was swept away and his guests fled in terror; when the wreckage cleared, it was found that the tunnel had worked well enough—though Claudius reneged on his agreement and took the salvaged land for himself.

Throughout antiquity (and indeed up through the Renaissance) the tools used in tunnel-building varied very little. The Egyptians developed copper saws and hollow reed drills, turned in an abrasive like carborundum, for cutting harder rock, and devised a means of controlled cleavage: first carving grooves along the rock's surface, then drilling along the grooves a series of strategically placed holes; the holes were next filled with water and plugged with wood. The action of the water caused the wood to swell, forcing the rock apart along predetermined lines. Another technique, used more widely by the Romans, was "spalling" or "fire-quenching." In this procedure the face of the rock was heated by fire and then abruptly splashed with cold water. The sudden thermal shock caused fracturing. Though sometimes extremely effective, fire-quenching could be devastating to the laborers. Without excellent ventilation, which only large air shafts sunk at close intervals could provide, the "fire" of the method rapidly consumed the tunnel's oxygen, while the "quenching" flooded the passageway with steam and scalding fumes.

Nowadays, of course, tunneling is assisted by such powerful machinery that few excavations short of the archaeologically delicate seem formidable. The routine use of nitroglycerine for blasting, in sequences scientifically controlled for maximum effect, mocks the hardness of almost any rock, while less adamantine strata crumble before the battering of pneumatic drills and the great boring forces of "mechanical moles." As the loosened earth or "muck" accumulates, it is swiftly removed by machines driven by diesel engines, or by power shovels coordinated with conveyor belts. We are a far cry from antiquity.

Indeed, if the great Roman tunnels speak eloquently to us of the grandness of imperial style, at least one of them, near Cumae, unashamedly reminds us of how difficult the work must have been. On the vault of the entrance, left pointedly to posterity as a sign, are carved a pick, a mallet, four wedges, and a stone-axe. If to these we add the simple chisel, we have roughly the full range of hand tools with which most tunnels of antiquity were made.

From the fall of Rome in the fifth century A.D. until the late seventeenth century, tunnel construction lapsed into its most primitive forms. Feudal lords provided their castles with subterranean escape routes, or secret passageways for hiding, and sappers continued to dig under fortress walls. Otherwise, as one engineering expert writes,

> in the Dark Ages no center of economic and political power strong enough to launch important enterprises existed in Europe. In the fragmented western world, the only great ventures demanding the cooperation of large numbers of men were marauding expeditions such as the Norman invasions of England and Sicily and the Crusades. At the same time, the decline of the cities removed the principal reason for digging tunnels—water supply and sewage disposal. Virtually the only tunnelling done in Europe during the Middle Ages was by the Moors in Spain, whose civilization was the most scientifically advanced in Europe, and who constructed water tunnels for irrigation.

The first breakthrough took place in Germany in 1613 when Martin Wiegel introduced gunpowder for blasting in mines. But it was not until the end of the century that explosives played a decisive role in the creation of a tunnel: when Pierre-Paul Ricquet blasted through the base of a hill at Malpas, France, during the construction of the Languedoc Canal linking the Atlantic with the Mediterranean. The tunnel portion of this canal was only 510 feet long, but it created an international sensation. The canal itself was widely regarded as the greatest feat of civil engineering in Europe since Roman times.

Over the next hundred years canal-building flourished on the Continent and in England to a degree never surpassed. By 1800 there were 12,000 miles of canals in Britain alone, many including tunnels along their routes. The point was to achieve a level course; as James Brindley, the great canal builder, put it: "Water is a giant, therefore, lay him on his back." Most of the important early canals were connected to mines and transported coal.

The tunnels took some getting used to. When the Tronquoy and Riqueval tunnels on the San Quentin Canal in France opened in 1810, the boatmen "refused to a man to enter them out of fear of the long dark passages. Canal authorities offered freedom from tolls in perpetuity to the first boat that entered. Even so, only one man came forward." On the average, these tunnels were not large—about 15 feet across—and some were extraordinarily small. A few were so low that boatmen had to lie on their backs on top of the freight and kick the roof of the tunnel with their feet to move the boats through.

Until the early nineteenth century, tunnel engineering—for all its variety, technical resourcefulness, and occasional splendor— was an arrested science. "In no other branch of civil engineering," according to one authority, "did empiricism so long resist the advance of theory, or remain largely independent of the realm of mathematical analysis." While tunnels were used for many purposes, they were all, in fact, quite alike in architectural idea. Every one of them was cut through "hard ground," or some form of rock, which meant that they were essentially self-supporting. The exception proves the rule: in mining, where timbering (wooden frames) often reinforced the work, the ground had to be firm enough to tunnel in the usual manner, firm enough to allow a heading from which to advance. In effect, timbering was an accessory support, insufficient—and indeed, hardly possible, as events would shortly show—in genuinely soft or fluid soil. Its prominent defect was that a portion of the heading was always exposed, above or in front, just before the next frame was set. Through that exposed area soil might come pouring in, destroying the tunnel and anyone inside. It was a common disaster.

In the history of tunneling, indeed, one paramount fact stands out: over the course of 5,000 years and, very likely, over the whole life of man, a true soft ground tunnel supported exclusively from within by human architecture, had never been built. That challenge had baffled even the most ingenious engineers. Somehow (and it was a real paradox) the making of the tunnel and the tunnel itself would have to be simultaneously achieved.

Until the early nineteenth century, the challenge lacked urgency. Then it appeared with a vengeance. By the 1800's, in London, England, it had become apparent that population growth and other pressures necessitated a traffic tunnel beneath the river Thames—though no soil could be softer, more fluid or treacherous than alluvial silt. The immediate task was clear; what was hardly foreseen was what the ultimate consequences of success would be.

THE BEGINNINGS

A PICTURE PORTFOLIO

A Tunisian mosaic depicting the poet Vergil between the muses of History and Tragedy. In the folklore of the Middle Ages, Vergil was known as a powerful sorcerer whose reputed deeds included spectacular engineering feats. One of the most famous was a tunnel through a mountain in southern Italy.

Above, an 18th-century watercolor of the entrance to the "Grotto di Posilipo." Above right, a photograph of one of the road tunnels built by the Romans near Cumae. Below right, a fresco of the Madonna and Child at the Posilipo entrance. From the first, wayfarers through this tunnel's gloom sought reassurance and protection in the presence of a guardian power. A small sanctuary dedicated to Mithras was carved by the Romans in the tunnel's center. In the 1500's it was succeeded by a chapel to the Virgin.

Sir Arthur Evans, whose excavations of the Palace of Minos at Knossos (shown in a view from the south side) turned up labyrinthine ruins that accorded convincingly with the Minotaur's legendary maze-like lair.

Left, a water tunnel built by Eupalinus on the island of Samos in the Aegean in the 6th century B.C. The Greek historian Herodotus regarded it as one of the wonders of the world.

Right, a corridor in the Roman catacombs—perhaps the most intricate of all ancient labyrinths—showing loculi, or horizontal burial niches, along the walls.

Below, the first picture of a railway ever drawn, 1530, depicts a miner pushing a wagon along tracks leading out of the mouth of a mine.

Left, a horse-drawn railway in an 18th-century coal mine. Below, a colliery near Leeds with an early locomotive in the background.

Left, the Dannemora Iron Mine, in a contemporary aquatint, c.1809. Below, heavy traffic over London Bridge, when progress was so slow that merchants often had to stand helplessly by as their produce withered in the sun.

Painted by H Wyatt   Engraved by H Adlard

Marc Isambard Brunel, who invented the
tunneling shield and built Thames Tunnel,
the first subaqueous tunnel in history.

*Operations from a diving bell after the
roof of the tunnel caved in. Inundations
by the river were a chronic tribulation.*

Top, cross-section view of the completed tunnel.
Left, interior view. Above, Brunel's shield
in operation. Under its protection, 36 men could
work back to back. Here, the propelling screws
and moveable stage are clearly shown.

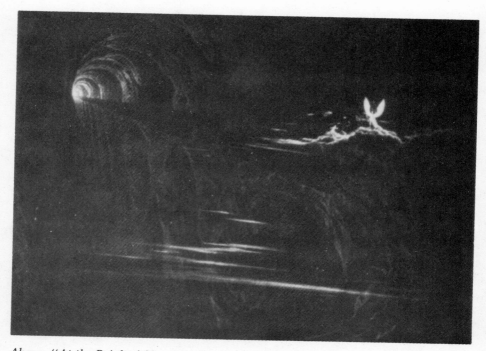

Above, "At the Brink of Chaos," one of John Martin's mezzotint illustrations for Milton's Paradise Lost, was inspired by Brunel's tunnel. Below, the tunnel's twin archway as adapted for use by the London Underground in the 1860's.

CHAPTER 2

Hades Hotel

For as long as anyone could recall, Marc Isambard Brunel had been uncanny at deciphering how things work. In his early teens he had constructed a ship's quadrant from sight, after observing one in the cabin of a naval officer. "When it is remembered," wrote Richard Beamish, his one-time assistant and devoted biographer, "that this instrument demands in the constructor a knowledge not only of geometry, trigonometry, and mechanics, but of optics, one is filled with astonishment and admiration at such intuitive sagacity." After his third lesson in trigonometry, Brunel reportedly devised an instrument to measure the height of the Rouen Cathedral spire.

As a boy he had resisted his father's determination that he train for the priesthood. When he was sent to the seminary of St. Nicaise at Rouen, he manifested such distaste for patristic study that the abbé sent him home. His real pleasure lay in watching artisans at work, particularly wheelwrights and joiners, and in sketching—"the alphabet," he would later write, "of the engineer." By the time he was twenty he was an able painter of miniatures and could draw a perfect circle freehand.

This combination of talents was to save his life. In 1785, when he was sixteen, he was appointed to the frigate *Marquis de Cast* and sailed for the West Indies. When he returned in 1792, France was in its third year of revolutionary turmoil. Brunel's royalist sympathies put him in grave danger (he openly called his dog "citoyen"), and in January 1793, just four days before Louis XVI was beheaded and the Reign of Terror began, he fled Paris for Rouen where his cousin, M. Charpentier, was the American vice-consul. He lingered in Rouen for six months, undecided what to do next. He lingered almost too long. Word reached him that he was marked for arrest and on July 7, 1793, he rode at breakneck speed for Le Havre, where the American ship *Liberty* was about to hoist sail. In his pocket was a passport (provided by Charpentier) identifying him as a government official on errand to buy provisions for the army. As he neared the town's outskirts, his horse stumbled, throwing him to the ground. Bruised and in a daze he continued on, unaware that his passport lay uselessly behind him in the dust. The ship was hardly out of port when a naval patrol of the new revolutionary regime appeared on the horizon. Brunel reached for his passport—and discovered it was gone. He had only a few short hours in which to improvise a new document. The gendarmes came on board; his passport was demanded; he presented it. It was returned to him without question. Somehow, with his phenomenal memory and calligraphic skill, he had created an exact replica of the original, with all the official markings reproduced down to the fine significant details.

When Brunel arrived in New York, French agents were all over the city. With two other emigrés, he headed north through Albany and found work surveying the wild terrain around Lake Ontario and the route for a canal between the Hudson River Valley and Lake Champlain. French expatriates, particularly former aristocrats, abounded in the wilds of America at this time. One afternoon, canoeing up a small stream, Brunel encountered the Duc d'Orleans (later King Louis-Philippe) vigorously working the oars of a tiny boat.

Yet Brunel had come to America with useful connections. Through Charpentier he had an entrée into influential circles; Alexander Hamilton, New York's chief banker and a major political power, took special interest in him. Under Hamilton's patronage, Brunel's considerable abilities as an architect and engineer flowered. He designed a number of New York's buildings, including the imposing Park Theater (destroyed by fire in 1821), and redesigned the city's defenses. He also proposed the winning design for the new Capitol Building in Washington, although another blueprint was ultimately adopted as more economical. Within five years of his arrival, he was New York State's Chief Engineer.

One evening in 1798, when he was dining with Hamilton, he overheard a guest complain of the time-consuming process involved in making ship's blocks, or pulleys, which he had recently witnessed at an English naval yard. It seemed to Brunel that the procedure might be simplified. He had a keen desire to go to England, for his English fiancée, Sophie Kingdom, imprisoned for many months in a convent making artificial flowers, had finally managed to get out of France. As it happened, her brother was an undersecretary to the English Naval Board. It would make a fine impression indeed to come to England for her hand with an invention beneficial to her nation. Some months later, as he was wistfully carving Sophie's initials into the bark of a tree, the shape of the letter "S" suggested to him the mechanical design he had been looking for. On January 20, 1799, he set sail with a high heart for England.

The Naval Board took his ideas under consideration. It would take time and politics before the contract could come his way. Meanwhile, his prolific ingenuity as a mechanical engineer led to a number of contributions to industrial design. In May 1799 he invented a duplicate writing and drawing machine; shortly thereafter, an exquisite apparatus for twisting cotton thread and forming it into balls. It "measured the length of the thread it wound, and proportioned the size of the ball to its weight and fineness." Each "was very elegant in form, and from the manner in which the thread was wound, presented the appearance of networks of ribbons of lace." He next devised a machine for hemming and stitching, then another for shuffling cards.

Brunel's prospects before the Naval Board improved dramatically when master mechanic Henry Maudslay—who, more than any other man of the age, established new and exact standards for the fashioning of machine parts and tools—agreed to make models of the block-making machinery. Though it took several years to set the machinery up, its historical importance went far beyond its usefulness to the English navy. It was, historians agree, the first example of mechanized mass production. In forty-two separate operations, it cut the mortises and shaped the outside of the shells in such a manner that, as one contemporary pointedly observed, "without requiring dexterity on the part of the workman," each one turned out the same. Ten men could do the work of one hundred and ten, turning out 160,000 pulleys a year. Another contemporary remarked: "The machinery is so perfect that it appears to act with the happy certainty of instinct and the foresight of reason combined." The unhappy certainty in its aftermath, however, was the decline of the handicraft industry, and the rise of a new kind of unemployment—men out of work because they had been replaced by machines.

Brunel's plant, established at Portsmouth dockyard, became a prominent tourist attraction, and was visited by many of the famous and renowned, including the novelist Sir Walter Scott and the more earnestly curious Czar Nicholas I of Russia in 1814, who put a diamond ring on Brunel's finger and invited him to St. Petersburg. Indeed, by 1814 Brunel had demonstrated in a number of other ways how productive his genius could be for a nation. In 1805 he had invented machines for bending and sawing timber (which stimulated a boom in shipbuilding) and during the War of 1812 he supplied the entire army with shoes. His factory, employing just twenty-four men, turned out four hundred pairs a day in nine sizes. The equipment was so simple to operate that disabled veterans managed the process from beginning to end.

The gratitude of the government, however, was short-lived. With the armistice, Brunel found himself with a surplus of eighty thousand pairs, only half of which, at a fraction of the original cost, the government agreed to buy. Brunel had to unload the rest for practically nothing. This profound reversal to his fortunes came at the worst possible time. The year before, fire had completely destroyed his celebrated sawmills at Battersea. "In two short hours," the London *Times* reported, "those most valuable machines, which in point of execution and perfection, exceed everything we know ... presented the awful sight of a heap of fragments." Brunel had met that blow like a stoic. When a messenger arrived in a sweat, barely able to tell him the news, he merely asked, "Is anybody hurt?" "No," the messenger replied, whereupon Brunel turned to a companion and said, "I can build better machinery now." But when his financial reserves perished utterly with peace, he was not only bankrupt but deeply in debt.

In some ways Brunel had had a hand in his own undoing, for he was a terrible businessman. His accountant, after going over his books, wrote to him: "It was a most extraordinary jumble, which you certainly have not understood; and I should have wondered if you had. I should hardly have been more surprised if one of your saws had walked to town." Creditors now shadowed him constantly, banging on his door at night and calling after him in the street. His life was miserable. On May 14, 1821, he was arrested and cast into King's Bench Debtors Prison. Though spared one of those squalid chambers made famous by Dickens in *Little Dorrit* and *Pickwick*, his fall was hard. "My affectionate wife and myself," he wrote to his friend and influential ally Lord Spencer, "are sinking under it. We have neither rest by day or night. Were my enemies at work to effect my ruin of mind and body, they could not do so more effectually."

Brunel's affection for the English was vanishing. He remembered the Czar's solicitations, and the two men began to correspond. Nicholas was particularly interested in a crossing for the River Neva. Brunel worked out the design for a bridge but then astonished the Czar by suggesting a tunnel instead. Although the idea was almost without precedent, Brunel had been thinking about subaqueous tunnels for years. Ever since that afternoon in Chatham dockyard in 1816 when he observed the little bivalve mollusk boring nonchalantly through the fragment of oak, his special study had been "to imitate (by some mechanical means) the action of this animal."

A subaqueous tunnel had been tried only once. In 1802 the Thames Archway Company undertook a tunnel from Rotherhithe to Limehouse, with Robert Vazie, an experienced Cornish miner, as engineer. Confident pronouncements were made by the company's directors and Vazie, who should have known better, let himself be carried away. His optimism faded, however, when it took a full year to sink an 11-foot-diameter shaft just 42 feet. By that time all the money for the entire undertaking had been consumed. Additional funds were raised and a smaller shaft was sunk instead. Then Richard Trevithick, the great locomotive engineer, was hired as superintendent and a small driftway or exploratory cutting, 5 feet by 3 feet, was begun on August 17, 1807. The cutting was to serve as a drain for the tunnel proper, planned for later. The method of support was timbering.

Remarkable progress was made at first—by Christmas about 950 feet; then workmen hit a pocket of quicksand and part of the roof fell in. Bags of clay were dumped on the riverbed from barges to stanch the breach and by the end of January Trevithick was just a few hundred feet from the opposite shore. From that point onward, however, the work proceeded with exasperating difficulty. There was another cave-in; then another; and then (after repairs) the water burst in with such violence that in fifteen minutes the whole driftway was filled. It became obvious to all that the task was hopeless; the driftway disintegrated like a castle in the sand. "In five years," as Beamish summed up the affair, "they had not even been able to complete their drain, not a single brick had been laid, and everything which had been done was irretrievably lost."

In 1809, a "committee of learned men" sought to determine whether construction of a subaqueous tunnel was actually possible. They offered a prize of £500 to anyone who could come up with a workable plan. Forty-nine proposals were submitted, but the judges found them all preposterous. "We consider," they announced, "that an underground tunnel is *impracticable.*" Brunel, who had followed the controversy with great interest, regarded this conclusion as absurd.

His observation of the shipworm's boring technique sparked his imagination, and then later he worked on plans for a machine that would prove the learned committee wrong. In 1818, he patented the design for a large, circular cast-iron machine which he called a shield. It was divided into "augur-like cells (for miners) which were forced forward with a rotary motion by hydraulic presses, displacing only so much ground as the machine would occupy in its place." The machine provided a mobile backbone to support the tunnel it excavated. Construction of a permanent tunnel structure would take place under the shield's protection. Like the shipworm, the shield lined the passageway as it bore ahead.

Brunel's financial collapse and subsequent imprisonment had prevented further development of the design; but his correspondence with Czar Nicholas, intercepted by British government censors, provided sufficient details to bring the Duke of Wellington to his aid. Wellington, an ardent advocate of a Thames tunnel for military and defense purposes, had many government supporters who regarded such a tunnel as a commercial necessity as well.

Indeed, between 1800 and 1820, the Thames dock system had undergone extensive development and the waterside population had greatly increased on both sides of the river. Each day thousands of people crossed the Thames by ferry or by a roundabout route across London Bridge. Traffic on the bridge was so congested and progress across it so slow that many merchants stood helplessly by as their produce withered in the sun.

The Duke of Wellington brought Brunel's plight—and his scheme—to the attention of the government, which released him at once and helped him out of debt with a "public service acknowledgement" of £5,000. Thus, in August 1821, at the age of fifty-two, Brunel began anew. Famous and admired throughout Europe and America, he was nevertheless quite poor. His son wrote in his diary: "We have neither a horse, a carriage or a footman." But Brunel looked at it this way: "A man who can do something, anything, and keep a warm sanguine heart will never starve."

Still, Brunel was never just after "anything." Over the next three years he revised his shield design (making it rectangular) and rallied support for a Thames tunnel project. He hoped its novelty and daring would redeem both his fortune and his reputation. On February 18, 1824, a meeting of all those interested was held at London Tavern, and after a number of ambitious toasts, the assembly moved to incorporate. The Thames Tunnel

Company was born. As a gesture of confidence—and defiance to all those in doubt—it was decided to drive the tunnel between Rotherhithe and Wapping, not far from where the earlier attempt had failed. Shares were offered, £160,000 were raised, and the tunnel design—a large double archway suitable for vehicular traffic—was approved. Soon thereafter Parliament unanimously passed a bill authorizing construction and on June 24, 1824, the project received Royal Assent.

Brunel estimated that the tunnel, projected to be 1,200 feet long, would take at the most three years to build—by modern standards certainly a very long time. But no one thought so then, not even the company directors whose interest in its engineering significance was as nothing compared to their hopes for financial gain. They announced with satisfaction that *"thirty-nine borings* made upon two parallel lines across the river" had found *"a stratum of strong blue clay of sufficient depth to assure the safety of the tunnel."*

Brunel, buoyed by optimism, moved from his residence in Battersea to No. 3 Bridge Street, Blackfriars, near the site chosen for sinking the first shaft. As he busied himself with "making accurate experiments on the adhesive properties of Roman cement" for the brickwork, Henry Maudslay labored on the gigantic shield at his Lambeth works.

On February 16, 1825, an acre of ground was cleared next to Cow Court, Rotherhithe, 141 feet from the shore. Two weeks later, the first stone for the shaft was laid. A large crowd gathered and the steeple bells of Rotherhithe "rang out their joyful acclamations." For two hundred specially invited guests, a lavish open-air dinner was spread at a table decorated with a model of the tunnel in sugar. During the next three weeks, the shaft rose in place like a small tower: 42 feet high, 50 feet across, and weighing 912 tons, it had an iron curb at its base and was made to descend into the ground by its own weight. Workmen within loosened the gravel uniformly all around and heaped it up in the hollow center, whence it was raised by bucket and windlass. Many dignitaries gathered by the riverside to watch, including the Duke of Wellington, the Duke of Gloucester, the Duke of Somerset, the Duke and Duchess of Cambridge, General Ponsonby, the Duke of Northumberland, Prince Leopold, and Sir Robert Peel. It could hardly be doubted that the tunnel was now regarded as a national undertaking.

But Brunel was uneasy, and found omens in unremarkable events. As the iron curb dug into the gravel it produced a striking sound, at once thunderous and harsh, which reverberated "like the rattling of multitudinous chains" from the walls of the hollow shaft. The tower slipped and tilted and seemed biased for a fall—and would have fallen but for constant realignment. The ground seemed stubbornly to resist its descent. One afternoon a workman arrived drunk, clambered up to the top and fell in, and was killed. About this time, Brunel received a visit from August Pugin (père), the famous architect, who asked him for help in organizing a vast new cemetery to be called the "Necropolis of London." Its secular character—divorcing burial from the place of worship—went over badly with the public and revived misgivings about Brunel and the tunnel itself, which some clergymen had earlier cast in the darkest light by calling it a flirtation with the Underworld.

It was not until mid-October 1825 that the shaft was sufficiently deep and the shield's installation could begin. It was an immense rectangular construction, consisting of twelve massive cast-iron frames jointed together and subdivided into three stories each, forming a sort of iron honeycomb in which thirty-six men could work in individual cells. A team of bricklayers, standing on projections of the outer cells, back to back with the miners, bricked up the walls from behind as the shield was thrust forward by powerful screw-jacks braced against the end of the lining. The cells were protected in front by narrow poling boards which the miners removed one at a time to excavate the earth 6 inches deep. Each board was then fixed forward. When this procedure was completed for all the boards in a frame, the whole frame was advanced and the same series of operations began again. The idea was that at no time would the tunnel be exposed to roof-falls, and only briefly to influxes of soil or water from in front—and then from only a very small area. Almost simultaneous with the excavation, the lining would be laid up in place. Thus, the tunnel could be absolutely secured, inch by inch, without fear. A long platform for the removal of dirt followed like a tail and the whole shield stood on flat soles like feet.

William Hazlitt once said of Nicholas Poussin, the great French painter and Brunel's distant relative: "He applies nature to his own purposes, and works out live images according to the standards of his own thought." Perhaps it is not inappropriate to draw a comparison between the artist's severely organized and idealized landscapes and the mechanical engineer's adaptations from organic life. As Brunel's contemporaries never tired of remarking, the traveling shield operated "like a living thing." On November 28, 1825, it began its long walk toward Wapping.

The tunnel was designed as a rectangular mass of brickwork $22\frac{1}{2}$ feet high by 38 feet wide, subdivided along its entire length into a double horseshoe archway with a wall of open arches in between. By starting the tunnel at a depth of 63 feet (taking into account the incline from the shore to the river's center), Brunel hoped to ensure that at no point would the floor of the tunnel be more than 55 feet below the riverbed. In laying out this course he had followed the best advice available, for every geologist he consulted warned him of a layer of quicksand reported to be farther down. Trial borings in fact had seemed to bear this out. He was led to believe that if he kept his tunnel as close to the riverbed as possible he would encounter only "homogeneous blue clay."

But no sooner did the miners strike forward with their picks than water spurted into the frames. The survey had been all wrong. Blue clay there was indeed, but it was cut by silt, gravel, gypsum, indurated sand, and sand so fine and waterlogged "as to have become absolutely fluid"—quicksand. As one of the engineers noted, with restraint, "the variety of the strata was not foreseen." But it was too late to turn back. The company investment was already large; a year had been spent in the preparations; public doubt about the project was still deep. Brunel hoped it was just an unlucky beginning. But two months later, on January 16, 1826, he could boast an advance of only 14 feet; and on that day water came in again, flooded the heading, and rose to 12 feet in the shaft. Initial efforts to remove the water failed when "the feed pump of the steam engine became deranged." Twelve days later, water and gravel again broke in and a worker nearly drowned.

It was obvious to all it was going to be a long, hard road. Over the next several months, progress was piecemeal—never more than 14 feet in a week. By mid-August 190 feet were done, but under such duress that the resident engineer, Armstrong, had a nervous breakdown and quit. Brunel replaced him with his twenty-year-old son, Isambard, and hired Richard Beamish as his assistant.

The company directors were growing impatient. At the rate the tunnel was going, it would take twice as long as the original maximum estimate, or about six years. They held a meeting and voted for "piece-work"—work paid by how fast it was done. Brunel, foregoing his usual diplomacy, told them point blank that this was folly, that the faster the work went, the more liable it was to hazards of all kinds, since all the men would care about was how much ground they could cut through or how many bricks they could lay in a shift. The whole point of the shield would be undermined. And if there were disasters, no time would be saved after all. He left the meeting in anger, overruled.

Though a compassionate man, Brunel's opinion of the workers was touched with aristocratic disdain. They were the "rudest hands possible," incapable of ingenuity and care. He also shared vicariously in the Englishman's bigotry toward the Irish, which most of the workers were. Their lack of fortitude under stress seemed to him as formidable a problem for the undertaking as the instability of the ground. Beamish, concurring, called it a "moral evil," and complained that "any sudden gush of sand or rattling of gravel upon the frames, would drive them precipitously from their posts." In their flight, they would douse the lamps, as if the Thames were a living thing with eyes that could find them out more easily in the light. Perhaps this was a superstition; more likely it had to do with a religious reminiscence, a sense of the river as a ghostly presence, active and animate and angry in seeking entrance to its own abode. "It is a widespread belief," Sir James Fraser wrote, "that when ghosts return home people light lamps for them as a guide." As inhospitable intruders beneath the Thames, which they could barely keep out with a citadel of iron, the miners had incentive enough to beware the river's wrath.

With regard to "piece-work," however, Brunel was psychologically right. Not long after meeting with the directors, he wrote in his diary: "The miners were reckless. They took out two, three, sometimes four polings at a time." This made the advance uneven; under the unequal strain (for the river pressed down on the shield at 2,000 pounds to the square foot) frames "tipped and skewed out of alignment," iron plates "buckled and broke."

On Friday morning, September 8, 1826, water began cascading down through a fissure in the ceiling of two frames. The breach was stuffed with oakum, but two hours later silt appeared and the men had to work all day to hold it back. At one point during the night, "it burst in with considerable force," and almost resisted the united efforts of three men. From sunset to sunrise Beamish managed only "a feverish dose" of three hours' sleep. Saturday was given over to preventing disaster. On Sunday, leave was canceled for all the men. On Monday, things went from bad to worse. Planks, capped with clay, were braced across the front of the heading while others were forced upward by powerful screw-jacks; but just when this seemed to be making a difference, "gravel and broken pieces of yellow mottled clay" plunged in through a new breach behind. As the men whirled to stop it, "water suddenly appeared again in front in such abundance, as to threaten them with utter destruction." They began running around in pandemonium. Holes were drilled in the brickwork overhead to drain water out of the soil, planks were rushed forward and back, and the men found themselves drawn into a circle, like a wagon train under seige. Meanwhile the deafening sound of water falling in a broken descent 22 feet along the iron floor plates was unnerving.

Shift after shift, the struggle went on for ten days. Beamish sustained extraordinarily long periods of work without sleep—fifty-three hours, twenty hours, twenty-four hours, twenty-one hours. Isambard's shifts were even longer.

On October 22, Isambard collapsed; a week later Beamish had to be carried out of the frames. Brunel went to the board of directors and asked for two more assistants. In November, a Mr. Gravatt, "a trained engineer whose father was a Colonel of Sappers," and a Mr. Riley were taken on. In his first fortnight, Gravatt worked two shifts of forty hours each. Within three months, Riley became delirious and died.

Brunel himself was beginning to go under. He wrote in his diary: "Little do others know of my anxiety and fatigue day and night . . . We have not a period when we can think ourselves safe except when we have connected these arches with a shaft on the other side." He noted his own hours: "Seven days out of the last ten in the tunnel. For each of nine days an average of $20\frac{1}{2}$ hours per day in the tunnel, and $3\frac{2}{3}$ to sleep."

If the roof above was treacherous, like the wall ahead, so was the ground below. Beneath a fragile crust, there was often nothing but quicksand. Efforts to consolidate it by ramming down rubblestone and short piles met with only partial success. One night as Beamish was testing it with a 5-foot crowbar and a 10-foot rod, he cut through a layer of gravel and both implements disappeared right out of his hands.

About 300 feet of the tunnel were now complete and on February 26, 1827, the company directors tried to make some money out of it by admitting visitors during certain hours of the day at a shilling a head. Brunel thought they were mad. In mid-March he wrote: "There being no clay above us, there is much to apprehend from the springs." And a few days later: "Things are getting worse every day . . . We have nothing above our heads but clayey silt." Nevertheless, on April 10, the directors actually staged a concert in the tunnel as a publicity stunt.

The shield was now just short of the middle of the river. Brunel found the faces of the heading "extremely tender . . . we run imminent risks . . . We shall have to fight it out until we have a stronger or thicker stratum of clay." On April 20 a "shower of bones" came down into the tunnel along with pieces of coral and fragments of china and glass. An inspection party searched the riverbed from above in a diving bell and, probing it with an iron rod, struck the top of the shield.

On May Day the workmen went on strike for higher wages and picketed the shaft. Their wages were small—from three shillings three pence to three shillings nine pence a day, less than one dollar. But the directors refused to negotiate and after a week and a half the strikers gave in.

Several days later, when a workman removed a poling board, a shovel plunged right at him into the frame. Someone from the diving bell had left it behind. It was an ominous sign. The "head of earth from 12 to 17 feet in thickness quite undisturbed" that Brunel had counted on above the shield was no longer there— nor anything like it. Dips and pockets in the riverbed had not been taken into account nor had the tendency of the soil to sink above the shield. It was now obvious that nothing but an inch or two of sand lay between them and the Thames. Indeed, it looked as if the tunnel itself might soon be in the river and everything lost.

At two o'clock in the morning on May 18, Beamish relieved Isambard at his post. At five o'clock, as the tide rose, the ground "seemed as though it were alive." Diluted silt came into two of the frames in bursts, like cannon; at six o'clock, when a new shift of men arrived, they milled about the shaft and at first refused to go down. Though that day passed, to everyone's surprise, with "not more than the usual amount of alarm," with the flood-tide the ground again seemed to be swaying. "A strong feeling of apprehension," Beamish wrote, "took possession of my mind." He changed his holiday coat for a "strong weatherproof," his polished Wellingtons for greased mud boots, and put on a large-brimmed southwester—his battle gear.

The tide was now rising fast . . . The miner Goodwin, a powerful and experienced man, called for help. For him to have required help was sufficient to indicate danger. I immediately directed an equally powerful man, Rogers, in No. 9 to go to Goodwin's assistance; but before he had time to obey the order, there poured in such an overwhelming flood of slush and water, that they were both driven out; and a bricklayer (Corps) who had also answered to the call for help, was literally rolled over to the stage behind the frames, as though he had come through a mill sluice, and would have been hurled to the ground, if I had not fortunately arrested his progress. I then made an effort to reenter the frames, calling upon the miners to follow; but I was only answered by a roar of water, which long continued to resound in my ears. Finding that no gravel appeared, I saw that the case was hopeless. To get all the men out of the shield was now my anxiety. This accomplished, I stood for a moment on the stage, unwilling to fly, yet incapable to resist the torrent which momentarily increased in magnitude and velocity, till Rogers, who alone remained, kindly drew me by the arm, and, pointing to the rising water beneath, showed only too plainly the folly of delay...

... On we now sped. At the bottom of the shaft we met Isambard Brunel and Mr. Gravatt. We turned. The spectacle which presented itself will not readily be forgotten. The water came in a great wave, everything on its surface becoming the more distinctly visible as the light from the gas-lamps was more strongly reflected. Presently a loud crash was heard. A small office, which had been erected under the arch, about a hundred feet from the frames, had burst. The pent air rushed out: the lights were suddenly extinguished, and the whole work, which only a few short hours before had commanded the homage of an admiring public, was consigned to darkness and solitude. It only remained to ascend the shaft, but this was not so easy. The men filled the staircase; being themselves out of danger, they entirely forgot the situation of their comrades below. For the first time I now felt something like fear, as I dreaded the recoil of the wave from the circular wall of the shaft, which, if it had caught us, would inevitably have swept us back under the arch. With the utmost difficulty the lowest flight of steps was cleared, when, as I had apprehended, the recoil came, and the water surged just under our feet. The men now hurried up the stairs, and though nearly exhausted, I was enabled to reach the top, where a new cause of anxiety awaited us. A hundred voices shouted, a rope! a rope! save him! save him! How anyone could have been left behind puzzled and pained me sorely. That someone was in the water was certain. With that promptitude that ever distinguished Isambard Brunel, he did not hesitate a moment. Seizing a rope, and followed by Mr. Gravatt, he slid down one of the iron ties of the shaft. The rope was quickly passed round the waist of the struggler, who proved to be old Tillett, the engine man. He had gone to the bottom of the shaft to look after the pumps, and being caught by the water was forced to the surface, from which he would speedily have disappeared, but for the presence of mind and the chivalrous spirit of his officers.

The roll was now called, when, to our unspeakable joy, every man answered to his name.

At one o'clock I threw myself on my bed; and, breathing forth a grateful thanksgiving for the protection which a beneficent Providence had extended to me and to those placed under my charge, I sank, utterly exhausted, into a profound sleep, having been twenty-three hours under unusual anxiety and continuous activity.

The next day two company directors accompanied by a few miners went into the tunnel in a boat One director, who apparently had never been in a small boat before, stood up suddenly, the boat overturned, and one of the miners drowned. Brunel was anguished when he heard about it. Somehow, whenever the directors became involved, they caused some misfortune—by demanding piece-work, which had helped bring on past floods through shoddy work; by insisting on starvation wages, which brought on the strike and made the men chronically surly; and now, after everyone had miraculously been spared in the inundation, their carelessness in a little boat had killed a man. The following Sunday the curate at Rotherhithe denounced the disasters in his sermon as "but the just judgment upon the presumptuous aspirations of mortal man."

It took most of the summer just to pump the tunnel out and get it clean. The archway was seldom dry; on the best of days it was an unwholesome environment. It was like a sewer, a conduit of the Thames which was then the great public sewer of London. Beamish relates that one day when he was inspecting the bottom cells of the shield "a peculiar and indescribable sensation came over me—a haze rose before my eyes and, in the course of half an hour, I lost the sight of my left eye." It was never completely restored. Men became dizzy or outright sick. In early September another man died. Beamish contracted severe pleurisy and was ill for a month.

In spite of these trials, Brunel's faith did not flag. His public remarks were steady, even buoyant at times, and we know from his diary that this was not just a pose. On September 30, he wrote:

How slow our progress must appear to others: but if it is considered how much we have had to do for righting the frames, and for repairing them—what with timbering, shoving, shifting, and refitting, all executed in a very confined situation—the water occasionally bursting in upon us—the ground running in like slush—it is truly terrific to be in the midst of this scene. If to this we couple the actual danger—by the report made by large pieces of cast iron breaking—it is no exaggeration to say that such is the state of things. Nevertheless, my confidence in the shield is not only undiminished; it is, on the contrary, tried with its full effect.

Indeed, his shield was slowly accomplishing what had never been done before; and it could not be denied that it was just about all that stood between the workers and demise. Yet mechanical contrivance is not the only hero of the tale. The image of Isambard dashing bravely through the darkened archway is a recurrent one. It was largely due to his heroic actions in emergencies that some sense of discipline and *esprit de corps* was maintained.

The tunnel had been in progress now for almost two years, and on November 10, it was decided to hold a banquet in it to reassure the public and investors. It was believed that the low point of the riverbed had been passed. The side arches were draped in crimson, and tables were lighted with candelabra "mounted on decorative urns containing patent portable gas." The band of the Coldstream Guards was engaged to play through dinner. Fifty guests of honor sat at one table, while in the adjacent archway a table was spread with warm beer mixed with gin for about a hundred workmen. After toasting their implements, they presented Isambard Brunel with a pickaxe and spade as symbols of their craft. But that evening was almost the swan song of the enterprise.

On January 12, 1827, Isambard Brunel came in on the morning shift with two of his most able assistants, a Mr. Collins and a Mr. Ball, men of skill, courage, and exceptional physical strength. The tide was rising. Collins entered the first frame and began to remove the side-shoring. The exposed ground bellied toward him like a balloon, then popped like a plug in a dike, as an overwhelming torrent of water washed him right out of the cell. A sudden rush of air extinguished the gas lights, cutting the three men off from each other in the dark. As they splashed about in the tunnel, heavy barrels, planks, and tools swept along by the rising tide battered against them like wreckage in a storm. Isambard was momentarily pinned by something thrown against his right leg. By the time he pulled himself loose, water was swirling above his waist. He called out for Ball and Collins, but they did not answer. When he got to the shaft, at the end of the east arch, he found the workmen's staircase crowded. The "morning shift had not all come down, the night shift had not all gone up." Other men, stunned by what was happening below, had simply "stopped and blocked up the passage." Opposite he could see that the visitors' staircase was completely free, but the water was coming on with tremendous force and speed. He did what a swimmer must do in the sea when he is caught too far from the beach: gave himself up to the wave. It "bore him along on its seething, angry surface" toward the far wall, but instead of crushing him against it, raised him like a great pair of hands to the top of the shaft. The recoil of the wave under the arch shattered the ladder and lower staircase to pieces.

Meanwhile Beamish, above, who had been writing out orders for warm beer and gin for the men just coming off the night shift, became aware of the confusion. A watchman rushed in shouting, "The water is in—the tunnel is full!" "My head," Beamish wrote, "felt as though it would burst." He rushed to the workmen's staircase and, finding it blocked, knocked in the side of the visitors' staircase with a crowbar. He had taken two steps down when the wave delivered Isambard into his arms.

For hours afterward Isambard lay in a delirium. Over and over he repeated the names of his two friends, Ball and Collins; but their "well-known voices answered not—they were forever silent."

In all six men died, and Isambard was so badly wracked up that he couldn't work for months. The hole in the riverbed was so large that 4,500 bags of clay and gravel had to be lowered from boats to fill it. Thereafter, though the work went on, it was with a sense of doom. Funds for the project were exhausted; few visitors would dare risk their lives in the tunnel for a shilling's glimpse.

An appeal was made to the country for support. On July 5

friends and promoters of the enterprise gathered at the Free-Mason's Tavern, and a debenture scheme was concocted. Although £18,000 were at once subscribed, it was not enough. Apparently, the tunnel had failed.

The shield was bricked up in place. A mirror was erected at the end of the visitors' arch, and the arch stuccoed and lighted with gas. Eventually, pedestrians were drawn back to it as a "site" and in this way it yielded the company a small investment return.

It was a sad time for all who had been involved. After two and a half years, the work was barely half done. Brunel's spectacular career of brilliant public undertakings appeared to have climaxed in defeat.

The tunnel became an object of derision. Journalists nicknamed it the "Great Bore," and Thomas Hood, the rhymer, suggested it be turned into a wine cellar:

> *I'll tell thee with thy Tunnel what to do;*
> *Light up thy boxes; build a bin or two,*
> *The wine does better than such water trades,*
> *Stick up a sign, the sign of the Bore's Head;*
> *I've drawn it ready for thee in black lead,*
> *And make thy cellar subterranean—the Shades!*

But Brunel had no apology to make. In fact, in 1829 he declared proudly:

> We have completed and secured the work as we proceeded and in spite of the difficulty we have encountered, we have never lost a single foot of what has been completed. We have a substantial structure, the strength of which has been proved beyond a doubt; whereas with regard to the driftway heading of 1808, nothing remains but the recollection of it.

Thus was the Thames Tunnel to remain for seven years, solid and permanent in what Beamish wryly described as "vegetable mould and loamy sand." Brunel's own good spirits during this period baffled his acquaintances. One, Charles MacFarlane, wrote: "What I most admired of all about him was his thorough simplicity and unworldliness of character, his indifference to mere lucre . . . Evidently he had lived as if there were no rogues in the world." Not quite, but his essential nobility of mind had somehow prevailed.

Revival of the project was largely the result of international interest. Taken seriously throughout the world, the tunnel assumed renewed importance in England. The Duke of Wellington obtained a government loan of £246,000 for the company and Brunel was showered with honors. In Paris, he received a silver medal from L'Academe de l'Industrie de Paris; the Viceroy of Egypt requested that he design a tunnel under the Nile; King William IV of England invited Brunel to come and discuss his plans; and the Royal Society formed a Tunnel Club.

The brick wall at the end of the tunnel was demolished and piece by piece the old shield was removed. It was a difficult procedure. One company director asserted he would eat any part of it that came out. By March 1837, however, it was out and the new shield in, with no more serious mishap than the crushing of a man's finger.

Time had brought change. Isambard, too caught up in his own accelerating career to return to the project, was destined to become one of the greatest railway engineers of the age. He would lay 1,000 miles of track throughout Great Britain and Ireland, and build bridges and enormous ships, including the first successful transatlantic steamer, the *Great Western*, which in 1857 made the journey in fifteen days. His *Great Eastern* of 1858—also known as the *Leviathan*—was the largest ship in the world until the beginning of the twentieth century. Beamish, Isambard's loyal lieutenant, was chosen to take his place.

The new shield (weighing 140 tons) was stronger and more versatile than its predecessor. But the river was the same. And so were the company directors, who rode Brunel hard. They introduced "contract work"—what Brunel called "piece-work on a large scale, . . . always done with as cheap materials and in as slight a way as can be admitted by the specifications." The renewed anxieties brought on a stroke. "An extraordinary stiffness has come over me," he recorded in his journal, "and a nervous irritability such as I have never before felt." He also began to have heart trouble.

For the first three months the work went fairly well. But on June 21, at high tide, it was the old story. "The whole ground above and in front seemed to be in motion," and then the water poured in, 500 gallons per minute into the top boxes alone. Nevertheless, by the end of August, 55 more feet of the tunnel were completed.

At this point Beamish, whose health had been in rapid decline, chose to retire. His successor, a Mr. Gordon, lasted a single month. He was succeeded by a Mr. Page. In the following weeks the progress was minute, on the average just a few feet a week. The river kept breaking in—on August 23, November 2, and on March 21, 1838.

There were other problems, familiar but now more intense. Beamish, even in absentia, chronicled the story: "The water from the springs came largely impregnated with poisonous sulphuretted hydrogen gas; the black mud which rolled in spread its foul, noxious, pestilential influence throughout the works." Disinfecting agents failed:

A sudden irrigation of sixty cubic feet of this mud and water at once neutralized all such appliances. The only mode of modifying the effect upon the health of the men, was to limit the number of hours of underground work, and to secure ventilation. Still, the men gradually sank under such overwhelming trials. Inflammation of the eyes, sickness, debility and eruptions on the skin, were the most prevalent symptoms; and if exertion were long continued, the men would fall senseless in the frames, often at a time when their efforts were most needed. An explosive gas, or firedamp, also spread dismay among the laborers. Large puffs of fire would pass from twenty to twenty-five feet across the shield.

Over the next two years Brunel's diary tells us all we need to know:

Works have been uneasy during the night . . . ground very tender . . . ground very threatening . . . things had a terrific appearance this morning, after a very serious struggle for the night.

. . .

Illness; the men complain very much . . . the effluvia was so offensive that some were sick on the stage.

. . .

Heywood died this morning. Page is sinking very fast. It affects the eyes—I feel much debility after having been some time below. All complain of pain in the eyes . . . On Sunday a bricklayer fell senseless on the top floor.

These frightful developments induced the most melancholy thoughts:

This night, viz, about 10 o'clock, walking as I did, up and down the arches which are lighted enough to give an exterior view of the work, I could not refrain from the reflection that the brave men who are agents for a work like this one are so many men that are sacrificed, and my assistants likewise; that in a few weeks, most probably they will be lingering under the influence of a slow and insidious poison.

During this period Brunel "lived within a few yards of the Rotherhithe shaft . . . Every night he went down to the tunnel for a couple of hours to see how things were going. When he reached his seventieth birthday, his wife insisted he spend his nights in bed." Thereafter, "at two-hour intervals throughout the night, a bell would ring beside his bed and, by hauling on a string, he would raise a little basket to the window"—containing either fresh samples of soil from the heading or a succinct report from one of the assistant engineers. Brunel would "scribble a note in reply"—emergency instructions, if necessary—and send the basket back down.

On April 4, 1840, the heading finally came within low-water mark, about 90 feet from the site of the proposed Wapping shaft. The ground over the shield was observed to sink. "People ran in crowds to the wharfs and warehouses; those that could obtain a boat pushed off to the nearest vessels in the river, with the vague idea that they might witness the destruction of the tunnel, and perhaps the struggles of those engaged in its execution. On an area of *thirty feet diameter* the ground had gone down bodily, leaving a cavity *thirteen feet in depth.*" Meanwhile, inside the shield itself, a noise was heard like "the roaring of thunder," immediately followed by a rush of air which extinguished every light. All but a few of the men fled, bewildered and amazed. Everyone expected the water to come pouring in. But the tunnel was spared.

In October, work began on the Wapping shaft. The ground was cleared and a wide assortment of ships' parts was unearthed—masts, iron ties, chains, tools, and timber. The spot turned out to have once been a ship-breaker's yard. It took thirteen months to sink the shaft just 7 feet.

Though it would not be until December 12, 1842, that the shaft and tunnel linked up, and an additional year before the whole work was perfected, everyone now knew the tunnel would be done. On March 24, 1841, Brunel was knighted.

Two years later, on March 25, 1843, the tunnel was officially opened, "greeted with an outburst of popular prints, medals and handkerchiefs." A "Tunnel Waltz" was composed for the occasion and the Lord Mayor headed the list of invited dignitaries. The band of the Fusilier Guards led the procession through the tunnel, according to the London *Times*, followed by the Standard-Bearer,

> and persons carrying various flags and banners, the clerk, the solicitor, the acting engineer, the surveyor, the chief engineer, the chairman of the board of directors, the directors, the treasurer, the auditors, the proprietors, and lastly the visitors, an immense number of persons, including ladies . . .
>
> The majority of the visitors went the whole distance, 1200 feet; many, however, proceeded only a little way, pausing and looking about with an air of suspicion every four or five yards, while some would not venture into the tunnel at all, but remained in the shaft or on the staircase, yet amongst the majority there was a perceptible anxiety, and notwithstanding the brilliance of the lights, the singular reverberations of the music, the shouting of the admirers of the undertaking, and all the means that were taken to give *éclat* to the event, and encouragement to the spectators, notwithstanding also the physical heat that oppressed them, it was evident that there was a lurking chilling fear in the breasts of many.

In the first twenty-four hours, 50,000 people passed through; by April 30, 495,000; within fifteen weeks, 1 million. On July 26,

Queen Victoria herself came down in a barge with Prince Albert to inspect the work.

The tunnel had taken eighteen years and one month to complete, at a cost of £600,000. From shaft to shaft, the total length was just 400 yards, for the Thames is by no means an exceptionally broad river. Even so, it was regarded as one of the wonders of the world. People asked about it as far away as Constantinople; and it is said that "in a remote Calabrian monastery, where the monks thought England rather smaller than Rome," it was a topic of earnest discussion.

The American writer Nathaniel Hawthorne, then a vice-consul in Liverpool, visited the tunnel in 1855, and described it as "an arched corridor of apparently interminable length, gloomily lighted with jets of gas at regular intervals—plastered at the sides and stone beneath the feet . . . It would have made an admirable prison . . . There are people who spend their lives there, seldom or never, I presume, seeing any daylight; except perhaps a little in the morning. All along the extent of this corridor, in little alcoves, there are stalls or shops, kept principally by women, who, as you approach, are seen through the dusk offering for sale views of the tunnel, put up with a little magnifying glass in cases of Derbyshire spar." Numerous frescoes depicting famous places around the world decorated the walls of the entry shafts.

Although the tunnel had been intended for vehicular traffic, with 40-foot-wide spiral roadways enclosed in enormous shafts, for twenty-three years it was used as a pedestrian crossing, with a toll of a penny a head. "By day the great tunnel was filled with stall-holders, like an underground street market, and sometimes the foot passengers' homeward journey was enlivened by an exhibition of paintings, or a fancy fair with games of chance, 'Mysterious ladies' and 'American Wizards.' When darkness cloaked the riverside streets the connecting arches became the refuge of the temporarily embarrassed and the chronically down-and-out. The tunnel was London's cheapest doss-house. The habitues, mindful of the flaring gas-lights, named it Hades Hotel."

Promotional engravings portrayed the archways in the most

convivial light: gentlewomen in bonnets and hoopskirts enjoy the promenade with their children; sunlight appears to be visible at the distant end of a perspective view, which of course was not the case. In other depictions, such as the German engraving reproduced on page 46, a more accurate image of the clientele comes through.

In 1865 the East London Railway Company bought the tunnel, and it became part of the London Underground system when the company built approaches for its trains. It was indeed a soundly made thing—Underground trains run through it today.

Vindicated as he was in the end, and in all his glory, Brunel aspired to a standard still higher than his success. When someone praised his tunnel, as he felt, overmuch, he replied: *"Neanmoins, si je l'avais à refaire je ferais mieux"*—"Nevertheless, if I had to do it over again, I'd do it better."

CHAPTER 3

At
the Brink
of
Chaos

Among the many remarkable illustrations that John Martin rendered for an edition of Milton's *Paradise Lost* during the years when the Thames Tunnel was under construction, there is one which portrays the bridge built by Satan, Sin, and Death from Earth over Chaos down to Hell. It is called "At the Brink of Chaos" and, in a manner habitual with Martin, adapts its subject to the contemporary scene: a land bridge traverses an abyss-like tunnel resembling a gigantic mine; horseshoe-shaped arches suggest multiple tunnels within its depths. Martin is said to have based his illustration on various promotional engravings which optimistically pictured how the Thames Tunnel would appear—only instead of showing a cheerfully well-lit, airy interior, his is deep in gloom.

Martin's prestige as an artist rivaled that of Turner at the time, but he was also a lay engineer. He proposed a method for ventilating mines and outlined a system for improving London's water supply, which received distinguished support. He was sensitive to developments around him and while he possessed, perhaps more than most, an apocalyptic turn of mind, his ominous vision was hardly extreme.

In 1825, when Brunel began to sink the first shaft of his tunnel beside the Thames, the course of the Industrial Revolution had already been critically determined. His adventure was one of its early culminations, as important in its own way as the inauguration of the Railway Age with the Liverpool & Manchester, the first passenger railway in the world, in November 1830. The Industrial Revolution came out of the mine. The mine was the womb; from it emerged, along with iron and coal, the steam engine—"like a giant," said Samuel Taylor Coleridge, "with one idea." The havoc wrought, in a thousand and one ways, was well on its blundering course toward prosperity when Martin cast about for a fitting image for his Miltonic parable.

Mining of course did not begin with the Industrial Revolution; its history is long. In all likelihood it has always represented the material aspect of man's immemorial quest for possessions of value: for knowledge and wisdom, silver and gold, precious gems and useful minerals of every kind. (The Greek verb *metallao* itself means "to search.") The twenty-eighth chapter of the Book of Job, inspired by an Egyptian copper mine near the Dead Sea, took this quest as its theme:

> Surely there is a vein for the silver, and a place for gold where they fine it.
> Iron is taken out of the earth, and brass is molten out of the stone . . .
> There is a path which no fowl knoweth, and which the vulture's eye hath not seen:
> The lion's whelps have not trodden it, nor the fierce lion passed by it . . .
> But where shall wisdom be found? and where is the place of understanding? . . .

Paths "which no fowl knoweth, and which the vulture's eye hath not seen" had been cut deep into the earth, from North America to the Far East; millennia before Christ gold and silver, copper and lead, mercury and tin, as well as key minerals like salt had been drawn out of mines in sometimes prodigious quantities. The search for tool-making metals other than bronze led to the mining of iron in 1200 B.C., probably in Armenia. Some early mines were extensive, and grew into veritable labyrinths, like the iron mines of Monte Valero worked by the Etruscans and Tyrrhenians. Known as the "hundred rooms," they were revived in the mid-nineteenth century, when the demand for iron reached an unprecedented height.

With only a few exceptions (primarily in Renaissance Saxony), mining was done by forced labor under appalling conditions. "In the confines of Egypt," wrote a Greek geographer in the second century B.C.,

> there is a place full of rich gold mines . . . Out of these laborious mines, those appointed overseers cause the gold to be dug up by the labour of a vast multitude of people. For the Kings of Egypt condemn to these mines notorious criminals, captives taken in war, persons sometimes falsely accused, or against whom the King is incensed; and not only they themselves, but sometimes all their kindred and relations together with them, are sent to work here . . . all bound in fetters, where they work continually, without being admitted any rest night or day . . .
>
> No care at all is taken of their bodies . . . they have not a rag so much as to cover their nakedness . . . These miserable creatures always expect the future to be more terrible than even the present, and therefore long for death as far more desirable than life.

Two thousand years later, when the great naturalist Carolus Linnaeus visited the Falu copper mine in 1734, he found conditions hardly more humane:

> The mine is more terrifying than Hades as described by classical writers and Hell as painted in the sermons of our clergy. The sulphurous smoke poisons the air and kills everything growing and fills the cavities of the mine with evil fumes, dust and heat. Here, 1,200 men labour, shut off from the light of the sun, slaves under the metal, less men than beasts, surrounded by soot and darkness. Fear of being crushed under falling rock never leaves them for a moment. These *damnati* work naked to the waist and have before their mouths a woolen cloth to prevent them from breathing too much smoke and dust. They cannot take a breath of pure air, and sweat streams from their bodies as water out of a bag.

Metal mining also had a destructive effect on the environment, mainly through its multitudinous consumption of wood for fuel. Three thousand years before Christ, incessant copper and tin mining had exhausted the forests of Egypt's Fertile Crescent, leading one modern historian to conclude: "The price of maintaining a culture built on metals is high: it means, eventually, complete collapse. The depletion of the timber range upsets the natural balance, and the land that began as an arboreal abode for foraging men and beasts finishes as a useless wasteland scourged by the sun and scoured by floods, with an interesting past but no future. To eat the apple of metallurgical knowledge is a sure way to close the gates of Paradise." By the mid-sixteenth century this process was being repeated in Europe. Georgius Agricola, in his account of metal mining in Germany, foresaw the full extent of the threatening disaster: ". . . when the woods and groves are felled, there are exterminated the beasts and birds, very many of which furnish pleasant and agreeable food for man. Further, when the ores are washed, the water which has been used poisons the brooks and streams, and either destroys the fish or drives them away."

The quest for coal, undertaken in part to deliver civilization from this extremity, led to the Industrial Revolution and gave it its distinctive character. Coal was not unknown to earlier ages. The Chinese apparently used coal as long ago as 1000 B.C.; Marco Polo in his wanderings through Cathay in the thirteenth century A.D. confirmed that the Chinese used a black stone, probably coal, for fuel. The Greeks and Romans may have been acquainted with it—Theophrastus in his *Treatise on Stones* seems to refer to it—and archaeological expeditions in England have uncovered coal ashes in Roman remains. A thirteenth-century chronicle written by a monk at Liège speaks of "black earth very similar to charcoal in use by metalworks," and other records from the same period disclose that shallow pits were being worked in England, Scotland, and on the Continent. But coal had an evil reputation. Henry III of England grudgingly allowed it to be mined on a limited scale, but shortly thereafter, by the reign of Edward II (1239–1300), its noxious fumes caused such distress that anyone caught burning it might be sentenced to death.

Nevertheless, by the seventeenth century feeling about coal had changed dramatically and its mining became the technological spearhead of an effort to save the woodlands. English poets such as John Cleveland, fired with nationalism, celebrated the Newcastle coal pits as a new "Indies" and "Peru" of boundless wealth. The mines soon fostered a technology that held out promise for the whole society.

In order to keep the pits productive, miners had to descend deeper and deeper into the veins. The more profound the quest, the more liable the works were to inundations, and correspondingly the harder they were to drain. After a time, bucket-chains driven by horse-powered waterwheels simply could not meet the need. As early as 1630 it was recognized that an engine would have to be devised that could, as one prophet of the steam engine put it, "raise water from Lowe Pitts by fire." Beginning in 1712, the challenge was successively met by the simple steam engine of Thomas Newcomen and the later improved models of James Watt. By the late 1700's the steam engine had become sophisticated enough to be used in other industries as well, such as weaving (e.g., the power loom), and ultimately to power the locomotive. Even with his shield, Brunel, of course, would not have been able to keep his tunnel clear of water without the steam pump.

During this period the iron industry, which had ample use for the steam engine, found a new use for coal. Abraham Darby, the master of Coalbrookdale iron works in the Shropshire Valley, discovered a technique for smelting iron ore with coke, a residual distillation of coal, rather than with lime and charcoal in the blast furnace. As the industry boomed, coal was also adopted for use in forging and rolling the smelted ore. Thus foundries followed the blast furnaces out of the wooded areas into the coal regions. In some places where iron and coal were found together, as at Coalbrookdale, a comprehensive industry of coal and iron mines, blast furnaces, lime kilns, foundries, and factories evolved to turn the raw materials into commercial products. A large proportion of the population shifted from agricultural districts in the south to the new mining districts of the Midlands and north.

This rapid march of progress had a retrograde motion that was more or less invisible at first to all but those who actually worked in the mines—or who had grown up in their shadow, like John Martin, for he was a Newcastle boy. In their depths the future—and calamitous past—might indeed be read. A man in a coal mine is set against the four elements of the world: "Fire menaces him in blasting, in the firing of the coal, and in the explosions of the damp; the air, by becoming rarefied, or mixed with mephitic or explosive vapours; the earth, in falling rock or soil; the water, by inundation." The Thames Tunnel miners came to know most of these perils well.

Fire damp, a constant hazard, is an explosive gas of hydrogen and carbon that accumulates in pores and fissures of the coal, often under very great pressure, and "bursts out with a gurgling sound like effervescing water." At a high temperature, or when subjected to flame, the hydrogen and carbon separate to combine with oxygen, producing an explosion. Fire damp is also liable to spontaneous combustion, from the heat generated by the decomposition of iron pyrites in the coal as they come into contact with moisture. Common practice was for one miner to go ahead of the rest and extend a flame, exploding away the accumulated gas. Such a man was called a *penitent*, wrapped as he was "in a covering of wool or leather, with his head enveloped in a hood like a monk's cowl." When fire damp explodes, it produces carbonic acid, the other deadly gas of the mine, not in itself a poison but simply irrespirable. Sometimes called "choke damp," it is also given off by the respiration of men and animals. From the gunpowder blasting came other unhealthy emanations, such as sulphuretted hydrogen and ammoniacal vapors. Thus, as one contemporary put it, "everything concurs to vitiate the air of a coal mine. Not only does the labyrinth of works sometimes oppose very considerable difficulties to the diffusion of fresh air proceeding from without, but the composition of this air soon becomes changed." Moreover, "the soil above a burning coal mine is barren and baked: hot vapours escape from it ... The sulphur deposits itself around vents in coatings of a citron-yellow colour, acid gases are evolved, and it is a sort of pseudo-volcano."

By the middle of the nineteenth century some mines had developed into virtual underground cities. Miners had to carry compasses to find their way about, and it was rumored that in the salt mines of Austrian Gallicia and the Czarist penal colonies of Siberia men passed their whole lives under ground from birth. One contemporary wrote after a visit to a French mine that its corridors diverged

> in all directions like the streets of a town with many turnings. There are crossroads and squares; each road has its name and destination, but as there are no sign posts, a stranger loses his way at first . . . Some of the galleries, which are long, wide, and well-ventilated, form the principal thoroughfares and great streets, constituting the fine quarter of the mine. The others, which are sometimes low, narrow, tortuous, ill-supplied with air, kept in bad repair, and liable besides to be in only temporary use, are like the old quarters which will soon have to disappear. This underground town is inhabited night and day; it is lighted, but with lamps. It has railways, traversed by horses and locomotives. It has streams, canals, and fountains—strong springs of water which, in truth, could very well be dispensed with. There are even certain plants and creatures which are peculiar to it, and life, as has been said, seems to assume special forms in it. It is the black and deep city, the city of coal, and the lively center of labour.

Gradually the terrain above took on the character of the mine below. When Arthur Young visited Coalbrookdale in 1776 he found it "a very romantic spot," despite the "variety of horrors art has spread at the bottom." The striking contrast of its "winding glen between two immense hills . . . all thickly covered with wood," with the "noise of the forges," "the flames bursting from the furnaces," and "the smoke of the lime kilns," struck him as "altogether sublime."

But time would wear away the romantic aspect. Around 1800, Charles Dibdin wrote in his *Observations on a Tour*: "Really, if an atheist who had never heard of Coalbrookdale could be transported there in a dream and left to awake at the mouth of one of those furnaces, though he had been all his life the most profligate unbeliever, that added blasphemy to incredulity, he would infallibly tremble at the last judgment that in imagination would appear to him." And when John Britton, the antiquarian and railroad enthusiast, traveled through the industrial heartland from Birmingham to Wolverhampton in 1850, he found "a region of smoke and fire filling the whole area between earth and heaven." Figures "of human shape—if shape they had—were seen to glide from one cauldron of curling-flame to another. The eye could not descry any form or colour indicative of country—of the hues and aspect of nature, or anything human or divine." The landscape had become a living hell. Perhaps the most telling description was given slightly later by James Nasmyth, the inventor of the steam hammer and very much a man of the new industrial age, when he paid a visit to Dudley Castle:

> The Black Country is anything but picturesque. The earth seems to have been torn inside out. Its entrails are strewn about; nearby the entire surface of the ground is covered with cinder-heaps and mounds of scoriae. The coal, which has been drawn from below ground, is blazing on the surface. The district is crowded with iron furnaces. By day and night the country is glowing with fire, and the smoke of the ironworks hovers over it. There is a rumbling and clanking of iron forges and rolling mills. Workmen covered with smut, and with fierce white eyes, are seen moving about amongst the glowing iron and the dull thud of forge-hammers.
>
> Amidst these flaming, smoky, clanging works, I beheld the remains of what had once been happy farmhouses, now deserted. The ground underneath them had sunk by the working out of the coal, and they were falling to pieces. They had in former times been surrounded by clumps of trees; but only the skeletons of them remained, dilapidated, black, and lifeless. The grass had been parched and hulled by the vapours of sulphureous acid thrown out by the chimneys; and every herbaceous object was of a ghastly gray—the emblem of vegetable death in its saddest aspect. Vulcan had driven out Ceres. In some places I heard a sort of chirping sound, as of some forlorn bird haunting the ruins of the old farmsteads. But no! the chirrup was a vile delusion. It proceeded from the shrill creaking of the coal-winding chains, which were placed in small tunnels beneath the hedgeless road.

This was the new Underworld of the earth, so like the mythological version even in its birdless or "avernal" aspect; and there were places like it growing up all over northern Europe.

The environment of the mine, which at first transfigured only the mining camp and those areas where mine-related industries were concentrated, eventually spread across the entire land-scape. Industrial towns were transformed into "dark hives, bus-ily puffing, clanking, screeching, smoking for twelve and fourteen hours a day, sometimes going around the clock. The slavish routine of the mines, whose labor was an intentional punishment for criminals, became the normal environment of the new industrial worker," inspiring Blake to write:

O Satan, my youngest born, art thou not Prince of the Starry Hosts
And of the Wheels of Heaven, to turn the Mills day & night . . .
Get to thy Labours at the Mills & leave me to my wrath . . .
Thy Work is Eternal Death with Mills & Ovens & Cauldrons.

Dickens created a composite portrait of the new settlements in his novel *Hard Times*. He called his prototype "Coketown."

It was a town of red brick, or of brick that would have been red if the smoke and ashes had allowed it; but, as matters stood it was a town of unnatural red and black like the painted face of a sav-age. It was a town of machinery and tall chimneys, out of which interminable serpents of smoke trailed themselves for ever and ever, and never got uncoiled. It had a black canal in it, and a river that ran purple with ill-smelling dye, and vast piles of buildings full of windows where there was a rattling and a trembling all day long, and where the piston of the steam-engine worked monot-onously up and down, like the head of an elephant in a state of melancholy madness . . .

Nature, he goes on, "was as strongly bricked out as killing airs and gases were bricked in," and among "the labyrinth of courts upon courts, and close streets upon streets, which had come into existence piecemeal—the whole unnatural family, shouldering, and trampling, and pressing one another to death," even the chimneys wanted "air to make a draught." Thus Coketown, seen from a distance on a sunny summer's day,

. . . lay shrouded in a haze of its own, which appeared impervious to the sun's rays. You only knew the town was there, because you knew there could have been no such sulky blotch upon the prospect without a town. A blur of soot and smoke, now confusedly tending this way, now that way, now aspiring to the vault of Heaven, now murkily creeping along the earth, as the wind rose and fell, or changed its quarter: a dense formless jumble, with sheets of cross light in it, that showed nothing but masses of darkness:—Coketown in the distance was suggestive of itself, though not a brick of it could be seen . . .

The streets were hot and dusty on the summer day, and the sun was so bright that it even shone through the heavy vapour drooping over Coketown, and could not be looked at steadily. Stokers emerged from low underground doorways into factory yards, and sat on steps, and posts, and palings, wiping their swarthy visages, and contemplating coals. The whole town seemed to be frying in oil. There was a stifling smell of hot oil everywhere. The steam-engines shone with it, the dresses of the Hands were soiled with it, the mills throughout their many stories oozed and trickled it. The atmosphere of those Fairy palaces was like the breath of the simoom; and their inhabitants, wasting with heat, toiled languidly in the desert. But no temperature made the melancholy mad elephants more mad or more sane. Their wearisome heads went up and down at the same rate, in hot weather and cold, wet weather and dry, fair weather and foul. The measured motion of their shadows on the walls, was the substitute Coketown had to show for the shadows of rustling woods; while, for the summer hum of insects, it could offer, all the year round, from the dawn of Monday to the night of Saturday, the whirr of shafts and wheels.

Older, more established cities like London did not escape some aspects of Coketown's fate. "In a greater or lesser degree," writes Lewis Mumford, "every city in the Western World was stamped with archetypal characteristics of Coketown. Industrialism, the main creative force of the nineteenth century, produced the most degraded urban environment the world had yet seen; for even the quarters of the ruling classes were befouled and over-crowded." The new manufacturing turned large areas into factory slums, and there were fiery furnaces and cauldrons enough to send over the metropolis a semi-permanent pall of smoke, gases, and fumes. Overcrowding aggravated the squalor, for in the rough and desperate scrimmage for space people squeezed into nooks and crannies otherwise not deemed fit for habitation. A large proportion of the populace came to live in jerry-built houses leaned back to back or in unventilated courts, cellars, and basements. The new industrial town and the old town newly industrialized—with its air, its rivers and streams (become sewers), its people, thus transformed—was on the verge of becoming a town underground.

Indeed, it is a large question whether this is not, after all, the critical fact in our story: that as life above came to resemble life below, modeled on the mine, it became possible for people to reconcile themselves to living in the Underworld. With our late twentieth-century toxic wastes, vehicular fumes, and threatened nuclear fallout, we still maintain this sad psychological adaptation, though its original cause has by now almost vanished from memory.

The agent of transformation was the railway, hauling the products of the mine to and fro, connecting industrial settlements and creating new ones where none had been before. "Wherever the iron rails went," Mumford has written, "the mine and its debris went with them . . . The rushing locomotives brought noise, smoke, grit, into the hearts of the towns." They also brought people, building up populations at a tremendous rate. Congestion during this period, all historians agree, can be traced to one overriding cause: the iron horse. Its fifteen-year gallop across England culminated but did not end with the so-called Railway Mania of 1845–46. George Stephenson, one of its prime movers, was himself appalled and astonished at its headlong pace. He had once declared proudly: "The strength of England lies in her iron and coal beds; and the locomotive is destined above all agencies to bring it forth. The Lord Chancellor now sits upon a bag of wool, but wool has long ceased to be emblematical of the staple economy of England; he ought to sit upon a bag of coals." Yet in 1830, when there were just eight railway bills before Parliament, he was moved to write: "It is really shameful the way the country is going to be cut up by railways"—a sentiment echoed by Isambard Brunel: "Here the whole world is railway mad. I am really sick of hearing proposals made."

Whence had the railway come? The earliest depiction we have

of a railway is from a sixteenth-century engraving of a mine in Saxony; it shows a wagon on wooden rails leading out of the tunnel's mouth. Although the locomotive or self-propelling steam engine (itself a derivative of the mine) would eventually give the railway hegemony overland, the railway itself, powered by human and animal labor, was born underground. The standard gauge of its tracks, fixed at 4 feet 8½ inches, was the "coal wagon gauge," as Isambard Brunel dubbed it in scorn; and it was for the mines of Cornwall that the first iron rails were forged. Aptly enough, the locomotive that on June 13, 1842, pulled the train carrying Queen Victoria on her first ride—thus christening the new invention with Royal Assent—was called the "Phlegethon," after one of the rivers of the Underworld.

The first railway had in fact been a sort of subway, serving the underground cities of iron and coal. It emerged from the mine, carried its message aross the land, then plunged back into the earth, in time taking much of the rest of the world along.

CHAPTER 4

St. George
and the
Fleet Ditch

I n the history of the world's subways, the Thames Tunnel must take a major place. First, because it stimulated an invention that would later figure prominently in subway development; second, because it proved that tunnels could be driven through any kind of ground; and third, because it introduced tunnels—particularly transportation tunnels—into the urban environment as a solution to traffic congestion. In London, its immediate impact was immense: it put the idea of road tunnels "in the air." The railway interests then moved swiftly to give it "a local habitation and a name."

The Thames Tunnel euphoria coincided almost exactly with the Railway Mania at its height. Though rails had begun to "cut up the countryside" of England without much governmental interference, they had not yet been able to get in through the city gates. In a takeover metaphorically reminiscent of the time-honored use of tunneling to besiege a town, they now tried to invade the precincts of London like sappers, underground. The suddenness of this maneuver had all the advantages associated with a military surprise.

In 1825, when Brunel was about to embark on his subaqueous adventure, there was no local transportation service in London of any kind. The first line of horse-drawn coaches was introduced in 1829 by George Shillibeer, who hoped to duplicate the thriving business he had established in Paris ten years before.

London's burgeoning population certainly warranted this first stirring toward "mass transit," although the city government had not yet adapted its ordinances to facilitate its growth. It was still illegal, for example, to pick up or set down passengers in the streets; since this was necessary for any real service, gypsy lines operated in constant violation of the law. To avoid arrest, drivers sometimes chained themselves to their seats. The government soon acquiesced and made a virtue of necessity. In 1832 it passed the Stage Carriage Act.

Coach service thereafter grew quickly. By 1835, nearly eight hundred carriages were in operation. During the snowy months these were replaced by huge sleighs drawn by four- and six-horse matched teams. The drivers, unusually burly men of great girth, went to extreme lengths to ensure patronage. According to Dickens, they would sometimes seize a hesitant pedestrian by force and just throw him in. Shillibeer soon saw his competitive advantage disappear, and within a few years he was doing time for his debts. After his release from prison, he tried smuggling French brandy into England. Eventually he found modest prosperity as an undertaker with a funeral carriage of his own, patented design.

The development of railways in England, however, was so rapid that by the time coach service had established itself in London, large railroad termini were already on the city's fringe. Many arguments were advanced for letting the railroads in, especially the non-argument of the doctrine of progress. This peculiar idea, still so much with us, was favored equally by liberal reformers and industrial tycoons. Among its more imposing advocates was Thomas Babington Macaulay, the great English historian, who singled out the recent history of public transportation as sound evidence for an optimistic historical view. In his *History of England* he heaped scorn on all who might disagree.

During the years which immediately followed the Restoration, a diligence ran between London and Oxford in two days. The passengers slept at Beaconsfield. At length, in the spring of 1669, a great and daring innovation was attempted. It was announced that a vehicle, described as the Flying Coach, would perform the whole journey between sunrise and sunset. . . . At the close of the reign of Charles the Second, flying carriages ran thrice a week from London to the chief towns.

This mode of travelling, which by Englishmen of the present day would be regarded as insufferably slow, seemed to our ancestors wonderfully and indeed alarmingly rapid. In a work published a few months before the death of Charles the Second, the flying coaches are extolled as far superior to any similar vehicles ever known in the world. Their velocity is the subject of special commendation, and is triumphantly contrasted with the sluggish pace of the continental posts. But with boasts like these was mingled the sound of complaint and invective. The interests of large classes had been unfavorably affected by the establishment of the new diligences; and, as usual, many persons were, from mere stupidity and obstinacy, disposed to clamour against the innovation, simply because it was an innovation. It was vehemently argued that this mode of conveyance would be fatal to the breed of horses and to the noble art of horsemanship; that the Thames, which had long been an important nursery of seamen, would cease to be the chief thoroughfare from London up to Windsor and down to Gravesend; that saddlers and spurriers would be ruined by the hundreds; that numerous inns, at which mounted travellers had been in the habit of stopping, would be deserted, and would no longer pay any rent; that the new carriages were too hot in summer and too cold in winter; that the passengers were grievously annoyed by invalids and crying children; that the coach sometimes reached the inn so late that it was impossible to get supper, and sometimes started so early that it was impossible to get breakfast. On these grounds it was gravely recommended that no public carriage should be permitted to have more than four horses, to start oftener than once a week, or go more than thirty miles a day. It was hoped that, if this regulation were adopted, all except the sick and the lame would return to the old mode of travelling. Petitions embodying such opinions as these were presented to the king in council from several companies of the City of London, from several provincial towns and from the justices of several counties. We smile at these things. It is not impossible that our descendants, when they read the history of the opposition offered by cupidity and prejudice to the improvements of the nineteenth century, may smile in their turn.

Perhaps. But "cupidity and prejudice" were not the only responses evoked; and after more than a century of living with our industrial inheritance, a smile is not the only response we may be allowed.

In the mid-1840's a Royal Commission on Metropolitan Termini was established to consider proposals for building new lines into the heart of London. London Bridge, Fenchurch, Shoreditch, Euston, Paddington, and King's Cross were just some of the sites for which main-line stations were planned or on which they were already going up, and each aspired to be a center of a circle of commerce. The scrimmage of corporate appetite was so unseemly, in fact, that the Royal Commission postponed their consideration with disgust.

The most ardent advocate of a city railroad, however, was not a corporate schemer, but a radical—Sir Charles Pearson. And this was to make all the difference. City Solicitor since 1839, Pearson had marched in the procession inaugurating the Thames Tunnel. He had made his mark in city politics early on as a reformer. Sent to the Common Council in 1817 as a representative of the radical ward of Bishopsgate, he had been instrumental in abolishing the packing of special juries for political trials and in outlawing sheriff's fines and the sale of public offices. One of his proudest accomplishments was the establishment of equal rights for Jews as free citizens of London. With similar fervor he campaigned for the abolition of the slave trade, the emancipation of blacks, and an end to the persecution of Catholics "before the names of Wellington and Peel gave it grace, favour and fashion." He was personally responsible for having the inscription around the plinth of the monument commemorating the Great Fire of 1666 removed, because it blamed Catholics for the disaster. With Samuel Favell, he also helped eliminate the famous "sanguinary laws," which imposed harsh punishments for petty crime. During his term as under-sheriff he had hated "having to be present at the savage whipping of little pilfering urchins, scarcely tall enough to be seen over the dock by the judge."

Pearson was an eloquent man, whose long periodic sentences

had a fine Ciceronian roll even when he was not speaking out on behalf of a cause. Despite his radical views, he was popular with his colleagues and often won them over by sheer urbanity and wit. In an amused analysis of a public dinner to which twelve hundred guests had been invited at city expense, he remarked, "Looking at it in the mass, without considering the number of persons who partake, it would seem to denote a series of gastronomic preparations rivaling the days of Apicius: but brought down to the sober subdivision of each separate table, it exhibits such a homely banquet as I am sure, Sir, if you had a party of friends at your house, to whom you desired to show particular respect, you would hardly think it becoming your station to place before them such a meagre entertainment."

When Pearson was first elected to the Common Council, the financial condition of the city corporation was so desperate that the city baker had refused to supply the prisons with bread "except upon the personal guarantee of the Chamberlain." As much as any man, Pearson helped restore the city to solvency. His numerous contributions to the moral and financial health of London, together with his reputation as a man of impeccable integrity, gave his opinion on any matter of civic interest considerable weight. So it is not surprising that his revolutionary advocacy of a city railroad stirred the issue up. Indeed, he has sometimes been called the Father of the Subway.

Pearson didn't really want an overland railway into the city, nor was he especially a railway partisan. But he saw the compelling issue in humanitarian terms: the poor must have some rapid, inexpensive means of getting out of the city into the countryside. In 1846 he said: "A poor man is chained to the spot. He has not the leisure to walk and he has not the money to ride to a distance from his work." On another occasion he declared: "The desire to get out of town is not a mere desire, it is not a passion, it is a disease ... The passion for country residence is increasing to an extent that it would be impossible for persons who do not mix with the poor to know. You cannot find a place where they do not get a broken teapot in which to stuff, as soon as spring comes, some flower or something to give them an idea of green fields and the country."

For a time, Pearson got caught up in the Utopian Movement for New Towns: preplanned, precisely populated communities supposed to ensure for their inhabitants the humanitarian conveniences rapidly vanishing from industrial settlements. One of his proposals was for a congregation of ten thousand cottages, just for artisans. Others suggested similar communities for power-loom workers and clerks. Pearson's most cherished scheme, however, was for a majestic eight-track "covered way"—which he imagined as a cheerful arcade—running the length of the Fleet Valley from King's Cross to Holborn-Cheapside as part of an overall valley improvement plan.

The Fleet Valley was a slum. As early as the thirteenth century the river which ran through it was so befouled that the Prior of the House of Carmelites at Whitefriars reported that "many of the brethen" had died from the stench, which "overwhelmed even the incense of the altars." Restored for a time, it was known in the sixteenth century as the "River of Wells," from its "divers fair wells and fresh springs" on which the city of London drew with thirsty gratitude. By the end of the century, however, its waters had again "decayed" and for two hundred years thereafter it precipitously declined toward its destiny as a sewer—the "King of Dykes," Alexander Pope called it, "which rolls the large tribute of dead dogs to Thames." By the 1840's the whole valley "had descended to one of filth and degradation where thousands of people were jammed together in an indescribable squalor, to die from starvation or consumption or from one of the frequent cholera epidemics." Slatternly little houses and poorly thatched shacks were heaped together along tiny alleyways that could hardly be called streets. It was a refuge (if refuge it was) for every kind of vice and illegal trade. The Fleet—by then known as the Fleet Ditch—ran through the whole area, in some places open to the air, infesting the atmosphere with malodorous vapors that mingled with the acrid scent of slaughterhouses to the east.

Pearson wanted the valley cleaned up. Though his "covered way" plan fell by the wayside, it set in motion the subway debate. And once started, the railway companies kept it fueled. They were sure they had time on their side since London was growing at a frightful rate. Prior to 1836, the year the railway arrived at the city's outskirts, the average population increase was 100,000 per decade. Thereafter, it was 200,000 or more. Between 1811 and 1851, the population doubled, from 1,138,000 to 2,362,000; in addition, according to Pearson, "Two hundred thousand enter the City each day on foot by different avenues, and about 15,000 by the river steamers, and . . . besides the cab, cart, carriage and wagon traffic of the streets, omnibuses alone perform an aggregate of 7,400 journeys through the City."

In the face of hostility and ridicule, Pearson untiringly pressed his campaign, and by 1851 the issue could scarcely be in doubt. Isambard Brunel began building his great Paddington Street Station and placed the tracks at basement depth, because he was sure that "one day there would be an underground railway running round London at about that level."

Two years later, Pearson introduced a bill into Parliament for an underground City Terminus Railway from King's Cross to Farringdon Street. At the same time, a rival company, the North Metropolitan Railway, sought an underground line from King's Cross to Edgeware Road near Paddington. The second bill outmaneuvered the first, whereupon the North Metropolitan, to enlarge its franchise domain, worked out a merger with the City Terminus and on February 1, 1854, petitioned the House of Commons for what amounted to a combined route—from Farringdon in the east to Paddington in the west. This bill passed and received Royal Assent on August 7. The company changed its name to the Metropolitan Railway and began to raise funds. It negotiated with the Great Western Railway for capital in return for the use of its track, and with the Post Office, from which it hoped to obtain heavy traffic. The Great Western at once agreed to subscribe £175,000; the Post Office encouraged the scheme.

But the fund-raising effort soon stalled. In 1854 England was on the verge of war. The previous July, Czar Nicholas had crossed the Pruth into the Turkish principalities of Moldavia and Walachia; and in December France dispatched two fleets into the Black Sea to hem in the Russian fleet at Sevastopol. On September 14, 1854, an allied force of fifty-seven thousand men landed on Crimean shores. The conflict dried up speculative capital and England was plunged into a depression.

Another problem was that the public was simply not yet won over to the subway idea. Apprehensions of all sorts abounded, and some were aired in 1855 before a Select Committee of Parliament. The sharpest questioning had to do with ventilation in the tunnels, a not unnatural concern since even in the open air the locomotive was considered a hazard to the environment.

John Fowler, the Metropolitan Railway's chief engineer, was called upon to respond. He disarmed the committee almost at once by announcing that he planned to build a "fireless engine"—a locomotive that would burn no fuel. "What we propose to do," he stated, "is . . . to start with our boiler charged with steam and water of such capacity and of such pressure as will take its journey from end to end and then, by arrangement at each end, raise it up again to its original pressure." A reservoir of cold water would condense the steam, instead of allowing it to be released into the tunnel. Isambard Brunel, chief engineer of the Great Western Railway, and Fowler's friend, endorsed the plan. With customary wit, he remarked: "If you are going a very short journey, you need not take your dinner with you or your corn for your horse." This was a little too off-hand for the committee to accept, especially since, however tenable in theory, a fireless engine did not yet exist. Fowler was thus forced to declare that "the line could be worked by ordinary locomotives if need be." Brunel again backed him up: "Generally speaking, the passage of a train through a tunnel creates such a commotion and change of air that I do not know of any difficulty in any tunnel I am acquainted with."

This was a remarkable statement. There were a number of tunnels in England where the ventilation was so atrocious— Brunel's own Box Tunnel near Bath was a prominent example— that several deaths had been plausibly attributed to asphyxiation. The issue had been raised in the first place because most of the evidence was on the other side. Nevertheless, Brunel could almost get away with it. In 1854 he was regarded as an engineering giant and it was almost an insult to differ with him. Only a fellow engineer of similar standing might demur, and one did: Joseph Locke, whose Woodhead Tunnel through the Pennines was absolutely infamous on the ventilation score—its air was said to have "the taste of cheap port" and was acknowledged to have caused "a nightmare of tracheal and colonic complications." Locke hated tunnels, and avoided building them whenever he could. (Nevertheless, in 1845, when his Woodhead Tunnel was complete, the Board of Trade had pronounced it "the finest piece of engineering ever seen.") He now came forward to say that if ordinary locomotives were used in the London tunnels, the smoke would be so thick that grease deposited on the rails would make it impossible for locomotives to drag the trains.

As the committee deliberated on this murky question, several members became captivated by a strange and exotic alternative proposal placed before them by Sir Joseph Paxton, creator of the monumental Crystal Palace of iron and glass that had caused an international sensation at the Exhibition of 1851. He suggested a Great Victorian or Crystal Way, an immense boulevard of glass, 11½ miles long, encircling London. Ribbed with iron, "houses and shops were to be built under its cover, with an ordinary railway between them. Above, eight lines of railways, four being for express trains, were to run on the top of a raised corridor twenty-six feet high." The trains were to run on the "atmospheric principle" recently tried with mixed success by Isambard Brunel on the South Devon railway. In this arrangement,

a train was attached to a piston passing through a cast-iron pipe laid between the rails. The train, outside the pipe, was attached to the piston, inside, by an arm passing through a longitudinal slot rendered air-tight by a continuous flap valve. Steam engines housed in brick buildings sited at intervals along the line, created a vacuum in front of the piston which was impelled along by the pressure of the atmosphere, drawing its train behind it.

The whole operation was exquisitely clean; Paxton promised that the air in his translucent boulevard "would be as sweet as that in the country ... In the month of July, during the very hot

— 95 —

days, it would be the most cool and airy place in the dense parts of London."

The committee nearly went for it; Prince Albert found it "both ingenious and useful"; the Queen herself expressed interest. The House of Commons, however, thought it was preposterous. It was an aristocratic dream.

Reluctantly reconciled to the Metropolitan, the committee urged Fowler to go ahead with hir fireless engine. It also emphatically expressed the hope that the new underground would serve "to accelerate the mails, and take all through traffic not only of passengers, but, *in a still more important degree*, of goods off the streets."

The idea that the line might turn out to be mainly for freight was widely held, and did much to win it adherents. Company executives were careful not to dispel the impression, which seemed fairly convincing given the Metropolitan's increasing alliances with commercial lines. Nevertheless, Fowler personally expected the line would be of "omnibus character"; and William Malins, the Metropolitan's first chairman, predicted it would be the beginning of an underground passenger network that would spread throughout the city. "It must be obvious," he remarked, "that the constantly accumulating number of omnibuses, wagons, and conveyances of all sorts would, if it continued two or three years longer, render London almost insupportable for purposes of business, recreation and all ordinary transit from place to place . . . Doubling the thoroughfares by means of *sub via* railways is the only mode of accommodating the increased traffic of London."

Three years later, however, funds were still not raised; indeed, it began to appear as if the Metropolitan might die of neglect. Pearson came to the rescue. On December 1, 1858, at a large town meeting presided over by the Lord Mayor, he made a dramatic appeal on the Metropolitan's behalf. Though the theme of his speech was the salvation of London's poor, his most effective argument outlined a financial formula designed to satisfy all parties involved: the City Corporation would subscribe for shares worth £200,000; in return, the Metropolitan would pay the city £179,157 for use of the Fleet Valley land. The company would also agree to link up with the Great Northern Railway, so that slaughtered cattle could be brought underground from Copenhagen Fields to a new meat market planned by the city for Smithfield. To offset the expense of this new link the original Post Office branch connection would be dropped. Once the Great Western's own subscription of £175,000 was added in, the sought-for capital would be in hand.

Pearson prevailed. The route, as adjusted, extended for $3\frac{1}{2}$ miles from Bishop's Road, Paddington (where the Great Western had its terminus), through King's Cross (where the line linked up with the Great Northern) to Farringdon Street. By the end of 1859 tunneling began.

The tunnels were kept shallow for two reasons: ventilation and the cost of real estate. Any locomotive, even a "fireless" one, would have to blow off steam at some point, if only to re-fire the engine. For this, "open cuts" were necessary at intervals along the route. Moreover, by making the route coincide with public roads, the Metropolitan would not have to purchase its right of way through private property, nor contend with the complex problems of passing under buildings which would have to be shored up. Even so, no amount of precaution was suffi-cient to prevent damage suits of all kinds; and one company di-rector was to "dwell bitterly" on having to "paper with bank notes the cracked walls of a chapel."

The tunneling method (an alternative to the shield, which was inappropriate for such shallow work) was "cut and cover," which involved digging an open trench, supporting the soil on either flank with sidewalls, and then roofing over the excavation and restoring the surface above. The result was a sort of covered way, reinforced with six-ring elliptical brick arches having a $28\frac{1}{2}$-foot span and a rise of 11 feet. Ordinary stock bricks and blue lias or graystone lime were used throughout, with an oc-casional set of cast-iron rings. Strictly speaking, there was only one conventional tunnel on the line—the Clerkenwell, 728 yards long, which passed through a hill near Farringdon Street. It would be some years before the tunneling shield, radically mod-ified, would give London its deep-level tubes.

In the meantime, Fowler had finally put together his fireless

engine—which had a firebox after all: "a large mass of fire brick
. . . in the boiler proper; the idea was to run the locomotive in
the ordinary way on open sections of the line, getting the bricks
really hot, then damping down the fire in covered sections, with
the fire bricks acting as a heat reservoir. The exhaust steam
would not be allowed to escape into the tunnel but would be
turned into an injection condensor fitted with an air pump."
This promising machine had a trial run in October 1861. It was
a disaster. "The condensing apparatus got so hot that steam
mixed with boiling water came out of the air pump pipe. At the
same time, boiler pressure fell and the bricks lost much of their
heat." Having built up a head of steam, it came to a stop. Fowler,
appalled at the spectacle of his incapable and frothing monstros-
ity, which after years of work had been brought to such imper-
fection, consigned it to oblivion. Only a photograph survives;
but around London it became an object of local forklore known
as "Fowler's Ghost."

Along with its demise went all hope that the underground
tunnels would be pollution-free. Daniel Gooch, the great locomotive engineer, instead devised a variation on the standard engine for the Metropolitan's use. It gave the appearance of being
a sort of compromise. It burned coke, but was arranged to con-
sume its own smoke, while "flap valves, worked by rods from
the foot plate, directed the exhaust steam either up the chimney
when the engine was running in the open or into tanks under
the boiler, between the frames, when it was working in the tunnel." As one historian has pointed out, even with these modi-
fications "the fumes were thus left to be consumed by the
passengers." Most of the locomotives were constructed at the
Vulcan Foundry in Liverpool.

As the tunneling went on, Pearson was in the eye of a continuous storm. He graciously withstood a good deal of partisan
abuse ("the fool who would bring down St. Paul's Cathedral"
was one of the things he was called), though his opponents were
just as unfairly portrayed as "wailing Cassandras," prophets of
improbable doom. Convinced that subways were a good and inevitable thing, most historians have echoed the latter view. Certainly Pearson was no fool, but there was much to intimidate the

pioneering engineers—at least, the engineers themselves thought so, and they were the ones to know. It amused them, in a wry sort of way, to hear their "allies" in government expound with imperturbable confidence how little risk or danger they had to face. It was not so. But just how delicate and novel the work actually was is suggested by the recollections of Sir Benjamin Baker, Fowler's colleague. "It was not known," he wrote,

> what precautions were necessary to ensure the safety of valuable buildings near to the excavations; how to timber the cuttings securely and keep them clear of water without drawing the sand from under the foundations of adjoining houses; how to underpin walls, and, if necessary, carry the railway under houses and within a few inches of the kitchen floors without pulling down anything; how to drive tunnels, divert sewers over or under the railways, keep up the numerous gas and water mains, and maintain the road traffic when the railway is being carried underneath; and, finally, how to construct the covered way, so that buildings of any height and weight may be erected over the railway without risk of subsequent injury settlement or vibration.

Nevertheless, even with such knowledge in hand,

> with the utmost precautions tunneling through a town is a risky operation, and settlements may occur years after the completion of the works. Water mains may be broken in the streets and in the houses, stone staircases may fall down, and other unpleasant symptoms of small earthquakes alarm the unsuspecting occupants.

At least the engineers knew what they were trying to do. To the unsuspecting occupants, however, or just the man on the street, the bewildering tumult appeared little short of bizarre. "A few wooden houses on wheels first made their appearance," remembered one eyewitness,

> and squat like Punch and Judy shows, at the side of the gutter; then came wagons loaded with timber and accompanied by sundry gravel-coloured men with picks and shovels. A day or two

afterwards a few hundred yards of roadway were enclosed, the ordinary traffic being, of course, driven into the side streets; then followed troops of navvies, horses and wagons arrived, who soon disappeared within the enclosure and down the shafts. The exact operations could be but dimly seen or heard from the street by the curious observer who gazed between the tall boards that shut him out; but paterfamilias, from his house hard by, could look down on an infinite chaos of timber, shaft holes, ascending and descending chains and iron buckets which brought rubbish from below to be carted away; or perhaps one morning he found workmen had been kindly shoring up his family abode with huge timbers to make it safer.

For all its numerous and, at the time, uniquely unprecedent perils, the building of the Metropolitan featured few adventures worthy of comparison with the Thames Tunnel ordeal. From an archaeological and geologic standpoint, however, the work could hardly have been of greater interest.

In some places the engineers found themselves working through 24 feet of ruins and dust, the deposit of bygone generations of Celts and Romans, Saxons, Danes, and Normans. The foundations of an old fort were exposed at the mouth of the Fleet, and at the Mansion House a masonry subway [underground passage] was discovered intact. Along the old riverbed the foundations had to be sunk in some places to a depth of 37 feet below high water. Beds of peat were encountered in the swamp of Pimlico. Below the peat is the London clay, and on this the railway walls between Gloucester Road and Victoria were made to rest ... The north section of the line was driven through gravel and sand beds of comparatively small dimensions, lying on top of the London clay ... great ochreous deposits were found [overlaying] the hills and valleys. At what period in the remote past the sand, gravel, and brick-earth, cut through by the railway in Westminster at a level of 8 feet and in Marylebone at 103 feet were deposited no one can tell. Geological speculation, however, suggests that England was united to the Continent, that the present site of the North Sea was dry sand, and the Thames a tributary of the Rhine, along whose banks disported themselves mammoths, wooly rhinoceros, and other extinct animals, and, possibly, also man.

Other things were discovered too: ancient wooden water pipes, consisting of hollowed-out tree trunks, and lead pipes used by the Romans; fragments of early pottery; at Highgate, a fossilized crab of great antiquity; Roman coins; pavement mosaics and archways; and an elephant's tooth, thousands of years old.

Fowler had predicted the line would take about twenty-one months to complete. When that forecast proved too optimistic, he hoped at least to have it ready for the Great Exhibition of 1862, scheduled for the fall. On May 24, various dignitaries, including Fowler and the Right Honorable William Gladstone (then Chancellor of the Exchequer), assembled in cattle trucks for a run over the partially finished track. All seemed well.

Then, a month later, there was a major setback. During one of several crossings the line had to make of the Fleet Ditch sewer, a retaining wall by the Farringdon Street Station collapsed and the sewer burst into the works. Ten feet of refuse flooded the tunnel as far as King's Cross. So it was not till the following year that London could celebrate the opening. On January 9, 1863, at noon, John Fowler (soon to be Sir John) left with his wife and eldest son for Bishop's Road Station. At one o'clock the train pulled out, packed with members of Parliament, city officials, company directors, and engineers. At each station the assembly paused to examine the premises in detail, till at length they reached Farringdon Street where an elaborate banquet was spread. But the occasion was a let-down. The Prime Minister, Lord Palmerston, failed to show up, excusing himself because of his age and affairs of state. His message added that, in any case, he wanted to keep above ground as long as he could. A member of Parliament, presiding in his stead, called on everyone to "drink a bumper to the success of the Metropolitan Railway," and saluted Fowler as "the modern Saint George, who had four times vanquished the Fleet Ditch." Fowler, piqued by this mock-heroic tribute (the work, after all, had required exceptional skill and nerve) made a speech in reply that was recalcitrantly matter-of-fact. In a depressed voice, he gave a brief history of the work and talked about the problems the company had had in raising money because of the Crimean War; then he thanked the city for its subscription of £200,000 and sat down.

Thirty thousand people tried the line when the Metropolitan was officially opened to the public the next day. On the whole, the cars were attractively done up, with heavy carpets on the floors, richly upholstered seats, and "highly polished" hardwood paneling on the walls. Here and there a mirror was placed "for decorative effect." Lighting was supplied by incandescent gas drawn from collapsible India-rubber bags mounted in cylinders or boxes on the roof. The gas, under pressure, flowed into individual fishtail jets "enclosed in wire-netted glass shades."

There were no straphangers; in fact, standing was forbidden, as the rule book of the line advised: "The company's officers and servants are not to allow any person to stand in any of the carriages, or wagons, but compel them to sit upon the seats or floors; should they refuse to comply, they must be removed and given into the charge of the company's police."

One of the more memorable features of the line was the "Workmen's Train"—for laborers and clerks—which ran at a reduced fare early in the morning and late at night. Brought about by way of a clause in the Chatham Act of 1860, through Pearson's initiative (he died before the Metropolitan service began), it turned out to be a profitable experiment and other railways soon began to build up their "poor man's line." William Burt, the general manager of the Great Eastern, regarded these arrangements with distaste: "The men all came into the station at whatever hour they might have left their work and accumulated in such large numbers and were such a constant source of annoyance by expectorating all over the station and smoking very much with short black pipes that we felt we had far better let them go home." Gustave Doré has left us an evocative engraving in which the Workmen's Train clientele are portrayed as miners.

The coaches of the regular trains were separated into three classes which differed mainly in space. Apparently, the third-class coaches attracted a bizarre crowd—"lower," according to John Fowler, "than originally travelled by omnibus," but also "many persons otherwise rarely seen." In 1868, smoking carriages were mandated by parliamentary act, largely as a result of the eloquence of John Stuart Mill, the Utilitarian philosopher, who spoke on their behalf with emotion in his farewell speech before the House of Commons.

The Metropolitan, of course, did not turn out to be a freight line at all. Its 3½ miles of double track linked up with the Great Western at Paddington, the London & Northwestern at Euston, and the Great Northern at King's Cross. Soon the Midland Railway was also connected to the line by means of an extension to St. Pancras. All these had passenger traffic of their own to coordinate with the Metropolitan's. Trains were scheduled every fifteen minutes on weekdays, from eight in the morning to eight at night, and almost as frequently at other hours and on weekends. Such heavy traffic did not augur well for the tunnels' atmosphere.

A few months before the line opened, the London *Times* had given voice to familiar doubts. Who, it asked, would of his own free will choose to travel in tunnels

> buried beyond the reach of light or life; in passages inhabited by rats, soaked with sewer drippings, and poisoned by the escape of gas mains. It seemed an insult to common sense to suppose that people who could travel as cheaply to the city on the outside of a Paddington 'bus would ever prefer ... to be driven amid palpable darkness through the foul subsoil of London.

Many, however, chose to do just that, mainly because the trains were fast. But they paid a price. The air in the tunnels was quite as bad as had been feared, and in a brash attempt to befuddle the public about it, the company directors got doctors to testify that the sulphurous fumes were actually therapeutic for asthma and other respiratory complaints. Fowler, whose jaunty disparagement of the whole issue in 1855 had raised eyebrows, now spoke as if the problem had never been in doubt. "Ventilation," he said in a speech to the Merchant Venturers' School, "has always been an objection and a difficulty ... No satisfactory ventilation can be obtained with the present type of engine, or any modification of it." In one experiment, blowholes were punctured in the roadway above the tunnel between Edgeware Road and King's Cross; this had no appreciable effect on the tunnel atmosphere, but had a powerful effect on the travelers on the road, who were frightened by the sudden, miniature volcanic bursts of smoke and steam. As one engineer put it, "It is not enough just to make a hole in the roof." Eventually, large and costly exhaust fans had to be erected in the tunnels to keep the air from becoming absolutely sour.

Not long after the Metropolitan opened, it became embroiled in a dispute with the Great Western. The latter had invested heavily in the line, furnishing much of the capital and all the locomotives and cars. Accordingly, it ran its own trains as frequently as possible, cutting into the traffic of the Metropolitan, which saw its profits decline. The result was a struggle for control of the line.

The Metropolitan was at a distinct disadvantage. In the middle of July 1863, as the dispute heated up, the Great Western threatened to repossess all the Metropolitan's trains. The Metropolitan appealed to the Great Northern and the London & Northwestern for help and at the same time contracted with the Manchester firm of Peacock & Company for permanent replacements. These were furnished within just a few months, by mid-October. The Great Western was completely trumped.

The Metropolitan's new locomotives, "painted dark green with large brass numerals," bore names "appropriate to the stygian gloom of the tunnels they inhabited." One by one they rolled majestically forth—Jupiter, Mars, Juno, Mercury, Apollo, Medusa, Orion, Pluto, Minerva, Cerberus, Latona, Cyclops, Daphne, Dido, Aurora, Achilles, Ixion, and Hercules—as formidable a fleet as any mythologist dare conjure up. The Great Western promptly made amends.

The Metropolitan presaged the future; after 1863, there was a "giant onslaught on the metropolis by the railway promoters." Two hundred and fifty-nine proposals were submitted to Parliament for some 300 miles of railway inside London in 1864 alone. Opposition was fierce. In one neighborhood "every resident agreed to pay 5 percent of the rental value of their houses towards a campaign fund to fight the proposed railways." One citizen prophesied: "Next year we are to have a revival of the Railway Mania which will surpass in intensity the celebrated season of 1846. London is to be burrowed through and through like a rabbit-warren, and its main thoroughfares and rivers bridged over in every direction . . . If London is to be cut up in such style, London will have to move elsewhere."

In order to give some coherent shape to the various proposals and organize the best of them toward a common purpose, Parliament set up a Joint Committee in 1864 which decided that what London needed most was an "inner circuit" line to link up the main-line termini. This was a logical compromise and emminently satisfactory to corporate hopes. The circuit would be formed by extending the Metropolitan in both directions—eastward from Moorgate Street and westward from Paddington, while the new extremities would be connected by a line along the north bank of the Thames. At the same time, the Metropolitan won the right to extend its track from Paddington to Brompton (South Kensington) and from Moorgate to Tower Hill, with additional track between King's Cross and Moorgate for an increasing suburban clientele.

In a significant move, Parliament gave the contract for the line that would round the circle out to the Metropolitan District, a new company. The District, as it was called, set to work on June 29, 1865.

The building of the early London subways coincided almost exactly with the overhaul and ramification of the city's complex drainage system. In the course of London's growth river after river had been polluted and covered over to carry waste underground. First the Walbrook, flowing north to south, then the Fleet, the Tybourne, the Westbourne, and their tributaries evolved into a network that branched like arteries and veins through London soil. The Metropolitan met up with many of these streams, as did the District to an even greater degree. The problems of maneuvering around them constituted perhaps the chief overall challenge of the work:

> When constructing the District at Blackfriars the Fleet had to be diverted and re-diverted, carried temporarily in syphons, and otherwise carefully guarded, as the large volume of water coming down it necessitated. No less than five crossings of the Fleet had to be dealt with, namely, two at King's Cross over the junction

curves with the Great Northern Railway, one at Frederick Street over the Metropolitan Railway, another at the same spot over the widening lines, and finally a fifth under the District Railway at Blackfriars Bridge. The first four crossings were in cast-iron tubes of tunnel section, ranging in size from 9 feet by 8 to 10 feet by 10, and the latter in two brick channels 11 feet 6 inches by 6 feet 6 inches high, with flat iron tops.

At Kensington the District passed precariously under a number of dwellings, before proceeding eastward to Gloucester Road, South Kensington, and Sloan Square. When Westminster was reached in December 1868, it was feared that the Houses of Parliament might be in peril and the engineers had to go to great lengths to demonstrate the safety of their plan. In the process they apparently reassured themselves, and eventually connected Westminster Station to Parliament by an underpass. This had the unforeseen effect of foreshortening legislative debate: "Its convenience," as Prime Minister Gladstone once remarked, "had an influence of remarkable efficiency in removing the members of the House of Commons from their seats at a certain hour of the evening."

Though the District appeared to be an independent firm, it was in fact virtually a branch of the Metropolitan. Fowler was its chief engineer, and the chairman and three other members of the board also sat on the District board of directors. It was really just a "device for splitting the fund-raising effort"; and it was assumed that before long the two companies would merge.

But in 1870 they had a falling out (after the pattern of the Metropolitan and Great Western) and the District acquired its own engines. For years the two companies argued fiercely over rights to different portions of the shared circle line. The Aldgate to Mansion House stretch, supposed to be built jointly, went forward under duress. Progress on the whole line dragged. When it was completed in 1884, animosities came to a head. On August 30, the *West London Advertiser* reported:

A right to a siding is in dispute ... The District, in order to enforce their right, have run an engine and train into a siding and have actually chained it to the spot, notwithstanding that the engine's fires are kept alight, steam kept up, and night and day a driver and stoker are in charge. A day or two ago the Metropolitan sent three engines to pull the train and a tug of war ensued in which the chained train came off the winner.

Whether the public stood to win either way is a question, for the District, like the Metropolitan, turned out to be a mixed blessing at best for the traveler. "A journey from King's Cross to Baker Street is a form of mild torture," reported the London *Times*, "which no person would undergo if he could conveniently help it." To blunt this impression, the directors resuscitated their old claims that coke fumes were therapeutic for asthmatics and even tried to make people believe some of the stations were unofficially used as sanitoriums by bronchitis victims. As for the sulphuric acid gas, it merely "acted as a disinfectant." In truth, smoke in the tunnels was occasionally so thick that the signals could not be seen.

Nothing was done about it. Almost a decade later one journalist who went around the circle line on the footplate of a locomotive filed this neurasthenic report:

> The sensation altogether was much like the inhalation of gas preparatory to having a tooth drawn. I would have given a good deal to have waited just a minute or so longer. Visions of accidents, collisions and crumbling tunnels floated through my mind; a fierce wind took away my breath, and innumerable blacks filled my eyes, I crouched low and held on like grim death to a little rail near me. Driver, stoker, inspector and engine—all had vanished. Before and behind and on either side was blackness, heavy, dense and impenetrable.
>
> I looked ahead. Far off in the distance was a small square-shaped hole, seemingly high up in the air, and from it came four silver threads palpitating like gossamers in the morning breeze. Larger and larger grew the hole, the threads became rails, and the hole a station, Blackfriars, with rays of golden sunlight piercing through the gloom.
>
> Off again, a fierce light now training out behind us from the open furnace door, lighting up the fireman as he shovelled more

coal into the furnace, throwing great shadows into the air, and revealing overhead a low creamy roof with black lines upon it that
seemed to chase and follow us . . .

From Farringdon Street to King's Cross is the largest stretch
without a station, and the driver here gave us an exhibition of full
speed, and No. 18 came into King's Cross at the rate of some 40
m.p.h. The average speed of trains between one station and another is 20 to 25 m.p.h.

The road now began to be uphill, and at the same time the air
grew more foul. From King's Cross to Edgeware Road the ventilation is defective, the atmosphere on a par with the " 'tween deck
forrud" of a modern iron clad in bad weather, and this is saying
a good deal. By the time we reached Gower Street I was coughing
and spluttering like a boy with his first cigar.

An American engineer, who was in London at about this time,
had something else to criticize about the system. The locomotive, he pointed out, was an utterly uneconomical use of power
on short runs, particularly when running at grade or coming into
a station on an incline.

In London the trains run at full speed to a point within a short
distance of the station, when the brakes are whistled down, and
down they all go, by the prompt use of well-trained brawny arms
scotching many of the wheels, and at night creating a most magnificent display of fireworks as each wheel planes off a part of
their 84 pounds steel rail. Now this system of starting and stopping involved, in the first place, the entire loss of the *"vis viva"*
(momentum) existing in the train, the sum of its weight and
speed; it is annihilated by the brakes, and lost forever, thrown
away as if it did not cost anything to create it. In addition to this
loss there is from their excessive use of the brakes another serious
loss from the destruction of the rails and cars and engines, the engines being often reversed, and the system used to de-assist in destroying what it had created.

The era of the underground locomotive was obviously running
out; the time of the deep tunnel was at hand.

The reported advantages of the shallow "cut and cover" technique—ventilation and economy—had not panned out. It took

the Metropolitan and District twenty-four years and £10 million to build 17½ miles of track. Streams, gas mains, sewers, and other subsurface conduits constantly got in the way; and the excavation, once complete, had to be roofed over. A tunnel deeper down could avoid all this, by following a route of its own—under houses, monuments, rivers, pipes, and so forth—beyond the reach of public utilities or private property claims. Nobody owned the Underworld.

Renowned as the Thames Tunnel was, its multitudinous tribulations had the practical effect of discouraging a similar attempt at underwater tunneling for a long time. Engineers published numerous pamphlets in which they discussed how the procedure might be modified, but it seemed apparent that a new discovery was needed or some new way of using what was known.

Then in 1862, during the building of the Lambeth suspension bridge, Peter William Barlow, a little-known engineer, saw the problem in a new light. As he supervised the sinking of hollow cast-iron cylinder piers for the bridge's foundations, it occurred to him that by laying them end to end horizontally they would form a tunnel like a tube. When shortly thereafter Parliament rejected plans for a bridge over the Thames near the Tower of London, Barlow won approval for a new Thames tunnel using a lining of cast-iron rings.

Barlow designed a new, circular shield, smaller and more compact than Brunel's, in which the "multiplicity of parts" was reduced to "a single rigid unit." Instead of weighing 120 tons, with room for thirty-six miners, it weighed 2½ tons with space for three men. Working from both sides of the river at once, Barlow kept a minimum of 30 feet of ground above the shield. He bored through strong, blue clay—the thick, reliable anchor Brunel had sought in vain.

The shield had a cast-iron cutting edge in front, 7 feet across, with a wrought-iron face plate behind fitted as a watertight sliding door. The miners cut away the dirt by hand—methodically, without fail, 18 inches each eight-hour shift—and then the shield was forced forward by screw-jacks. The iron segmental lining had two advantages: it could be bolted together fast, and "unlike green masonry, could immediately bear the full force of propelling screws."

The cast-iron rings were caulked with oakum and painted at the joints with cement. Between the tube lining and the shield itself was a space of about an inch all around, which had to be filled by pumping in blue lias lime which solidified quickly and acted as a preservative to the iron.

The tunneling went so rapidly that it became a matter of wonder. Barlow's tunnel was, of course, much smaller than Brunel's. Brunel's had cost the life of a man on the average every 100 feet, with five major irruptions of the river; Barlow's—230 feet longer and finished in just about a year—was casualty-free. "The water," it was said, "encountered at almost any time could have been gathered in a pail."

In a way, however, the tunnel was a casualty of its own haste. Just large enough to accommodate one carriage (seating twelve) at a time, hauled to and fro by a wire rope drawn by single-cylinder engines at either end, the amount of traffic it could handle was negligible. Four months after the tunnel was opened to the public, in August 1870, the hydraulic lifts in the shafts were replaced by spiral wooden staircases, and the tracks were taken up. Like its predecessor, it became a pedestrian passageway with a half-penny toll. A million people passed through each year until the Tower Bridge was built in 1894. The tunnel was then threaded with water mains.

Yet the failure of the tunnel was balanced by the lessons to be gained. It showed how fast such work could be done using a lightweight shield, and how durable prefabricated cast-iron segments were as an alternative to building up arches brick by brick in the traditional way. In 1884, James Henry Greathead, fresh from developing the roller skate, built a twin-tunnel tube railway from King William Street, by London Bridge, under the Thames to Elephant and Castle using a revised version of the Barlow shield. His model was virtually the perfection of its form: 12 feet in diameter, its hydraulic jacks had an awesome 210-ton thrust to move it through the ground. Greathead also had at his disposal new tunnel technology, including a mechanical digger called the "Thomson," which tore into the clay heading with saw-edged buckets strung on an endless chain. Even more important, compressed air caissons, exerting 15 to 25 pounds of pressure to the square inch, kept out water and sand as men and material passed in and out through airlocks. Near Stockwell, where the tunnels plowed into the path of an underground river, the caissons saved the work.

No expense was spared. The crypt of the Hawksmoor Church of Saint Mary Woolnoth was appropriated for one station over the objection of the Bishop of London, who had to be appeased by a charitable contribution of £250,000. The station memorialized its origins: one stairway led past a wall adorned with George I angels carved in stone.

Greathead had resigned himself, as had Barlow, to cable traction; but by the time the line was completed in 1888, experiments with electric traction—first by Werner von Siemens in Berlin, then by Magnus Volk at Brighton, and by the Bessbrook and Newry Railway in Ireland—had come of age. In June 1889, it was decided to electrify the line. On November 4, 1890, the Prince of Wales (later Edward VII) presided over its successful inauguration.

The City and South London, as it was called, was London's first "tube." Its heavily upholstered cars, windowless except for tiny apertures near the roof, were known as "padded cells" and conductors had to shout out the name of each station as the train pulled in. The trains were hard-riding and noisy: the projecting ribs of the cast-iron lining plates picked up sound and sent it echoing from ring to ring. But the ventilation marked a great advance, as the trains acted like a plunger in forcing forward a column of air. There was only one passenger class, and each train had a smoking car from which women were barred.

The complete success of the tube accelerated subway development. Over the next decade two more tubes—the Waterloo & City and the Central—were hollowed out of London clay. In most respects they were like the City and South London, though the Waterloo & City became known as "the Drain" because of its shoddy upkeep. Because of its low fare, the Central was everybody's favorite—the "Tuppeny Tube." On July 27, 1900, it "glided with an ease that was almost magical, out of the brilliantly lit Bank Street Station," shot deep into the ground, "slipped through brightly-lighted white-tile stations, one after the other, until . . . it climbed smoothly up into the sunlight once more at Shepherd's Bush."

The success of the Central represented a crisis for the Metropolitan and District, which continued to use locomotives and offer their patrons the old bottled gaslight and sulphurous dark. As their ridership fell off, they moved, with impecunious delay, toward electrification, hoping in whatever way they could to stint expense. At length, negotiations were begun with the Hungarian firm of Ganz for a system of overhead trolley wires.

There now appeared on the scene an American tycoon who is remembered in the annals of high finance as one of the most cynical and unscrupulous "robber barons" of the age—Charles Tyson Yerkes, whose life has been elaborately retold in Theodore Dreiser's epic trilogy of novels, *The Financier*, *The Titan*, and *The Stoic*. Yerkes was a "public utilities" magnate, one of a group of financial adventurers who would enter city after city, "purchasing the scattered street railway lines and lighting companies, equipping them with electricity, combining them into unified systems, organizing large corporations, and floating huge issues of securities." Philadelphia, Chicago, Pittsburgh, "and at least a hundred other towns and cities in Pennsylvania, Connecticut, Rhode Island, Massachusetts, Ohio, Indiana, New Hampshire, and Maine," were taken over and plundered by a single group of men among whom Yerkes was perhaps the dominant figure.

Born in 1839 in Philadelphia, he began his business career at seventeen as a clerk for commission brokers. A few years later he opened his own office and joined the stock exchange. By 1862 he had his own banking house, and by 1871 he had the financial dictatorship of Philadelphia almost within his grasp. When the Chicago Fire brought panic on the Philadelphia exchange, he was caught overextended, and was sentenced to two years and nine months in the penitentiary for "technical embezzlement." Released after seven months with a pardon, he reestablished himself in the wake of the Panic of 1873. In 1882, he decamped to Chicago and with the help of Peter A. B. Widener and William L. Elkins, "the Philadelphia traction kings," ob-

LONDON

A PICTURE PORTFOLIO

Sir Charles Pearson, the indefatigable champion of underground transit for London. He has sometimes been called the "Father of the Subway."

"Over London by Rail," a Gustave Doré engraving which not incidentally gives a vivid picture of the cramped living conditions of London's poor.

John Fowler

Left, Sir John Fowler, chief engineer of London's Metropolitan Line and the "St. George" who vanquished the Fleet Ditch Sewer that many times intersected the route. Above, "A City Thoroughfare" by Doré, showing crowds in the streets.

Iron-ribbed tunnel vaulting, viewed from above. Nearby, buildings are being shored up to prevent their collapse.

Left, two views of the excavations, showing miners carting away debris, and a stretch of "open cut," where trains ran in the open air to blow off their smoke and steam. Above, in history's first subway disaster, the Fleet Ditch Sewer ruptured and flooded the works. This delayed the opening of the first line for several months.

Dignitaries ride in cattle cars on a trial run of the Metropolitan Railway at Edgeware Road, on May 24, 1862. They include the Chief Engineer, John Fowler (#15), and the Right Honorable W.E. Gladstone, M.P. (#16). It was the first subway ride ever.

Above, left and right, two chromolithographs by Samuel J. Hodson showing aspects of the London Underground—the Baker Street Station in 1866, and the tunnel near Paddington, 1863, with a broad-gauge train on the tracks.

Below left, "Fowler's Ghost," the fabled "fireless engine" that didn't work.
Below right, Doré's famous engraving of the "Workmen's Train," which ran at a
reduced fare at special hours. The workmen are portrayed as miners.

Above, Skew Bridge, Clerkenwell. The Clerkenwell tunnel was the one "true" tunnel on the first line. Right, persisting chaos in the streets, as rendered in a contemporary engraving of the crowds on Ludgate Hill.

Above, the Prince of Wales at Stockwell Tube Station, City & South London Railway, November 4, 1890. Below, tube-tunneling by Greathead shield, showing cast-iron rings in place and a tank of compressed air.

tained an option on a North Chicago street railway line. After further borrowings, with the stock as collateral, he was soon in majority control of most of the public transport in the city. Over the next decade and a half he consolidated his position: among other things, he replaced forty-eight horse-car lines with cable traction, increased the surface lines by 500 miles, electrified 240 miles, and built the ingenious Downtown Union Loop. The prestidigitation of his dealings evolved such a maze of corporate entanglements that no financial historian has ever been able to satisfactorily sort them out.

During the 1890's, the Chicago daily papers were filled with pitiable reports of poor service, double fares, overcrowding, cars that broke down, and cars that never came. Yerkes probably furnished the worst transportation service a city has ever had. His corporate witticisms openly revealed his contempt for the public. "Straphangers pay the dividends," he once pointed out to a journalist; and on another occasion he remarked: "The secret of success in my business is to buy up old junk, fix it up a little and unload it upon other fellows." Which is just what he did. In 1897, when the "Boodle Aldermen" of Chicago gathered to ratify a law that would have extended Yerkes' franchises for a century, thousands of people armed with shotguns and nooses poured out of their homes in a homicidal rage and surrounded City Hall. The aldermen had second thoughts and shortly thereafter Yerkes sold out his holdings and fled to his New York City mansion with $15 million in cash.

There, virtually an exile within his own country, he cast about for new adventures and new worlds. His Italianate palace provided him with an opulent setting for European fantasies. It had two immense art galleries hung with paintings acquired from abroad—including three Rembrandts, a Franz Hals, a Van Dyck, a Hobbema, several Turners, and works by Corot, Claude Lorrain, Brugereau, Delacroix, and Millet. The windows of his study were medieval stained glass and he slept in a bed that had once belonged to the King of the Belgians. But his eyes were on England.

He arrived on the *Teutonic* in January 1901. For several months his agents had been buying up all the Underground stock they could. "No block was 'too small,'" reported the *Daily Express*, "and none too big." Within a short time he possessed the franchise rights of the Charing Cross, Euston & Hampstead, and the Brompton & Piccadilly Circus tube railways (both as yet unbuilt), as well as a controlling interest in the District.

His next move was his customary one at this stage of the syndicate game. He formed a utilities company to which he issued contracts on behalf of his own growing conglomerate, and he began building a power station for the electrification of his lines. The power station, on Lots Road in Chelsea, on the bank of the Thames by Chelsea Creek, was enormous and was widely regarded as an aesthetic offense. It had four great belching chimneys, and seemed designed, wrote one observer, to spoil "the bend in the river made famous by Turner." The painter James Whistler led the outcry.

Yet Yerkes had his way—and more. By the end of 1901 he had not only gained control of the Great Northern & Strand and the Baker Street & Waterloo but, repeating his Chicago schemes, a number of surface transport and lighting concerns as well. His utilities company, reorganized and given a new name, floated large new issues of watered stock.

Fortunately for London, Yerkes did not live long enough to milk and degrade the system in his usual manner. In the fall of 1905 he returned to the United States in ill health and died that December. His mourners were few. Four carriages, one filled with hired detectives, followed the casket from his Fifth Avenue mansion to his $50,000 tomb. He left a vast estate but London creditors attached it all.

In histories of London transport, however, Yerkes is remembered with some gratitude. In his hands the Underground railways were well on their way to being united under a single directorate. In fact, unification of the lines, and their coordination with surface transport, has long been regarded as one of the system's notable strengths.

The London Underground was the pioneer subway in the world. It was supposed to have a recoil effect on the city's population, withdrawing to the rural outskirts many of those who had come in by overland rail. However, the convenience of the system itself supplied a new enticement for coming to London, and especially for settling permanently in the suburbs on the way. At the same time, the diffusion of the population outward, even as it increased, had the overall effect of enlarging the diameter of the city's congested center without bringing relief. Large-scale housing developments closely followed the new lines, and occasionally anticipated their advent. Choice districts like Earl's Court, Baron's Court, and Brompton were drawn into the urban moil.

Coming as it did during a revival of the Railway Mania, the subway's local service was entangled from the start with cross-country and suburban main lines. The Great Western, the Great Northern, the London & Northwestern, the London, Chatham & Dover, and the Midland railways were just some of the lines that at one time or another used the early Underground tracks. Autonomous service for the city would not become a reality until the twentieth century.

The interdependent relationship was accepted early on, but with misgivings. In 1863 Parliament had opposed a large city terminus, yet in 1874, the Metropolitan's new chairman, Edward Watkin, announced to the shareholders that he hoped to turn the Metropolitan itself into a main line and run it out to "Northampton and Birmingham and many other important towns." As the years passed, this ambition took hold of his mind and became the subject of megalomaniacal outbursts. In 1881 he declared: "I do not intend to be satisfied, if I live a few years, until I see the Metropolitan Railway the grand terminus for a new system of railways through England." Two years later he took steps to initiate this scheme by arranging for the Manchester, Sheffield & Lincolnshire Railway (of which he was a former chairman) to use the Metropolitan tracks. A few months after that he disclosed a fantasy even more extreme, for "a great trunk railway from Lancashire and Yorkshire through London to the South Eastern Railway, and thence to Dover and by means of a Channel tunnel to the continent of Europe." The Underground would go all the way to France!

A Channel tunnel was not a new idea. In 1802 Albert Mathieu, a French mining engineer, had suggested it to Napoleon, and in the late nineteenth century work on it was in fact begun twice. The plan included, among other curiosities, an artificial island in mid-Channel on top of an undersea formation known as the Varne Bank. Here horses hauling carriages and wagons under the sea could come up for air and a rest. Pipes sticking out of the water would ventilate the tunnel itself. In 1875, seven thousand seabed soundings were taken and three thousand samples of Channel soil obtained. In 1881, the British began blasting through the Cliffs of Dover and the French began digging from Calais. However, the military potential of the tunnel was profoundly disquieting to the British, who with ample historical reason distrusted the French. The project was dropped.

As Watkin's Napoleonic fantasy reminds us, warfare tunneling and subway history have some common ground. From the most ancient precedents through the Thames Tunnel—and beyond—military interests were never quite out of sight. In London, the theme keeps a relatively low profile, since the underground onslaught was military mainly by analogy. But as we cross our imaginary Channel tunnel to France, the situation undergoes a dramatic change. Perhaps we should call it an about-face.

CHAPTER 5

Le
Style Métro

The directive came down from the Ministry of War and
settled the matter once and for all. After more than a
quarter-century of negotiations it had taken that grave,
blunt intervention over the last detail to bring about a meeting
of minds. Nevertheless, the ratifying handshakes were perfunctory and stiff. There was a subdued feeling about the moment,
as if each party suspected it had after all been tricked.

The settlement was not between two nations, or even between
the divided parties of one nation who had fought a civil war—
although probably neither party, as they left the room that
afternoon, would have argued with such comparisons. They
would have been in harmony with their own acrimonious exchanges over the years.

The city of Paris and the state of France had at last made
peace. The negotiations had involved nothing more than the
building of a single railroad. The final difficult detail had concerned the track gauge.

The animosity between city and state had deep and bloody
roots, and the controversy over the building of a city railroad
was more than just a curious inflection in their quarrel. Since the
late fourteenth century, when Charles VI had erected the Bastille and crushed the tax revolt of the Maillotins, Paris had pe-
riodically risen against the government as a revolutionary
commune. Even during those intermittent periods when Parisian

feeling was in conformity with that of the rest of the realm, her demands often had a decisive effect on national policy far out of proportion to her population and geographical size.

On May 12, 1588, the city had set itself against Henry III in a bloodbath remembered as the "Day of Barricades." His successor, Henry IV, tried for four months in the summer of 1590 to subdue the population by seige, without success. In January 1642, Louis XIV, the "Sun King," had to retreat with his coterie of idolators from Paris to Versailles because of persistent social unrest. Exiled from his capital for three years, he did not really become the all-powerful monarch of divine right until after 1661, when Paris completely embraced him.

The vicissitudes of this historical struggle culminated on July 14, 1789, when the insurrectional town council of Paris led the storming of the Bastille, setting in motion the French Revolution. One of the first revolutionary demands was that the king and his family take up residence in the Tuileries, in Paris, rather than at Versailles. The city felt sure that the views and interests of her citizens would sway all debate. It had always been the view of Paris that she was the fountainhead of national power.

The Revolution, of course, was not the act of Paris alone. Lyons, Bordeaux, Marseilles, the great manufacturing and shipping centers of the south, and large provincial towns all over France had their own Bastilles to storm, and storm them they did. But Paris spearheaded the thrust, and it is doubtful whether the Revolution would ever have come about without her leadership or been sustained without her help.

The Napoleonic *débacle*, and the restoration of the monarchy in 1815, by no means laid the struggle to rest. Over the course of the next three-quarters of a century there would be many reenactments, many strikes and barricades, and long bloody days of fighting in the streets: in July 1830, *les trois glorieuses*, the insurrection that toppled Charles. X; the Revolution of 1848, which overthrew Louis-Philippe and temporarily restored the Republic; and in 1870–71, the tangled, frightful series of events that began with the defeat of Napoleon III by the Prussian army and culminated in *la semaine sanglante*, seven days of slaughter during which the army of the Republic systematically cut down its own most ardent loyalists in the capital.

When the issue of a railroad for Paris first arose, it was in regard to the movement of troops. Although this was clearly in the interests of the national government, it wasn't the direct impetus for the idea. By the 1870's it had become clear that Paris needed a more advanced system of public transportation than the omnibus and tramway companies could provide. The state favored an arrangement whereby the main-line railroads, poised as in London on the city's outskirts, would extend their lines into the city. But ultimate control would repose with the state, because of the system's strategic value to national defense.

The city didn't see it that way. It wanted a system of its own, to serve its own special needs—a local system for the relief of traffic congestion and for the simple convenience of its citizens. It also looked with disfavor upon what it regarded as a flagrant attempt by the main-line railroads to commandeer its financial terrain. The golden prize of transit revenue, represented by the urban working population, glittered very bright.

The issue, in debate, turned on a legal formulation: whether the railroad was of "local" or "general" interest: if local, then it would fall by law under the jurisdiction of the city; if general, then of the state. As the controversy heated up, the rhetoric recalled the entire fratricidal background of French political history. The city accused the state of "Versaillism" and of trying to "take over." The state charged that the city was trying to keep its own citizens captive within its walls—a particular affront, since the walls of Paris, ranged alongside her gates, were quite literally fortifications. Physically, legally, and psychologically they stood for the city's independence.

There is no question that Paris needed a new transport system. She had been grappling with congestion for some four hundred years. As early as the end of the 1400's ordinances were aimed at bringing order to her thoroughfares. In February 1487, "All mule drivers, wagoners and carters" were forbidden "to let their horses trot and gallop" because of danger to pedestrians. In 1508 they were further forbidden to drive more than two horses at a time. Casualties in the street were frequent—like one Marguerite Crispin, a fourteen-year-old girl whose "thigh was run over" by the wagoner Jacques Ferrand in 1537. Ferrand, one of those unhappy individuals officialdom marks out as an example to others, was taken off to the Place de Grève, stripped, and flogged.

Three years later the following regulations went into effect:

> Since the city and its suburbs have already a great many carts, drays, wagons and horses, both harnessed and led, and since by evident malice they are driven on the run through the streets to pass each other, and since frequently the harness of one catches that of another in such a manner that the streets are so full of carts and vehicles that one cannot pass on foot or horseback, and since there are so many grave dangers and inconveniences and so many men and beasts are injured, We are obliged to forbid wagoners, leaders and drivers to run or foul another, and We enjoin them to lead their horses by hand and travel on foot under penalty of prison, confiscation of horses and vehicles, and of arbitrary fine.
>
> And under the same penalties, We forbid wagoners and drivers, whether of carts, drays, wagons or other vehicles, to turn in the streets, but they are to turn at the intersections and corners of said streets to avoid the inconveniences that might arise, such as wounding children or other persons and interfering with other passers-by along the road.

Most of the vehicles were slow-moving carts or wagons carrying garden produce or other merchandise; but the number of carts required to handle street sweepings, horse manure, excavated material, and refuse of all kinds made a sizable addition to those already in use. It was, in fact, primarily due to a crisis in sanitation—the most neglected field of civil engineering in the Renaissance—that the problems of traffic congestion in Paris first came into focus. The garbage men had to get through.

Public transit as we know it—that is, conceived as a system—was the idea of the philosopher Blaise Pascal. In 1662 he asked Louis XIV for permission to establish a system of carriages that would operate according to a fixed timetable along fixed routes. Although his primary aim was to raise funds for the famine-wracked poor in the Loire Valley, he hoped at the same time to provide a service for the Parisian lower classes at a price they could afford. In keeping with his ardent love of charity, half of his own interest in the enterprise was to go to the hospitals of Paris and Clermont.

In January 1662 he obtained his letters patent from the king, and by March 18 his company was ready to start. The first line, from the Porte Saint-Antoine to the Luxembourg, caused a sensation. The coachmen, liveried in blue, sported the colors of the realm with the heraldry of the king's arms embroidered on their jacket fronts; the carriages were escorted by a royal guard, to prevent riot and disorder. Large crowds gathered to watch the carriages go by, and on the first morning of service even Pascal's sister, Gilberte, had to wait for the sixth carriage before she could get a ride. The king was so enthusiastic about the scheme that to silence all ridicule he declared he'd be happy if a line ran past the palace. Pascal took him up on this, and in April opened a palace route. By May he had a third line going.

These promising beginnings did not last. Within a year the aristocracy took over the system and restricted its clientele to the rich. Carriages were stoned and overturned by gangs of unemployed footmen; routes were blocked by debris thrown down by the poor. The "service" faded out.

Pascal's *carosses à cinq sols*, or "coaches at a five sous fare," were a revolutionary innovation, well before their time. Not until the early nineteenth century would a comparable idea be tried: at Nantes, where a M. Baudry started a carriage line that realized a large profit. His depot happened to be opposite a shop run by a M. Omnes, who cleverly turned the Latin of his name into a slogan for his merchandise: *"Omnes Omnibus,"* or "Omnes has something for everybody." By association or propinquity, the name came to be applied to the first public carriages. And since the carriages were "for all," it stuck.

In 1828 Baudry moved to Paris, where he opened a line called *Les Dames Blanches*, which caught everybody's eye. According to the London *Times*, it featured carriages "painted white with a motto in gold upon a red ground; and at the back of each coach sketches of Scotch scenery from Boildieu's recent opera *La Dame Blanche*." The horses and harnesses were white and the drivers wore white hats and embroidered white coats. A "kind of trum-

pet under the seat of the coachmen, played by pressure, executed the principal airs of the opera."

Baudry founded twelve lines in rapid succession and called his
monopoly the Entreprise Générale des Omnibus. But, like his
London counterpart, George Shillibeer, he was soon hard-
pressed by competitors. In the Malthusian skirmish over lucrative inner city fares, he lost his early advantage and went
bankrupt. In February 1830 Baudry committed suicide in the Canal Saint-Martin across from his omnibus stables.

In the middle of the nineteenth century Paris nearly doubled
in geographical size and tripled in population. No multiplication
of omnibus lines, horse-car tramways (which soon made their
appearance), or for that matter even streets could possibly keep
up with the traffic growth. As in England, the proliferation of
industry on the heels of the Railway Mania was the main force
behind these developments. The first railway in France opened
in 1832, near Saint-Etienne. By the end of the reign of Louis-
Philippe, tracks radiated in all directions from the outskirts of
the capital. This radial configuration represented the only conscious government effort to impose order on an otherwise anar-
chic situation. At the same time, it had as its end the
establishment of Paris as the major manufacturing center of the
nation. In its own methodical way it brought Paris into pandemonium.

The railway, and the new industry, transformed the landscape. In an optimistic serenade of the new mobility one journal
wrote: "Fresh air, green fields, the song of birds, the ever chang-
ing panorama of the countryside, the quickened sensibilities of
mind and body are all accessory pleasures of the wheel." But if
"the wheel" ran on rails, such pleasures were often its accessory
casualties. "When a railroad station is built on the outskirts of
a city," Victor Hugo wrote, "it is the death of a suburb and the
birth of a town." Guy de Maupassant's account, in his novel *Bel
Ami*, of a suburban journey vividly portrays the change:

They looked down on the immensely broad long valley through
which the glossy river flowed from one end to the other in sweep-

ing curves. It could be seen coming from the distance, dotted with numerous islands and swinging around as it entered Rouen. Then on its right bank, slightly hazy in the morning mist, there appeared Rouen itself, its roofs gleaming in the sun and its hundreds of spires, slender, pointed or squat, frail and elaborate, like giant pieces of jewelry, its towers square or round, crowned with armorial bearings, its belfries, its bell-towers, the whole host of Gothic churchtops dominated by the sharp-pointed spire of the cathedral, that sort of strange bronze needle, enormous, ugly and odd, the tallest in the world . . .

Opposite, on the other side of the river, rose the slim round chimneys, swelling towards the top, of the factories of the vast suburb of Saint Sever.

They were more numerous than their brothers, the spires, and their long brick columns stretched far out into the countryside, puffing their coal-black fumes into the blue sky. And the tallest of them, as tall as the Cheops pyramid, the second tallest among the man-made pinnacles, almost as high as its proud companion the cathedral spire was the "Thunderbolt"; as it pumped out its flames, it seemed to be the queen of the laborious horde of smoky factories, just as its neighbour was the queen of the pointed throng of ecclesiastical monuments.

Paris, of course, was not a new industrial town started along a railroad siding or with a factory; but as manufacturing proliferated, tens of thousands of new residents poured in and the city came to share more and more in the problems peculiar to the new industrial age.

The official policy of the government until Napoleon III was strictly one of laissez-faire, and the ensuing disarray is perhaps best measured by the extent of the Utopian reaction. It was, indeed, out of the social miseries of the period that Communist doctrine emerged. Serious, if frequently bizarre, schemes for correcting the abuses of unregulated capitalism flowed copiously from the pens of such thinkers as the Comte de Saint-Simon, Charles Fourier, and Louis Blanc. Yet even their most far-fetched fantasies (of a "voluntary association of producers in phalanxes," a government of enlightened industrialists, and so forth) found an energetic following and sometimes an unlikely chance at power. Louis Napoleon, successor to Louis-Philippe, read Utopian works in earnest and was a true believer in social engineering as an all-correcting tool. While in prison in 1844, he had published *l'Extinction du Pauperisme*, which intrigued advanced circles with its plan for providing the poor with land. (On May 26, 1844, his image was further romanticized when he escaped dramatically from the thirteenth-century fortress of Ham, disguised as a laborer.) After he came to power and assumed the title of Napoleon III, it is said that "one day at St.-Cloud, before a large company of guests, he told a story of how, during his exile in New York [in 1836] he had been sitting in a restaurant next to some down-and-out who unrolled a great scroll of paper on which he had designed a city for twenty thousand inhabitants, with churches, fountains, squares, monuments and, of course, a stock exchange."

A "real city of the future," Napoleon is reported to have remarked, "such as we shall have here in France. No longer will one house be built at a time, but the whole will be begun on the same day and all shall be finished at the same time."

Napoleon's chief architect for the renovation of Paris was Georges Eugene Baron von Haussmann, Prefect of the Seine Department from 1853 to 1870. One of his first steps was to consolidate all the omnibus companies into one, allot them fixed and unconflicting routes, and schedule their service according to a timetable—thus reviving Pascal's idea after almost two hundred years. He called the new government-supervised conglomerate the Compagnie Générale des Omnibus. He also cut large, straight avenues, on an axial or *grand croisée* design, running east-west and north-south through the tangled mass of small, meandering streets; and he connected the inner and outer boulevards by diagonal routes. The large avenues led right to the railroad termini: in effect, these stations became the new city gates.

Haussmann's "improvements" were substantial (he also created new systems of water supply and drainage and opened up parks on the English model), but they permanently destroyed a part of historic Paris. And they had an anti-revolutionary cast. The *grand trouvaux* of the *grande croisée* were ideal for impressive military parades, intimidating displays of military hardware *en masse*, and the swift deployment of large numbers of troops from one end of Paris to the other. They were also very difficult to barricade, and provided few opportunities for ambush and flight. While they undeniably gave Paris some breathing room— not least by driving thousands from the city's center to wretched outskirt slums—they also represented the military will of the state.

Within and without, Paris was now dominated by a system of roads potentially hostile to her autonomy. This was the situation when the long struggle began over the jurisdiction of a city railway. To Paris, at least, it seemed almost a last stand.

One municipal councilor would describe the struggle as "Homeric." But the Trojan War was scarcely an apt comparison: there were no heroes, no shots were fired; and the duress was in the duration, for the city suffered a war-like agony while nothing was done. Meanwhile, lesser questions had to be resolved, of a more practical nature, which served as a salutary distraction over the long run. What sort of city railroad should be built? Should it connect with any of the main lines? Should it be elevated, underground, or some combination of the two? What pattern of routes should it adopt?

Precedents were few. At the time London had the only subway in the world, but it was still new and regarded as an experiment. In New York, the world's first elevated railroad had failed, after only a brief trial, and had gone for almost nothing at a sheriff's auction. In Paris, during the 1840's and '50s, a few railroads of a specialized nature had been proposed without result. In 1845 an engineer named de Kerizouet had drawn up plans for a supply line to connect the central marketplace of Les Halles with the wharves of Lyons. He suggested cable traction, such as Russian engineers had successfully used for hauling coal wagons over the Caucasus. But before the project could be fully discussed, barricades appeared in the streets and red flags flew in the working-class districts as Paris rose against Louis-Philippe.

In 1855, two civil engineers, Brame and Flachat, revived de Kerizouet's idea but with a difference. The freight line was to run underground. Brame, who complained of "incessant accidents" in the streets, argued that an entirely new level of traffic had to be built. Nothing came of it.

A turning point of sorts was reached in 1867, when the city hosted the International Exposition to showcase the new Paris of the Second Empire. For all of Haussmann's work, crowds of visitors had trouble getting around, and the city was acutely embarrassed. Pride and, in particular, envy began to work on the French: across the Channel, as everyone knew, the arrogant English were going full steam ahead with expansions of their Underground.

On November 19, 1871, the General Council of the Seine asked a commission of about forty engineers to decide what should be done. After months of deliberation, the commission recommended a local underground network with a pattern of routes resembling a cross enclosed in a circle, the axial lines following the *grande croisée*. In imitation of the first English line, and by direct translation of its name, they called it the Métropolitain. On May 11, 1872, the Municipal Council endorsed the plan but the state turned it down in the first formal confrontation.

Determined to keep the idea alive, the council invited engineers to draw up alternative proposals, most of which turned out to be for els. One of the more prominent came from Louis Heuzé, an architect who favored a "transverse elevated railway, seven meters high, with a covered passage for pedestrians." The tracks, forming a continuous roof, would shelter a promenade lined with chic boutiques; the supporting columns, engraved with the names of important manufacturers, "would edify posterity with a page of imperishable history." Overall, the structure would appear "elegant, visually light, and as lofty as the grand arcades of Caroussel."

As a specimen of engineering, Heuzé's design was commonplace; but it achieved notoriety because he coupled it with an attack on the English. Underground travel, he wrote, might be alright for a people "used to the fogs of London," for whom "the obscurity of a tunnel is not a change." But Parisians are "people of the sun." They could not tolerate "descending by long staircases into veritable catacombs"; they could not tolerate a "Nécropolitain."

Heuzé, of course, was simply lobbying for his own scheme. His rhetoric could hardly be taken seriously. But it was; in fact, his pamphlet set the tone of the discussion for years.

In 1882 Heuzé introduced a new theme. Not only, he asserted, was a subway certain to be "cold, humid, gloomy, smoky, and fraught with danger," but "who knows what diseases and epidemics might be spread by stirring up the subsoil?" Others took up the cry. "The subsoil," wrote one, "is the repository of centuries of filth—the stinking inheritance of past generations." "Insulated cesspools," another pointed out, "are of recent origin. In the past all excretions were simply absorbed by the soil. What mephitic exhalations will not be released? Who can foresee what consequences may lie in mucking about in this putrefying earth?" In fact, cholera had been a chronic scourge, and memories of its ravages were fresh. Haussmann's whole legal authority for the reconstruction of Paris had derived from a sweeping sanitation law passed after the epidemic of 1849.

Most elevated railway advocates made as much of the fears and of the anti-English sentiments as they could. Thus, Jules Garnier wrote in 1884: "What difference does it make to an inhabitant of London if he is surrounded by vapor, darkness and smoke? Parisians, however, love gaiety, color, light; they don't want some form of transport that is a foretaste of the tomb." So also Charles Tellier (whose solution to the rapid transit problem was an elevated trestle supported by massive masonry pylons in the middle of the Seine): A subway, with its "permanent subterranean humidity and cold" will mean "chills, pleurisy, bronchitis, and other maladies"; passengers will have to contend with the "empyemic odor which impregnates the subsoil" and the "vitiation of the atmosphere by the collective breathing of the crowds"; "inherent darkness" will depress all Parisians, "who live so much by their eyes."

The celebration of Paris as a city of the sun was a little self-conscious, and to an alert Londoner not without irony. Even before the first shovelful of Métro dirt was overturned, Paris was, after Rome, literally the most underground city in the world. "The subsoil of Paris," Victor Hugo had written in 1862,

if the eye could pierce the surface, would offer the aspect of a gigantic madrepore; a sponge has not more passages and holes than the piece of ground, six leagues in circumference, upon which the old great city rests. Without alluding to the catacombs, which are

a separate cellar, without speaking of the inextricable net of gas-
pipes, without referring to the vast tubular system for the distri-
bution of running water, the drains alone form on either bank of
the [Seine] a prodigious dark ramification, a labyrinth.

From Roman times onward Paris had been tunneled for the
extraction of gypsum, limestone, and brick clay. The quarries, or
catacombs, as they were called from their use as burial chambers, furnished much of the building material for the city. Notre
Dame, Saint Germain-des-Prés, and Saint Severin are some of
the more famous churches built of local stone, as the tunnels
ramified under seven *arrondisements*, or districts. Some of these
galleries were the size of a gymnasium, divided into several stories like houses. Sebastian Mercier in his *Tableau de Paris* described the whole network in 1782 as an "underground city with
streets, crossings and squares." It is said that a deserter from Napoleon's army hid for a year in the caverns beneath the Place
Denfert-Rochereau, where he nourished himself on white
mushrooms that flourished along the walls in abundance. Today
these mushrooms, cultivated by industry, are known to gour-
mets the world over as "champignons de Paris."

By the end of the eighteenth century the galleries were so extensive that portions of Paris began to sink, and it was necessary
to strengthen the quarry vaults with masonry. About this time
they were also appropriated to contain bodies from the city's
congested cemeteries; it is estimated that six million skeletons
are today interred in their depths. Along the sides of the galleries the bones are arranged in various designs.

The drains or sewers of Paris were even more extensive, as every reader of Hugo's *Les Miserables* knows. "They are streets,
with lanes and squares," architecturally stamped by period and
style exactly like the streets above. The system is the city's
shadow self, "in the ground a species of dark polypus with a
thousand antennae, which grows below, equally with the city
above. Each time the city forms a street, the sewer stretches out
an arm." When the sewers were first systematically explored
early in the nineteenth century, they were still relatively small
in extent; nonetheless, their recesses yielded a number of sur-

prises, including objects of gold and silver, jewelry and precious stones, old dungeons, and the skeleton of an orangutan "which had disappeared from the Jardin des Plantes in 1800."

One historian has ventured that Paris, seen from underground, "is no less attractive and surprising than when viewed from the third level of the Eiffel Tower."

The sanitary condition of the subsoil was not the only part of Paris to come under hygienic scrutiny. "Scientific studies" were made of the quality of the air—around factories, above dung heaps, over sewer gratings, near tenements—to see what might be most responsible for what Hugo called the city's "bad breath." Horses came in for much criticism in the clinical literature. In 1881 there were 75,000 pack and draft horses in the city, most in everyday use. To Jean Chrétien, an influential engineer, it seemed as if their "baleful evacuations" were accumulating with such rapid abundance as to seem to be "leavening, like a sort of yeast." He wanted the horses off the streets, and at the same time to preserve the thoroughfares for essential traffic and pedestrians. This led him to design an elevated railroad carried on single-column supports. Though other designs showed a similar economy and were more striking, such as a monorail proposed in 1886 by Panafieu and Fabre, none taken in its entirety was more controversial. In the first place, it audaciously called for electric traction; second, for a signal system employing a sort of telephone, which Chrétien called an "acoustic horn." But what everyone noticed most about the plan was that its route crossed in front of the Opéra.

This kindled an aesthetic revolt, which took Chrétien by surprise. In his opinion, the Opéra was sure to appear by comparison the less imposing monument, certainly one less valuable to the public good: "The Opéra costs four to five million in a year, for a questionable result, to certain points of view, and is limited with regard to benefits (indirect, at that) which it procures for Parisian commerce. The aerial way will provide a magnificent means of conveying 30 million travelers, and the town will get out of it a million and a half per year." He also thought that his latticework girders would "enhance the Opéra's facade."

Underground and elevated railway advocates were galvanized

into factions. For the defense of historic Paris, a Societé des amis des monuments parisiens was formed, with Charles Normand (later head of the Commission Municipale de Vieux Paris) and Charles Garnier (architect of the Opéra) as its principal spokesmen. Victor Hugo, to whom the underground owed so much of its ambiguous romance, became the honorary president. In reaction, adherents of the el formed the Ligne parisienne du Métropolitain aerienne, whose avowed aim was "to create a movement of opinion in favor of the aerial solution by means of conferences, rallies, dissemination of brochures, etc. and to permit the public to manifest its will by the organization of a vast petition."

Some attempt at a compromise was offered by the Eiffel Society, a union of engineers and financiers with Gustave Eiffel at its head. The society came up with a plan which involved a circular line, mostly underground, with elevated crossings of the Seine. Both factions rejected it; so did the city and state—which served to remind everyone that the whole dispute was really academic until the larger question was resolved. The state objected that it did not link up with the large railroad termini; the city, that the route had nothing to do with the lines along which most of Parisian traffic flowed. Tension heightened in 1884 when the Minister of Public Works, M. Raynal, an importer of coal from Bordeaux, seemed to believe that the purpose of a new Métro was to carry his coal downtown. His transparently "self-interest" scheme (in "general interest" guise which won him the support of the state) provoked ridicule from the city. The prefect Poubelle, speaking for the Municipal Council, said that Paris would like a line it too could be "on familiar terms with."

In the following year, Raynal's successor, M. Baihaut, came up with a plan that had something in it for everybody: a circular line connecting most of the railroad termini; two cross lines, one parallel and one perpendicular to the Seine; and a route that would be alternately elevated and under ground. It would accommodate both downtown Paris and the main-line railroads, and it would be built by the state. Baihaut tried to ram it through committee and made blustering threats before the Commission des Chemins de Fer, saying he "wouldn't answer for what would happen if it wasn't approved." Even his allies thought he made a fool of himself.

The impasse notwithstanding, at least as early as 1885, when de Maupassant published *Bel-Ami*, it seems to have been taken for granted by many that the Métropolitain was somehow going to be built. In a scene depicting a gathering of journalists and politicians, one of the burning issues of the day—French colonial affairs in Africa—is preempted by the far more vehement feelings aroused by the transit debate.

> The men were now all talking together in loud tones and gesticulating. They were discussing the big project of the Paris underground railway. The topic was not exhausted until they reached dessert, because everyone had a great deal to say about the slowness of communications in the city, the disadvantages of the trains, the inconvenience of the buses and the boorishness of cabdrivers.

Indeed, the omnibus service on which most of Paris had to depend was laughable. M. de Saint-Martin, a director of the Compagnie Générale des Omnibus, compared his own network to "a mop of hair" from which it was "impossible to tease out a plan or order." "Just like a schoolboy," he said, "the omnibus goes, comes, turns to the right, turns to the left, comes back, goes about the squares and intersections, takes the freest route and the most congested—merely to vary the experience—and returns a different way." But service was not always a laughing matter. At the depots crowds were routinely degraded and harassed. "Under the rain, under the burning sun," wrote a contemporary,

> a resigned throng waits with meek patience for the omnibus to come—always full when it might have been able to take you somewhere on time. On the steps ... there is a nasty, brutish struggle in which strength always prevails. The weak are beaten back, to wait again, drenched to the bone, burned to the marrow. Every day this happens, and the old, the sick, women and children, are the inevitable victims.

The aesthetic argument won out against the el, which also received a fatal blow from the practical side. In 1892, the Chief Engineer of Bridges and Roads pointed out that the cost of buying up land for a right of way in downtown Paris was just too expensive. "When they appropriated the shanties between the rue d'Amsterdam and the Tivoli passage," he noted, "to create a carriage depot in front of the Saint-Lazare Station, each square meter of ground cost 3,500 francs. At this rate a road twenty meters wide would cost, for every meter in length, 70,000 francs for the land alone."

Meanwhile, the city was rallying behind a new subway plan put forward by M. Berlier, a celebrity in the engineering profession and the designer of the postal network of underground *pneumatiques*. He suggested connecting two of the city's gates, Porte de Vincennes to the east and Porte Dauphin to the west. At the same time, he recommended a special track gauge for the system to protect its local character. This inflamed the issue and nearly destroyed all hope of a compromise.

The International Exposition of 1900 was fast drawing near and Paris frantically began to prepare against the day. The London Underground by now had grown into a complex system with deep-level tubes; New York had an elevated railroad network the length of Manhattan island, with a subway apparently in the offing. It seemed that if the city–state deadlock dragged on much longer there might be a revival of "Haussmannism"— desperate "reconstruction" measures otherwise appalling to the majority. "We cannot," declared one alarmed citizen, "destroy all of Paris just to make our thoroughfares sufficient for the needs of modern life." The only practical solution "is to have circulation at two levels, to create . . . another road along which all those 'for whom time is money' can hasten on their way." As things stand, "every new vehicle is condemned to become part of the problem."

So it stood. Then on November 22, 1895, in the twinkling of an eye, the controversy was resolved. The Minister of Public Works, M. Barthou, recognized the right of the city to a system of "local interest." He conceded that the major railroad lines "might eventually be extended into Paris," and that the state "might be entitled to some peripheral urban lines." But all of these "mights" were not legally binding; they were mostly to save face.

Unlike the London Underground, which developed gradually in an organic way, the Métropolitain was conceived from the start as a system, and as such was far too ambitious to be undertaken without special financial arrangements. Over many months it was agreed that the city would build the infrastructure (tunnels, viaducts, and stations), while the superstructure and equipment (station access, rolling stock, power stations, etc.) would be supplied by a "concessionaire" who would lease and operate the system. In July 1897 bidding was opened to the public, and six companies applied. The choice fell to the most powerful—the Compagnie Générale de Traction, backed by the Belgian financier, Baron Empain. This outfit then organized a new company, the Compagnie de Chemin de Fer Métropolitain, specifically to fulfill its contract terms. The lease was to be for thirty-nine years (for each line built, line by line) with the option of renewal. Nine lines were projected in all. These would form a circle, with transverse lines and shorter interconnections. The first would follow the east-west axis of the *grande croisée*, between Porte de Vincennes and Porte Maillot, along the north bank of the Seine via the Gare de Lyons, the Louvre, the Place de la Concorde, and L'Etoile—a distance of 6 miles.

The agreement between the city and state was civil enough. But one of the parties had been tricked after all. The city had wanted a special track gauge of 1.30 meters rather than the standard gauge of 1.44, and had made this a prominent issue ever since Berlier first raised it a decade earlier. When the city finally gave in, upon demand of the Minister of War, it seemed as if the long stalemate had actually resulted in a draw: the city got control of the road; the state got its gauge—with all that that implied for the future. Indeed, the state might even have been said to have won, for it was likely that eventually the main-line railroads would somehow connect up with the Métro tracks. But, in fact, the state had lost: secretly, the city designed its rolling stock narrower than the norm, so that it could build abnormally small tunnels—too small, in fact, for the main-line cars to use. These were banished forever from the system, while the little Métro cars could run anywhere on any track in France.

Work on the Métro began in November 1898, and among the

engineering staff the feeling was widespread that it would be neither more nor less difficult to build than a new system of sewers. Manageable and recalcitrant by turns, the subsoil was of the same consistency and variety in all its quirks—liquid clay, running springs, hard rock, calcareous layers, and shistose strata encrusted with oyster shells; bottomless sands, green sandstone between chalk and Jurassic limestone (for Paris lies in a basin formed by white chalk from the Crustacean epoch); lacustrian and marine deposits of various kinds, left by the ebb and flow of the sea—all covered by alluvia deposited by the Seine. In addition, there was the constant danger of "asphyxia by miasmas," "interment by slips," and "sudden breaking in of the soil or bursting in of streams." Nevertheless, the engineers were familiar with all of this—which meant that they knew, more or less, they were in for a hard time. Given the heterogeneity and treachery of the soil, in fact, the work went extraordinarily well. This was largely due to the guidance of the chief engineer: Fulgence Bienvenue.

The son of a notary, Bienvenue was born on January 27, 1852, in the little village of Uzel on the northern coast of France. At eighteen he entered the École Polytechnique, and two years later began working in the Department of Bridges and Roads at Alencon as an engineer third class. By 1875 he was involved in the construction of railroads, and by the time he came to Paris nine years later, he was a master railroad engineer.

Shortly after his arrival, he was almost killed in an accident. One afternoon as he was conducting a tour of one of the railroad yards for a "jury d'expropriation" (a committee that decides questions regarding the acquisition of property for public works), a train suddenly started up behind him and threw him to the tracks. Before it could be stopped, a wheel passed over his left arm, crushing it above the elbow. Immediate attempts to save it failed and the arm had to be amputated. In the official photographs of his later years, Bienvenue is customarily shown posing from the right, with the amputation concealed; nevertheless, he preferred to make a joke of the mishap, and used to say: "In front of a group of expropriators I managed to expropriate my own arm."

In 1886, Bienvenue supervised the design and construction of aqueducts for bringing water into the city from the Aube and Loire rivers. Subsequently, he built a cable railway near the Place de la Republique, and created Buttes-Chaumont Park. Promoted through the ranks, in 1891 he became Engineer-in-Chief of Bridges and Roads, as prestigious a post as an engineer could hold in all France. Hence, when the Métropolitain became an imminent reality, it was natural enough for city officials to turn to him.

The impending crowds of the Universal Exposition of 1900 had a tonic effect on the plans. To speed up the work, the shield method, which had been preferred from the start, was discarded in favor of the cut and cover technique. Bienvenue, however, devised a new procedure less disruptive to life on the street: he built the crown of the tunnel first and the invert, or flooring, last, thus more or less reversing the construction norm:

A pilot gallery is cut following the line of the upper part of the main tunnel. Shafts are dug to this at intervals for removal of the soil. From this gallery, by digging sideways and supporting the earth above by props and wooden planks, space is obtained for building the roof of the tunnel with masonry (of dressed stone blocks). Under this roof the gallery can be widened into a covered trench along the line of the tunnel: from this trench, every few meters, side trenches are dug to where the walls are to be built. The walls, also of masonry, are built under the roof, giving a masonry arch tunnel resting on concrete footings. The whole of the tunnel cross-section is then excavated. The tunnel floor, or invert, of concrete is next added. Finally, liquid cement is injected behind the masonry work of the tunnel, to fill voids left by compression of the soil.

In this manner, a whole street could be excavated from several headings without having to be torn up all along its length, and could then be repaved for normal traffic while work continued underneath.

Early Métro labor gangs were sometimes a motley crew. In one contingent, there were several ruined businessmen, a group of acrobats, a dentist, and a marquis. The work was substantial: every twenty-four hours they had to remove about 1,000 cubic meters of dirt.

Built near to the surface, the tunnels systematically followed the course of the roads. As a result, they incorporated many sharp turns and steep gradients—including a hairpin curve on an incline near the viaduct over the Saint-Martin Canal, the one viaduct on the first line.

Despite Bienvenue's ingenious procedure, the work did create some havoc, and reaction was sometimes extreme. "Justifiably," attested one witness, "one heard everyone complaining that Paris was hatefully blocked up. The work sites of the Métro, which were erected everywhere like fortresses of clay and planks armed with an artillery of cranes, managed to tangle the roads and block the intersections. Not to mention that the tunneling undermined the city in every way and threatened Paris with collapse."

Paris was not really in danger of collapse, but the work did occasionally require extraordinary care. Near the Place Gambetta masonry shafts had to be sunk for support in quicksand; compressed-air caissons were brought in for tunneling beneath the Place de l'Opéra; near Buttes-Chaumont Park, among old gypsum quarries, progress was tentative at best in the cavernously unstable ground. Elsewhere, in dealing with marshy soil (as along the Quai Saint Michel) a vast refrigeration works was set up, bristling with tubes. These extended into the ground in every direction and artificially solidified it so it could be worked with tools.

The excavations were meticulously followed by the Commission Muncipale de Vieux Paris, created in 1898 with Charles Normand at its head. Those who anticipated a rich harvest of archaeological finds were not disappointed, for the shovels turned up Gallo-Roman and medieval artifacts as well as more recent objects of the city's past.

During the preliminary work of rerouting the sewers, the finds included Renaissance pottery shards, a medieval brooch, and the foundations of stables erected for Catherine de Médicis by Philibert de l'Orme. In 1899 a vaulted gallery was uncovered at Porte de Vincennes that once formed part of the ancient Roman causeway to the East. While building a terminal loop under Monçeau Park, the workers could hear the waters of a lost spring that had once irrigated the medieval garden designed by Carmentelle for the Duke of Chartres, of the Court of Orleans. As we know from other sources, the garden included a white marble temple, a Chinese bridge, and a little aqueduct. A Gallo-Roman sepulcher was also unearthed with a sarcophagus containing the skeleton of a young girl, whose head was laid to rest on a pillow of stone. More ancient still, at the Station Cité, charred remains from the original Roman settlement of Lutetia, razed in the first centuries A.D., were discovered. Also found were lapidary inscriptions, fragments of sculpture from the second and third centuries, funeral bas-reliefs, and a Christian tomb surmounted by a portrait in stone of two men and a woman in profile with the emblem of two fishes enclosed in a ring.

Charles Normand had wanted many of these finds preserved in the local stations, which he envisioned as museums of the city's past. Most artifacts, however, were transferred to the Musée Carnavalet.

At one point the Métro passed under a canal that had been formed by enlarging the ancient moat of the Bastille. Here, portions of the building from various stages of its history turned up: the cornerstone laid by provost Hugue Aubriot, on April 22, 1370, during the reign of Charles V; a parapet from one of the four towers added by Charles VI; and remnants of the outer bastion created by Henri II to serve as a garden for the king and a cemetery for non-Catholic prisoners who died.

Excavations for Station Jussieu revealed the foundations of the Abbaye de Saint Victor, one of the city's oldest abbeys. Its schools had edified many illustrious men, including Saint Bernard, Saint Thomas of Canterbury, and Peter Abélard. In the sixteenth century the church had been reconstructed and its burial crypt transformed into a chapel to the Virgin. But fragments of its supporting pillars were discovered beneath a wine cellar and today as travelers descend one of the stairways in the station, they pass through the place where this crypt once was.

The remains of many other ancient churches came to light,

among them that of Saint-Jacques-la-Boucherie and Saint-André-des-Arts. But perhaps the most remarkable find of all was an Egyptian oushabti, or funerary statuette, of Osiris, with arms crossed. Dating from the fourth century, it lent credence to an obscure tradition that there had once been a temple in Paris dedicated to Isis—perhaps on the site of Saint-Germain-des Prés, the city's oldest church.

On July 19, 1900, twenty months after the work had begun and only three months late, the first line of the Métro opened. It went from Porte Maillot in the east to Porte de Vincennes in the west, from one largely symbolic city gate to the other. The opening had originally been scheduled for July 14, Bastille Day, but was postponed by the Prefect of Police for fear of disorders. The precaution proved unjustified. The ceremony took place in late afternoon with only a few local dignitaries present. Still smarting from defeat, the state conspicuously snubbed the event: the previous day President Loubet had left Paris with the principal members of the government to attend a naval review in Cherbourg.

Le Figaro honored the occasion with a small paragraph announcement, tucked between two items of incidental news—one about an apoplectic fit of the Czar, the other about a charity sale. Reporters who attended noted slight things: that the stations resembled "cellars," for example, or that they smelled of disinfectant. All the articles did stress that the tunnels were pleasantly cool, for it happened that the day was a particularly hot one.

Most of the public was cynical. After almost a half-century of waiting they could hardly believe the Métro was real. Far more real seemed the *manifestations realisées* of the Exposition of 1900, which stretched from the Champs de Mars to the Esplanade des Invalides, and included such diverting auguries of the future as the "whirring dynamo" that fascinated Henry Adams.

Throughout the world the Métro would come to be symbolized by two cast-iron lampposts twisted upwards like gigantic rearing cobras, with a yellow sign hung between them lettered in a thick, black angular hand. If this image did not leap readily to mind, one thought of a variety of wired-glass and iron pavilions, inspired by orchid leaves and the wings of dragonflies—all painted a pale, eerie green resembling the patina of corroded copper.

The architect of these *édicules,* the original Métro entrances, was Hector Guimard, one of the foremost proponents of Art Nouveau. When he undertook the design commission he was already famous for his apartment house, the Castel Béranger, among other achievements. Yet so prominent did his *édicules* become that for a time Art Nouveau was actually known as "le style Métro."

Guimard's designs exhibited most of the qualities that advocates of the style proclaimed for it: evocative form, functional ornament, and abstract naturalism. Its myriad manifestations— from bookbinding to furniture to the graphic arts and architecture—can hardly be covered by a single descriptive epithet; but if its various exfoliations had one thing in common it was the "serpentine line." And indeed the serpent was a favorite image.

It is a style of many beauties, with a sinister cast, as writers were the first to recognize. In J. K. Huysman's *À Rebours,* an 1884 novel which did much to define *fin-de-siècle* sensibility, the hero sequesters himself in order to cultivate exotic tastes and sensations, and finds that his moods are subtly adjusted by (among other things) the typography of his books. In particular he is affected by one typeface "whose peculiar hooks and flourishes, curling up and down, assume a Satanic appearance"—clearly a precursor of the Art Nouveau designs then coming into vogue. Today similar typefaces are routinely exploited on the jackets of "Gothic" novels, murder mysteries, and tales of the supernatural and the weird.

Guimard daringly created a series of structures that harmonized, in a disquieting way, with their purpose as portals to the Underworld. Most Parisians were not happy about this. Some condemned the *édicules* as "Germanic" because of their green tint; others likened them to the "spines of ichthyosaurs" and the "waving tentacles" of creatures from the deep; and a large proportion of the population claimed to have trouble reading the lettering.

Le Figaro spoke of "contorted railings" and "enormous frogeye lamps," a "neurasthenic" and "hallucinatory" style. *Le Temps* agreed, and in particular attacked the typography: "These disorderly hieroglyphics are dismaying to little children trying to learn their alphabet in school. They are also confusing to foreigners. To calm our children and reassure the tourists, and above all for the honor of French taste, these ridiculous inscriptions must go." One outraged citizen branded Guimard the "Ravachol" of architecture, after the notorious political anarchist executed in 1892 for bombing churches.

Guimard's commission had come to him on the sly. In August 1899 an open competition had been held for choosing the stations' architect. But the winning design—for a neoclassical pavilion using freestone and glazed enamel reliefs—had left André Benard, President of the Municipal Council and an *aficionado* of the new style, cold. He went over the heads of the jury and hired Guimard. Nevertheless, consensus favored a traditional aesthetic. While many agreed with Charles Garnier that Paris must not "transform itself into a factory" with art of an "industrial character," Garnier for one had hoped for "stone and marble," "bronze sculptures and triumphal columns"—such as might harmonize with his own palatial Opéra facade. When Guimard submitted his design for the Opéra Station there was a terrific public protest because it did not "harmonize" with its setting. He wrote sarcastically in *La Presse*: "Must one harmonize the station at Père-Lachaise with the cemetery and construct it in the form of a tomb? Or that of the Place Mazas with the morgue? Or place a dancer kicking up her heels before the Place Blanche, to harmonize it with the Moulin-Rouge? Why put the station there in the first place? Why not put it behind the Opéra out of sight?"

Nevertheless, to the lasting credit of the city, one hundred forty Guimard *édicules* were installed all over Paris between 1900 and 1913. Most were simple cast-iron railings divided by two long stalks with a floral tip holding a lamp. Others, more elaborate, covered the stairwell with a glass roof, or were whole pavilions. In a few places, such as l'Etoile and Bastille, they even had a monumental character, and were exalted as the "flower of Baroque architecture."

Only a handful remain today. On July 27, 1967, the city designated seven for preservation as historic monuments.

When Franz Kafka visited Paris in 1923 he used to take the Métro out to the races on Sundays. He savored the paradox of being at once in a tunnel and in the reassuring company of a crowd. Nevertheless, he was amazed at the "unnatural indifference" with which most of the passengers submitted to the ride, and observed that whenever possible they seemed to prefer to "face the door."

Anxiety about traveling in the Métro was more manifest in its early years. A random encounter with a dangerous stranger seemed somehow both more likely and more sinister underground. "Only those condemned to death," remarked one contemporary, "and women who have to sit face to face with a ruffian in the darkness, know how long a minute can be." Nor was the Métro, in other respects, regarded as a wholesome place to be. Ezra Pound, in one of his more famous poems, "In a Station of the Métro," gives us its image:

The apparition of these faces in a crowd:
Petals on a wet, black bough,

while a M. Jolibois, in more prosaic testimony before the Municipal Council in 1900, offered this impression: "The Métro is a badly ventilated cellar, recalling at times a sewer. One is grabbed at the throat, on descending the stairs, by a succession of unnameable odors, unbreathable emanations, a mixture of sweat, coal-tar, carbonic acid, metallic dust, etc. . . . the whole of a heavy warmth like that of air on a stormy day."

There was also the danger of some terrible accident.

On August 10, 1903, just as the clock struck seven in the evening, a train of eight cars was passing through Barbes Station when flame flared suddenly from the cab in front, followed by a great gust of smoke. The motor had shorted out. As it happened, the train had a second motor car, and after a moment of alarm the conductor and his assistant evacuated the train and sent it on ahead to the Nation stop for repair.

But as the train approached Combat Station, on the way to Nation, its power faltered and a message for help was transmitted down the line. The next train, already loaded with its own passengers as well as those evacuated before, was emptied in its turn. The crowd began to grumble.

Meanwhile at Combat Station, the cab that had shorted out was smoldering with concealed flame. The second train now linked up with the first, forming a ghostly convoy of twelve deserted cars. On they glided, past Belleville Station, past Couronnes, to Menilmontant, where just as they arrived there was an explosion. Suddenly the smoke was intense. Thick flames flowed backwards along the cars, engulfing one after the other twelve boxes of resinous varnished wood, twelve empty boxes of kindling.

At the same time a third train was pulling into Couronnes Station with awful punctuality, carrying all the passengers previously stranded as well as its own. When the motorman saw a whirlwind of smoke coming toward him through the tunnel he exhorted the passengers to leave the train at once. They refused, saying they'd had enough; if they had to get off it would only be after a refund of their fare. Someone started to shout "nos trois sous," and soon others took it up as a chant. As their frivolous, fatal cry grew louder, they beat their fists on the rattan seats and rhythmically pounded the sides of the car.

The smoke swept into the station and extinguished the lights. Everyone rushed out blindly onto the platform. Matches flared and died; almost at once the oxygen was consumed.

At Menilmontant, where the twelve cars were burning, the heat was so intense that firefighters couldn't even get in to battle the blaze. As the evening wore on, a column of smoke four stories high rose from the mouth of the station.

It was not until dawn the following day that the casualties could be counted. Little more remained of the cars than ashes and their frames. Eighty-four people had perished: seventy-five at Couronnes, seven at Menilmontant, two in the tunnel—most from carbon monoxide poisoning. Some strange wrong instinct had guided most of them awry: the bodies were piled up at the opposite end of the platform from where the exit was.

An inquiry blamed the electrical equipment in the cars: the insulation was inadequate and was made of a material bound to give off a great quantity of smoke when burning. Henceforth, it was announced, all stations would be furnished with great paraffin lamps along passageways leading to exits, and portions of the stations would be reconstituted with incombustible material; wires for new protective lighting would be sunk in ballast, and alarms put in all of the stations and in the tunnels every hundred meters; trains would be limited to fewer cars; and so forth.

Such safeguards had little immediate psychological effect. The catastrophe cohered in the anxious hearts of many that special terror reserved for death underground. *L'Assiette au Beurre*, the "hardest-hitting and most visually compelling" of the contemporary social commentary magazines, rushed into print a special issue with a photogravure on the cover by Theophile Steinlen, showing Death as the ticket-taker in a Métro station. Dimitrios Galanis, another well-known artist, contributed zinc etchings that revived the word "Nécropolitain." Heuzé's prophecy of a quarter-century before had come to pass.

Like the Promethean gift of fire to man, the Métro was an ambiguous gift to the people of Paris: now a firetrap, now a refuge. In January 1916, bomb-laden dirigibles began to float over Paris in the first aerial bombardment of a city in history. On the evening of January 29, a bomb plunged through the Boulevard de Belleville into the tunnel near the Couronnes Station, inflicting the first wartime damage on the system. Perhaps in acknowledgment of the history of the site, the cavity was converted into a ventilation shaft.

The Métro was an obvious target. With the disruption of surface transport, it was called upon to bear an increasingly heavy load. Some stations were fitted out as air-raid shelters. When the invasion of northern France interrupted the supply of coal, it was necessary to cut the electricity on the lines; at the same time, lighting was virtually eliminated on elevated or open stretches of track. For awhile, underground trains were lit only by blue lamps, but the spectacle of these nearly invisible, eerily glowing caravans had an unsettling effect on the public. The authorities were forced to alternate the blue lamps with white.

When Fulgence Bienvenue retired as chief engineer in 1932 at the age of eighty, the Municipal Council held a special session in his honor. The words he spoke on that occasion revealed how completely his professional career had been consecrated to the Métro. He referred to himself in the third person, as "Father Métro," the spirit of the work. "The laborers," he said, "will no longer see his shadow silhouetted in the advancing tunnels. They will no longer catch sight of him outlined against the sturdy brick walls, where the mason goes about his patient toil, where the gouger of earth labors alongside the maker of vaults, abutments and pillars."

It was a touching farewell. Honors had come his way in abundance: in 1909 the Grand Prix Berger of the Academy of Arts and Sciences; in 1924 the Gold Medal of the City of Paris; in 1929 the Grand Cross of the Legion of Honor. Yet he was modest in his fame. He once remarked: "The work of an artist bears the stamp of his personality. But an engineer is the artisan of an impersonal work. For granted that the overall conception is an individual one, the execution of it brings together a great many separate efforts. In the Métro of Paris this impersonal quality is manifest to a high degree." Throughout his tenure he insisted on sharing his accolades with his staff.

Yet this self-effacement had its obverse side, and it is clear that in another way he had a large, perhaps heroic sense of his own accomplishment. It was said of him that he had done something "worthy of the Romans"—a tribute that could not have delighted him more. Bienvenue was a Latin scholar, with some skill at original composition; and the bronze tablet presented to him at his retirement was engraved with a hexameter verse of his own: *Jovis erepto fulmine, per inferus vehitus Promethei genus*—"The race of Prometheus has stolen the lightning of Jove and carried it into the Underworld."

PARIS

A PICTURE PORTFOLIO

*The elevated line proposed for Paris by Louis Heuzé.
The competition between subway and elevated railway
advocates was nowhere so fierce as in Paris, where the
elevated was regarded as an aesthetic offense, and the
subway as unsanitary, fostering all manner of disease.*

Above, Fulgence Bienvenue, "Le Père du Metro." It was said of him that his accomplishment in building the subway was a work "worthy of the Romans." Top right, a typical cut-and-cover scene in Paris. Bienvenue devised a special procedure for building the tunnels which was supposed to allow for swift repaving of the surface roads. Even so, some felt during the excavations that Paris was threatened with collapse. Below right, tunneling beneath the Seine.

Four varieties of Hector Guimard's Art Nouveau édicules, which for many years symbolized the Métro to the world. Although they helped foster an international style (Art Nouveau was once widely known as "le style Métro"), they scandalized much of the Paris population. Their green tint was criticized as "Germanic"; the lettering on the signs was said to be hard to read; and overall they were compared to the "spines of ichthyosaurs" or the waving tentacles of "creatures from the deep."

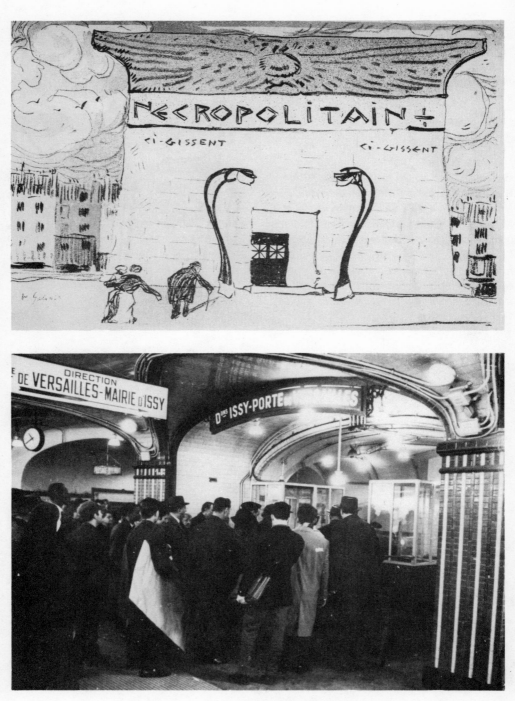

Art Nouveau sensibility curiously reflected in the sinuously curving electrical lines which follow the interior arches, above.

On August 10, 1903, 84 people perished in an electrical fire at the Couronnes Street Station. Theophile Steinlen's poster, below, was perhaps the most striking artistic comment on the event. It appeared, with the drawing by Dimitrios Galanis, left, in a special issue of L'Assiette au Beurre.

Above, a gathering of eminent citizens at the inauguration of the first Paris suburban subway line in 1934. Below, Jan Balet's brilliantly ambiguous lithograph of a modern Orpheus emerging from the Underworld. Note the musician's idiomatic resemblance to an "underworld character" with who-knows-what concealed in his case. In the distance, parallel lines of trees converge like railroad tracks, while above the stairwell a plaque advises "ENFER"—("HELL")—or (read as a pun) "IN IRON."

CHAPTER 6

The Lamp
and
the Ring

Everyone knows the story from *The Thousand and One Nights* about Aladdin and his magical lamp. By rubbing the lamp Aladdin could summon a genie to do anything he asked. When he desired a magnificent palace, the genie built it for him in a single night. We have already encountered this folk tale in another guise, at the beginning of our history, in the Faustian legend of the Middle Ages that ascribed the building of the first great road tunnel in history—the Roman military pass through Pausilypon—to the black art of Vergil, who completed the work "in one nighte's space."

In New York in the winter of 1870, the tale of Aladdin was on many lips. Word had it that under lower Broadway there was a secret room, furnished like a palace, connected to an underground railroad, the like of which had never before been seen. It was said that the trains were moved as if by magic by the wind, and that the railroad had sprung into existence almost overnight. It was a fabulous tale, and stirred the town with wonder. But it was also true.

This is the story.

In the early 1850's Alfred Ely Beach, co-publisher of the New York *Sun*, editor of *Scientific American*, patent attorney, and inventor, had an office on the top floor of the *Sun* building just below Printing House Square, where Fulton and Nassau streets intersect. Nassau Street was said to be "a good place to hide in." One of the narrowest streets in the city, its tall buildings shut out the light and cast it in perpetual gloom. The buildings were honeycombed with tiny offices, some hardly larger than a closet, many unidentified. A sort of back-alley of the financial district, the street became known as a "favorite place with persons who carry on unlawful trades, and do business by means of circulars and under assumed names."

On the face of it, Beach was not one of them. He was descended from a prosperous and respectable New England family whose forebears included a Plymouth pilgrim and Elihu Yale, the patron of Yale College. His father, Moses Yale Beach, owned the New York *Sun* and kept a house in Springfield, Massachusetts, where young Alfred was raised. Although he was sent to the best schools, he was not overindulged. When not at Monson Academy under the stern guidance of his uncle, the Reverend Alfred Ely, he was put to work in the family business, at first at the most menial jobs. In successive stages he worked as a newsboy selling extras, set type, sweated with the crew at the steam press, graduated to clerical work, and then went out as a reporter—with strict deadlines to meet. He mastered just about everything there was to know about his trade, and one thing that marked him as a man was his insistence on thoroughness and detail. When in 1848 his father turned the management of the *Sun* over to him and his brother Moses, he was suddenly, at the age of twenty-two, a person of considerable prominence.

From his top-floor office, where he occupied a sort of eyrie (the *Sun* building was one of the tallest in Manhattan at the time), Beach had a clear view southward to the tip of the island. He could see the new skyscrapers going up, seven and eight stories tall, mostly banks and insurance companies in the heart of the financial district. As yet—and for this he was glad—none could quite challenge the lofty imperial spire of Trinity Church in their midst.

Beyond, in the inner bay of the harbor, he could make out sailing vessels of every description crowding toward the wharves—the Indiamen, largest of all, with their huge white fin-like sails; sporty California clippers and little coasting sloops; turtle-like canal boats with their cargo from Erie; ice boats bearing their "crystal luxury"; oyster boats like floating sheds; barges and snorting bulldog tugs; and even an occasional European steamer, although most of these docked along the Hudson to the west. Outnumbering any of them at any one time were the ferries, operated by twenty-four different lines, linking Manhattan to Brooklyn, Staten Island, and New Jersey. They shuttled back and forth in waves, like a perpetual fleet. Across the East River, Brooklyn's uncluttered heights were arrayed with a diadem of stately mansions.

Over the past few years the ferries had multiplied their runs dramatically, as Manhattanites fled the island for the suburbs. This exodus had many causes—the prospect of cheaper rents, more open space, a more tranquil atmosphere—but beyond these allurements, the insult and injury of the city's crowded thoroughfares had become almost too much to take.

The stages or omnibuses were "clumsy, uncomfortable vehicles, inconvenient to enter, fatiguing to ride in, and dangerous to leave"; the cars of the street railroads were "dirty, badly ventilated, and full of vermin." Both ran constantly and in great numbers, and should have been fast. But the opposite was true. The volume of traffic was nearly paralyzing. As the New York *Tribune* put it: "We can travel from New York half-way to Philadelphia in less time than the length of Broadway."

A mere block from his office Beach could behold this morass in its epitome. There, where Broadway joined Park Row, stages, carts, and wagons might be seen at any time of day in hectic congregation, motionless for long periods of time, then in spasmodic motion, bunching together, lurching, stopping, crowding forward and jostling each other while drivers swore to the limit of verbal resources and sometimes lashed each other with their whips. Teams of horses reared, neighing wildly, terrifying pedestrians, while indignant passengers added their fulminations to the din. Often, policemen would appear in force, swinging clubs to restore order. One observer wrote that a pedestrian had to be a "sort of animated billiard ball, with power to carom from wheel to wheel," before he could safely "pocket" himself on the opposite walk. Most pedestrians, lacking such ballistic daring, were more like the futile boy in Horace's ode who waits all day long on the riverbank for the water to run by. Along its entire length lower Broadway was much like this; other thoroughfares offered a similar spectacle.

When Charles Dickens visited the city in 1842, he found the traffic as bad as London's, and in one respect even worse: wild pigs, "with scanty brown backs, like the lids of old horsehair trunks," mingled at will with the throngs of vehicles and pedestrians. Every decade from 1810 onward, the population increased by an average of 58 percent. Within a few years it would seriously be said that crossing Broadway was "as much as your life is worth." Nor were the ferry crossings themselves free of ordeal. Particularly in winter, when the rivers and bays were subject to ice floes and tempestuous gales, the short journey could seem "as treacherous as an Atlantic voyage."

First as a publisher, then as an inventor, Beach became involved in the rapid transit issue. The New York *Sun* added its voice to the chorus of complaint, and in 1849 Beach came up with a plan: "To tunnel Broadway through the whole length, with openings and stairways at every corner. This subterranean passage is to be laid down with double track, with a road for foot passengers on either side—the whole to be brilliantly lighted with gas. The cars, which are to be drawn by horses, will stop ten seconds at every corner—thus performing the trip up and down, including stops, in about an hour." Daring, almost unprecedented, the proposal was far ahead of its time: London would not have its Underground for another decade and a half.

Weary of his duties at the *Sun*, Beach longed to devote himself to scientific inquiry and publishing adventures in the scientific field. His loyalties were already divided down the middle of his working day. With his friend Orsun D. Munn, he had purchased the newly launched *Scientific American* in 1846, and soon became its editor. The magazine was ambitious, vowing to publish issues worth keeping long after "political and ordinary newspapers are thrown aside." In 1852 he left the *Sun* entirely to his brother Moses and the following year founded an illustrated monthly, the *People's Journal*, which carried items on agriculture, mechanics, and chemistry, as well as "useful knowledge" of a miscellaneous kind, including anecdotes and stories.

Meanwhile, he and Munn had set up a patent agency, known as Munn & Co., that was doing an enormous amount of business. Within a few years it would become the most important office of its kind in American history. Beach was extremely happy in this milieu, and in the company of inventors was generous, almost to a fault, with his time. Between 1850 and 1860 he traveled to Washington every two weeks at his own expense to look after his clients' affairs. At his New York office he offered free advice, and reputedly never turned an inventor from his door. Hour after hour he listened patiently to the famous and the obscure alike expound their sometimes fantastic conceptions in detail. Thomas Edison, Alexander Graham Bell, Samuel F. B. Morse, and John Ericsson (the designer of the Civil War ironclad, the *Monitor*) were among those who sought him out. Edison reportedly first demonstrated his phonograph in Beach's office. Beach turned the crank and the machine mumbled: "Good morning, sir. How are you? How do you like the talking box?"

If the history of American invention can claim a patron saint, it must surely be Beach. In 1846, the year he obtained *Scientific American* and started his patent service, less than six hundred patents were issued in the United States. By 1896, the year of his death, the number was more than twenty thousand. Moreover, some of the more notable patents were his own. One was a typewriter for the blind that featured a basket arrangement of the type rods and a spacing bar that moved the paper at each stroke. The forerunner of the standard modern office machine, it won First Prize and a Gold Medal at the Crystal Palace Exhibition in New York in 1856.

But Beach's greatest achievements as an inventor lay ahead.

The rapid transit problem had not faded from his mind. It was hard not to be aware of it. As the years passed, congestion had increased and service was deteriorating. "Modern martyrdom," wrote the New York *Herald* in 1864,

> may be succinctly defined as riding in a New York City omnibus. The discomforts, inconveniences and annoyances of a trip are almost intolerable ... It is in vain ... to seek relief in a [horse-drawn] car. People are packed into them like sardines in a box

with perspiration for oil. Passengers hang from the straps like smoked hams in a corner grocery . . . pickpockets ply their vocation . . . The foul, close heated air is poisonous.

The northern growth of the city had virtually stopped; the population, it was said, was "being driven across two rivers." In 1867 the state engineer pointed out that the number of passengers carried annually by the Third Avenue Railroad—twenty million—had remained the same for three years, proving that the road had reached the limit of its capacity. Other factors may have also played a part: "Personal violence," the engineer noted, was of "constant occurrence . . . At certain hours of the day the whole system of passenger transit can be compared to nothing save that of a mob in locomotion." Crossing the street had become a "passage of terror," and a force of police "had to be stationed at intersections to protect pedestrians from the attacks of drivers of vehicles." The New York *Evening Post* sketched in the larger picture:

New York has already nearly a million inhabitants, miserably accommodated for the most part . . . At present it is the most inconveniently arranged commercial city in the world. Its wharves are badly built, unsafe, and without shelter; its streets are badly paved, dirty and miserably overcrowded . . . The means of going from one part of the city to the other are so badly contrived that a considerable part of the working population . . . spends a sixth of their working day on the street cars or omnibuses.

The Department of Health had an interest in the matter too. The ill-paved streets, "broken by carts and omnibuses into perilous ruts and gullies," were further obstructed by debris, particularly "filth and garbage which was left where it was thrown to rot and send out its pestiferous fumes—breeding fever and cholera, and a host of other diseases across the city." As one writer observed, "The evils arising from the inadequacy of surface roads were almost as varied" in their sanitary and moral aspects "as a diamond with twenty facets"—unaccountably choosing a comparison that lent luster to the state of things.

With a kind of morbid fascination, countless studies were made of the exact volume of the traffic—ingeniously plotted by figure and chart, and calculated according to the season, the month, the week, the day, even the minute, then apportioned among the different kinds of transportation, in turn subdivided into the different lines. On a day in August 1852, Jacob Sharpe, a horse-car railway and ferry-line magnate (who would later die raving in a delirium after failing to secure a Broadway franchise), stood on the corner of Chamber Street and Broadway for thirteen hours and counted the number of omnibuses that went by, up and down. Every hour, on the average, 235 passed by each way, or 470 in all, with a mere thirteen-second interval between. In 1867 a reporter from the New York *Tribune* wanted to see how far things had progressed since Sharpe had made his count. He stood on the steps of Broadway's Astor House, also for thirteen hours, and added up the traffic. The numbers were astounding:

	7 A.M. UP	12 noon DOWN	12 UP	5 P.M. DOWN	5 UP	8 P.M. DOWN
Stages	714	691	710	683	442	432
Double trucks	397	616	512	476	173	194
Single trucks	1,151	1,213	1,355	1,214	287	782
Double carriages	158	158	191	205	94	124
Single carriages	70	93	101	85	45	25
Total	2,490	2,771	2,869	2,663	1,041	1,557

The total going uptown: 6,400; going downtown: 6,991—13,391 in all.

Something had to be done, or so it seemed; although a consensus as to the solution would have been hard to find. In addition to the misgivings about undergrounds and els that tormented the citizens of London and Paris, the issue in New York was entangled in politics in a way that set it apart. For while corporate and political power soon united in London to achieve the goal of rapid transit, and in Paris awaited only the resolution of the city-state feud, in New York these two forces—together far more powerful than public opinion—struggled in a conspiratorial way to delay the day of relief. Perhaps this is one reason why the engineers of the New York story emerge as especially appealing figures. Aside from some genuine personal virtues, the comparative simplicity of their mechanical aspirations appears even more candid and straightforward when set against the involved and devious stratagems of their foes. And this holds true even for those who were not without some aptitude for guile in accomplishing their ends.

Legislation for rapid transit could get nowhere in New York. The city had recently seen the rise of a most remarkable man whose name would become proverbial, even within his own lifetime, for big-city corruption. As a lowly alderman he and his confreres had been known, as "The Forty Thieves." Toward the height of his power *Appleton's Journal* called him a "Briareus of Plunderers," after the hundred arms of his ubiquitous graft. He was William Marcy ("Boss") Tweed, and he brought the corporate and political alliance in New York to undreamed-of refinements.

Tweed's financial base of power was inextricably bound up with transit revenues. As deputy street commissioner and later as commissioner of public works, he extorted vast sums from the various omnibus and street railroad lines in exchange for his patronage. With a covetous eye he watched out for their profit margins and guarded their franchises from competition. Many of the larger property owners in the city were also in league with the Tweed Ring. Others, honestly afraid that subway or elevated railway construction would devalue their real estate, played into the Ring's hands. After the election of 1868, when his candidates for city and state office won across the board, Tweed's power was almost absolute. Through his Tammany Hall protegé, Governor John T. ("Toots") Hoffman, he was able to exercise a grip on municipal legislation that was virtually complete.

The first rapid transit bill of any real importance was introduced into the New York State legislature in March 1864, on behalf of the Metropolitan Railway. The company proposed an underground line beneath Broadway from the Battery to Thirty-Fourth Street, and from there under Sixth Avenue, which merges with Broadway at that point, to Central Park. The promoter was Hugh B. Willson, a Michigan railroad man and financier who had been on hand for the opening of the London Underground in January 1863. He attracted several influential backers, among them John Jacob Astor, Jr. Within a short time about $5 million was raised.

The bill was defeated. A New York *Times* editorial fixed the blame:

> The defeat of the Underground Railroad in the legislature ... is a fresh and alarming illustration of the enormous power over our property and comfort which is now wielded by the omnibus proprietors, railroad corporations and political jobbers. The legislature on which we have been relying seems to have surrendered itself completely to their hands.

Willson didn't give up. He called in a consultant to make his proposal more convincing and hired A. P. Robinson to draft new plans. Robinson, today an undeservedly forgotten engineer, set to work with enthusiasm.

The advantages of an underground road appeared manifold:

> There would be no dust, there would be no mud. Passengers would not be obliged to go into the middle of the street to take a car. They have simply to enter a station from the sidewalk and pass down a spacious and well-lighted staircase to a dry and roomy platform. The temperature would be cool in summer and warm in winter. There would be no delays from snow or ice. The cars would not be obliged to wait for a lazy or obstinate truckman. The passenger would be sure of a luxurious seat in a well-lighted car, and would be carried to his destination in one-third the time he could be carried by any other conveyance. These would be the advantages to those who ride, and for that other great public using the streets there would be no collisions, no broken wheels or fractured axles, nor frightened horses or run-

over pedestrians. Everything would be out of sight and hearing, and nothing would indicate the great thoroughfare below.

This is how it would be during the day. At night, between midnight and six in the morning, the subways would be used for freight—the additional revenue helping the line become self-sufficient.

As in London, the engines were to be coke-burning locomotives made to condense their own steam. But there the resemblance would end. In London the route ran under a relatively minor thoroughfare, at some distance from the main business district; in New York "the field is open for a Grand Trunk line through the heart of the city since the great city movement is north and south, following either Broadway or parallel lines and not diffused laterally, or in every direction, as in London . . . We are therefore substantially commencing *de novo*, for we have different conditions to fulfill." It took courage to say this; the legislature would have preferred to hear that the project could be carried out along proven lines.

Great domed buildings, comparable to some London stations, would be impossible downtown, although they might be erected at the termini of the line and at two city squares, Union and Madison, along the route. A design for one of these stations survives, showing a handsomely proportioned cupola, with ground-level floors of wire and glass for admitting light directly to the tunnel.

The tunneling could be done economically, by building "as near the surface as possible" and following the watershed or ridge of the island. This meant, more or less, following Broadway all the way to Central Park. The coincidence of geography and commerce compelled the line of the route as well as the technique of its construction.

Robinson had a prophetic imagination. His cut and cover method, which involved constructing the floor, or invert, of the tunnel last, anticipated the procedure later credited to Parisian engineers. One of his other ideas was for synchronized trains, all moving in unison and coordinated by electric clocks.

Armed with this seemingly unimpeachable plan, Willson once

again applied for a charter. After a stiff floor flight, it passed, only to be vetoed by Governor Reuben Fenton, who favored an elevated railroad. Fenton was more than a little influenced by the testimony of Alfred W. Craven, the chief engineer of the Croton Aqueduct Board, who ruminated over the effect the subway construction would have on the city's sewer, water, and gas mains. Craven was their caretaker, and presumably knew more about them than anybody else. In February 1865, the year before, he had cautiously backed Willson's plan. He had written to him, "I have no doubt . . . that the works you contemplate can be so constructed, and the necessary removals and changes in the water mains, sewers, etc., be made in such a manner that, after this whole is completed, the public works will not be found to be permanently impaired, either in regard to their condition or efficiency of operation." Now he unfurled the prospect of a vast and intricate disaster.

> The extent of damage to individuals and to companies growing out of the construction of the suggested railroad is impossible to estimate with even approximate correctness. The area of population covered, the extent and variety of the interests involved and the different degree of inconvenience and loss sustained by each class of sufferers, all make up a whole so complicated that the actual experience alone of proved results could warrant any summing up of the total loss or damage. That the municipal government, which has guaranteed to consumers the use of this water, would be obliged to make good the losses growing out of the interruption seems probable. I do not advert to the cost to the city of making all these changes in the mains because the cost of removal and reconstruction would depend on so many contingencies that it is impossible to arrive at any degree of accuracy.

Such was the opinion he gave the state legislature on February 2, 1866.

Robinson was indignant. But Willson's support in the legislature had fallen apart. Origen Vanderburgh, formerly a Willson lobbyist, now pushed his own bill for the same franchise. Willson charged Vanderburgh with attempted "piracy"; Vanderburgh tried to buy Willson off with $112,500. The Vanderburgh bill had strong support, even though it was clearly founded on the documents and testimony Willson's company had supplied. The Senate Railroad Committee voted for it but then a senator revealed that each member of the committee had been paid $10,000 for his vote. In the ensuing scandal, the Senate Committee of the Whole killed it and everything else related to railroad rights on Broadway.

By 1866 there were twenty-nine omnibus and fourteen horse-car lines along major thoroughfares and subsidiary streets, carrying about 100 million passengers a year. Three steam railroads ran into the city as far south as Twenty-seventh Street—the New York & New Haven Railroad, the Hudson River Railroad, and the New York & Harlem Railroad—whose route included a quarter-mile tunnel through solid granite and a mile of open cut.

Most of this traffic traversed a rather small area, since more than half the population lived below Fourteenth Street in a zone roughly 2 miles square. Moreover, 40 percent of the tens of thousands of immigrants who arrived at the Port of New York took up lodging near the docks, which handled 75 percent of all imports and exports for the entire nation. Above Forty-second Street New York could "scarcely be said to exist, being only a dreary waste of unpaved and ungraded streets diversified by rocky eminences crowned with squatters' shanties."

This was the territory over which Tweed ruled. Of his many adversaries, the most resourceful by far was Alfred Ely Beach. Beach assessed his strength. The New York *Sun*, still controlled by his brother Moses, wielded substantial power. A working-class paper, its circulation of over fifty thousand (it was a pioneer penny daily) was among the largest in the world. Horace Greeley, editor of the rival New York *Tribune*, had called it "slimy and venomous . . . Jesuitical and deadly in politics, and groveling in morals." Be that as it may, more than half the city was then immigrant Catholic, and the laborers and servant girls who bought it helped make up the Tammany rank and file.

Beach also had powerful friends, including Henry Ward Beecher, the "Hercules of Protestantism," as he was called, whose stirring oratory from the pulpit of Plymouth Church in Brooklyn Heights had made him the most influential divine in the nation. The pulpit Beecher pounded for emphasis was made of wood that Alfred's brother had brought back from a pilgrimage to the Mount of Olives in the Holy Land.

Beach was obviously a man to be reckoned with. But Tweed somehow never took his measure. For a long time he affected to regard him with disdain. Having come up the hard way as a second-generation Scottish immigrant, without local pedigree, Tweed felt most at home with "big-handed, red-faced, boisterous men" like himself who had proletarian backgrounds. Beach, on the other hand, was rather small and delicate, with a professorial mien, while his character was almost proverbially upright, after the Benjamin Franklin mold. He went to bed early, got up early, exercised daily according to a fixed routine, attended church every Sunday, and worked very hard. It is said that he never took a vacation in his life. He was healthy (his only known illness was his last, pneumonia), wealthy (almost a millionaire), and, very possibly, wise. An acquaintance testified that "his only dissipation was the opera." It is not surprising that the palpably corrupt Boss Tweed disliked him. They were natural opposites.

Heady with power, Tweed comported himself like a potentate. His legislators-for-hire, or "Black Horse Cavalry," as they were called, closed ranks at command. Almost nothing could get through the legislature without his imprimatur. Beach saw that he would lose in an open confrontation. So he did what Tweed least expected: he dropped out of sight. He busied himself with inventions great and small and, in a manner not unworthy of the best of the Nassau Street confidence men, evolved a scheme that would one day cause them all to admire him.

The task Beach set for himself seemed impossible: to build a rapid transit line in New York City without anyone being aware of it—a line, moreover, that would be so convincing to the skeptical public that, once revealed, it would win them over to it en masse.

An elevated railroad was obviously out of the question. His line would have to be underground. The only precedent was the underground steam locomotive in London, then in its early phases of development. But Beach hated the locomotive. In *Scientific American* he had often inveighed against its noise and pollution—its "screeching whistles, smoke and cinders, and burnings from sparks." He was not out of sympathy with Broadway property owners like A. T. Stewart, the department store magnate, who was sure there was "scarcely a building that would not be materially damaged, if not destroyed" by an underground railroad. Even if a tunnel could be safely built, alarming reports were coming out of London about this time as to what travel in the tunnels was like. It was pointed out that the ventilation was not good, despite open cuts for air. Nevertheless, the lungs of many a Londoner on any given day were excoriated by scalding inhalations of steam. New Yorkers could read the firsthand reports of a correspondent like Francis Kirk, writing in the *Scientific American*: "What is at first merely unpleasant soon becomes unhealthy and eventuates in a subtle poison, first affecting delicate organizations, and afterwards visiting alike the weak and the strong, the unhealthy and the healthy, engendering pestilence, and this is the ready ally of all contagious diseases. Surely such a calamity should not be visited upon any people under cover of an enactment for their benefit." In Kirk's view, a subway might bring on cholera or yellow fever.

One day the New York *Post* announced: "A coroner's jury has just condemned the atmosphere of the underground railway." The jury convened to look into the death at King's Cross Station, London, of a woman named Dobrier attributed her death to a bronchial ailment accelerated by "suffocating air." The New York *Tribune* carried an expanded account, rather dramatically italicized:

A young woman, apparently in *good health*, entered the Bishop's Road station on Wednesday evening. On reaching the platform she said: "It is a very nice station but very hot." On getting into one of the carriages she said: *"What a dreadful smell there is here."* These were the last words she spoke! At King's Cross she was taken out by her companion in apparently lifeless condition. A physician being sent for, arrived in five minutes, and found her *dead*. An examination showed she had died from restriction of the aortic orifice.

An inquiry showed "that sulphurous and carburetted gases [had] gone on accumulating in the tunnels of the railway till the air had become dangerous to breathe, till the presence of choke damp, to be followed by fire damp, threatened a terrible explosion."

Occasional passengers complain of *headaches, sulphurous taste on the palate, and a stinging sensation in the throat, as of common occurrence. The employees at the station complain of the air, affirming that no man whose lungs are delicate can keep at work without suffering, and that a short, dry, hacking cough is common among all who are on duty.* At the first inquest the *coroner declared* that he avoided the railway as much as possible, *because of the depressing effect he experienced from the confined atmosphere. The jury returned a verdict,* in the words of the surgeon, that DEATH WAS ACCELERATED BY THE SUFFOCATING ATMOSPHERE OF THE UNDERGROUND RAILWAY.

In spite of such testimony, subway advocates abounded, while a touch of romance peculiarly American harmonized the idea of the underground with freedom: the legendary underground railway of the pre-Civil War years that had guided southern slaves through the North into Canada, out of reach of the Fugitive Slave Law. Some journalists wrote with opportunistic vulgarity about "the enslavement" of New Yorkers by their thoroughfares and how an underground road "would set them free."

For his own more refined reasons, Beach concurred—short of having to breathe the products of combustion. The intolerable problems of ventilation ruled out a locomotive. For a time he dabbled in cable traction, a cleaner sort of power. At length he hit upon his solution: a "rope of air." Such was the phrase recently coined by George Stephenson, one of England's foremost railway engineers. It referred to the pneumatic tube.

The idea of using pneumatic, or atmospheric, power for transportation was first introduced around 1800 by a Danish engineer, but it was in England that it matured. In 1805 George Medhurst, a Soho scale manufacturer, wrote an essay "On the Properties, Power and Application of the Aeolian Engine," in which he described how, within an enclosed space, the creation of a vacuum in front of an object could produce a tremendous atmospheric thrust behind it. He refined this notion over the course of twenty years, suggesting its practicality for moving the mails, merchandise, and even passengers through tubes. Brunel's South Devon Railway experiment (which, as we saw, lay behind the special appeal of Paxton's Crystal Way) had adapted Medhurst's idea to open air use. Indeed, all subsequent developments in the field owed Medhurst a considerable debt, but within his own lifetime his work was ignored.

In February 1844 the pneumatic-tube idea received a great boost when Prime Minister Robert Peel endorsed it in a parliamentary debate. A Select Committee backed it in April 1845, and a few months later the influential *Mining Journal*, in anticipation of the wave of the future, changed its name to the *Mining Journal and Atmospheric Railway Gazette*. In 1844–1845, plans for 300 miles of "open-air" atmospheric railway were submitted to Parliament. The idea was also catching on in France, and a 5½-mile stretch between Paris and Saint Germain was run on the atmospheric plan. At the same time, the British Post Office was making headway with related experiments. In 1842 W. A. James had proposed that hollow spheres sealed with plugs might be used for conveying the mails through tubes. In 1853 J. Latimer Clark linked two stations of the Electric and International Telegraph Company in London by a slender tube 220 yards long. By alternate use of a vacuum and compressed air, communications were whisked back and forth with remarkable celerity. It was only a matter of time before a similar attempt would be made on a grander scale. It came in 1861, two years before the opening of the Underground. After a trial run using dogs, thirty people were propelled in a carriage through a tube a quarter of a mile long in Battersea Field. The initial run was so promising that the Waterloo & Whitehall Railway was incorporated to construct a line on pneumatic principles from Charing Cross to the South Western Railway. The route was to include a tunnel under the Thames.

In New York, Beach was inspired. He could now envision a universal form of transit with all the blessings he thought it should have: it would be clean, quiet, and swift, "as swift as Aeolus, as silent as Somnus." By 1867 he had a working model of his own. At the Exhibition of the American Institute held that year in the Fourteenth Street Armory, he surfaced with his trial invention. A wooden tube, 6 feet in diameter and 107 feet long, was suspended from the ceiling and fitted with a car that seated ten. The car was cylindrical, with about an inch between it and the tube's inner sides. The tube had an elegant, light appearance; its walls were just an inch thick, but laminated in layers for strength. A large fan, powered by a stationary steam engine, stood at one end and blew the car through.

The contrivance was a sensation, drawing the largest crowds. One hundred thousand people took the ride. The newspapers reported it with excitement, and for a while there was a good deal of talk about pneumatic els. Tweed, of course, scoffed at the idea.

Beach next put out a little book on pneumatic power aimed at winning support among laymen. He kept the technical jargon to a minimum. "The mechanism," he explained,

> is of the simplest description: a tube, a car, a revolving fan! Little more is required. The ponderous locomotive, with its various appurtenances, is dispensed with, and the light aerial fluid that we breathe is the substituted motor . . . The velocity of the car is in proportion to the degree of atmospheric pressure . . . The car, in effect, is a piston moving within the tube.

Even as his book was coming off the press, he advanced another step. Since he had no chance of getting a subway bill past the governor, he sought permission instead for an underground mail dispatch line between Warren and Cedar streets near lower Broadway. The line was to connect up with the main Post Office near Liberty Street. He predicted that it "would rival the telegraph in speed." Tweed, who had expected Beach to begin compaigning for a pneumatic el, was delighted to see him so diverted. Beach nurtured his delight. The charter was above suspicion ("for the transmission of letters, packages and merchandise"), and its engineering specifications were disarmingly precise: two tubes would have to be built, each with a diameter of 4½ feet—obviously too small for a railroad car.

The charter went through.

It was a ruse. With act in hand, Beach then asked the legislature for an amendment. He wanted one large tube instead, to simplify the work and save expense. Although the Tweed Ring had made millions on amendments, somehow the Beach maneuver was overlooked—perhaps as unplunderable, perhaps as unimportant compared with other, more profitable legislation at hand. It passed.

Beach wasted no time. Working by night out of the basement of Devlin's Clothing Store at the corner of Warren Street and Broadway, he tunneled south toward Murray Street, carting away dirt in covered wagons rolling on muffled wheels. For the tunneling he had built his own hydraulic shield, one of the major inventions of the century. Although fundamentally modeled on Brunel's historic original, its cylindrical form, "which in shape resembled a barrel with the ends out," anticipated James Henry Greathead's slightly later design, which became the great standard. It gouged out 16 inches of earth at a time.

Just six men were needed to operate the remarkably compact machine: two to work the hydraulic rams, two to carry out the loosened earth, and two to lay the brickwork from beneath the rear hood. Eight horizontal shelves with sharpened leading edges extended across the front, while eighteen hydraulic rams, or pistons, were positioned at the rear and along the sides. Each of the pistons had a cock, so that they could be worked separately or in unison. By this means Beach could precisely control the direction of the tunneling—ascending or descending according to the required grade, or traveling on a curve of any desired radius.

Following the precedent set by Brunel in England with the building of the Thames Tunnel, Beach put his son Frederick in charge of the works. The historical analogy was a conscious touch: Beach understood very well the importance of what he was doing.

The soil was soft, and tunneling took just fifty-eight nights. In order to guarantee the accuracy of the route—in addition to the usual compass and survey—Beach had jointed rods of iron driven up through the roof of the tunnel to the pavement. The workmen were often jumpy. Even at night, when the Broadway traffic was intermittent, the sound of iron wheels on the cobblestoned road overhead was transmitted underground as a thunderous roar.

The one physical obstacle of any magnitude was a complete surprise: the stone foundations of an old Dutch fort, a pre-Revolutionary War colonial relic. But the shield held. One by one the stones were loosened and passed through its shelves into the night. An arched way was created and the shield continued on.

The completed tunnel was 312 feet long, cylindrical, arched with brick, laid with tracks, and furnished with a single car. For most of its length it followed the straight line of Broadway, but toward Warren Street it swept in a graceful curve into the station. At the point of the turn it was supported by cast-iron segments bolted together in rings. The tunnel was painted white throughout and brightly illuminated by rows of gaslights and Zircon oxygen lamps. The latter were a recent invention, highly touted for the clarity with which colors could be seen in their light.

At the Warren Street end, out of sight in a sort of alcove, stood a huge, 100-horsepower Aelor or Helix fan weighing 50 tons and christened the Western Tornado. One of the new Roots Patent Force Rotary Blowers recently developed for ventilating mines, it blew the car down to Murray Street gently, "like a boat before the wind," until, toward the end of the track, the wheels touched a telegraph wire which rang a bell back at Warren Street. There a waiting engineer pulled a rope which shifted an air valve, reversing the fan. The car was then sucked back along the tracks. The air for these operations was drawn through a ventilator shaft that opened out through a grate inside the grassy plot of City Hall Park, near Murray Street. Unwary passersby commonly had their hats snatched off their heads and loosely held objects plucked from their hands. (A circle of metal at the base of the Nathan Hale statue today marks the spot.) But the passengers waiting within hardly felt a draft, for the entrance to the tunnel was fitted with a double set of doors, one set always being closed.

In designing the station Beach saw to it that the requirements of his charter were, at least in principle, redeemed. In addition to propelling the car, the fan powered a sort of in-house postal dispatch: 1,000 feet of 8-inch-diameter tubing meandered about the premises, carrying letters and papers from one place to another at 60 miles per hour. The whole system was connected to a hollow lamp-post drop on the street above, in a manner then being proposed for the London mails.

The subway car itself, though small, was bright and appointed like a lounge. It seated twenty-two, and overall was shaped like a horseshoe. The ride was smooth. When the sliding doors of the car closed, "there was a noise like the approach of a squall at sea, and then a slight tremor as the car moved out of the station." It went about 6 miles an hour, but might easily have been driven at ten times that speed. Exerting just a few grains of atmospheric pressure to the square inch, the fan could deliver 100,000 cubic feet of air per minute to the tunnel.

The air in the tunnel was pure. "It is free," Beach wrote with feeling, "from that filthy, health-destroying street dust that runs over and collects in people's hats and coats, fills their hair, beards and eyes, and floats in their breath like the vapor of a frosty morning." Alternately blower and exhauster, the Western Tornado was like that fabled "fireless engine" never realized in London's lost battle against tunnel pollution.

Beach's subway was just an exhibition piece, of course. But he celebrated the achievement in high style. Remembering a warning he had once read in London's *Mechanics Magazine* that man has "a great and natural antipathy to being placed in a dark, cheerless tube and blown to his destination," he took care to make his tunnel bright, and built a waiting room 120 feet long and 14 feet wide, which he called "cozy." It was more.

Adorned with frescoes, illuminated with Zircon lamps, generously furnished with easy chairs and plushly upholstered settees, it had damask curtains in its blind window niches, oil cloths with pretty patterns on the floor, and chandeliers strung along the walls so that their light was spread through mirrors. Beach also installed an expensive grandfather clock, railed off a special section for the ladies, complete with a Chickering grand piano, and—after the fashion of the most prodigal salons—set a cascading fountain in its midst. The basin was alive with goldfish. The sound of falling water helped soften the roar of overhead traffic to a "hum like that of a cotton mill." Such was the dazzling opulence of this room that it recalled to many the Oriental luxuries bestowed upon Aladdin by his genie of the lamp. One reporter was to dub it "Aladdin's cave."

Nor was its further recess, the tunnel platform to which one descended by a flight of six steps at the eastern end, untouched by splendor. As the mouth of the tunnel came suddenly into view, the keystone arch which surmounted it announced in elegantly engraved letters: "PNEUMATIC (1870) TRANSIT," while on either side, poised on a pedestal, stood a bronze athletic figure of Mercury—messenger of the gods, symbol of the speed of winds—upholding a triform cluster of gaslights alternately enclosed by red, white, and blue globes.

Such grandeur took nearly two years to finesse; about $70,000 of Beach's own money went into it. Then, when the subway was almost complete, a reporter for the New York *Tribune*, disguised as a workman, gained access to it and broke the whole story. Along with a fairly complete description of the works, the *Tribune* published a small-minded editorial attacking the idea as impractical. To rebut this criticism, Beach opened his subway to the public on February 28, 1870. He charged twenty-five cents a head. To demonstrate that he was not out for personal gain, most of the money went to a charity, the Union Home for Orphans of Soldiers and Sailors.

The subway was a wild and immediate success.

In one stroke, Beach had blown away the strongest argument against a subway line—that it would undermine the foundations of the city's tallest buildings and bring them crashing to the ground. The tunnel was done; tall buildings still stood along its route above. And Broadway continued to bear up its twenty thousand vehicles a day. Moreover, that traffic had never even been disturbed.

Tweed was flabbergasted. He could scarcely believe this marvel had been installed right under his nose. Moreover, his options were now limited to the legal, which made him feel at bay. Through his confederates at City Hall, he brought suit for an injunction on constitutional grounds—but lost. The reasons why he lost are not clear, since his case was a sound one: the line was technically in violation of its own charter. But the degree of popular feeling was almost certainly a factor. The court decided to let the legislature decide.

Though Tweed's power was still large, his control had begun to slip, while squabbling among the Tammany faithful was growing. Moreover, the legislators had to contend with a passionate lobby of civic interest groups now united across a broad front. There was even some feeling that Governor Hoffman would have to go along with a strong majority vote if Beach could get it. He thought he could. "It will not be long now," he prophesied, "before New York will be provided with underground railways in all directions." He submitted a bill for carrying his subway through to Central Park, a distance of about 5 miles. In the next legislative session it passed the senate by 22 to 5, and the assembly by 102 to 9.

Hoffman vetoed it, alleging that certain engineering problems had not been faced. In particular, he said, he did not see how a tunnel could be driven beneath the intersection of Broadway and Canal Street without causing a flood. Eminent engineers responded with surprise. One of them, Douglas Fox, pointed out that the problems already overcome in building the London subway "dwarf into insignificance anything that can be encountered in New York."

As Beach prepared his lobbying effort for the next legislative session, he drew nearly unanimous support from the city's press. Among others, the *World*, the *Evening Mail*, the *Journal of Commerce*, and of course the *Sun* backed him. Alfred Craven, the engineer whose testimony had discouraged enthusiasm for the Robinson plan, said he was sure Beach's proposal was sound, as did another prominent engineer, J. G. Bernard, who assured Beach that his subway could be built "without endangering the foundations of any existing building."

Then, out of nowhere, another rapid transit bill appeared, with remarkably strong legislative support. It had all sorts of important people behind it. John Jacob Astor, Charles L. Tiffany, and August Belmont were among the incorporators and sat on the board of directors. But in conception it was most strange. It called for an elevated steam railroad mounted on massive masonry arches 40 feet high to be built through entire city blocks. If implemented, it would have leveled much of the city east of Third Avenue and west of Sixth. On the East Side, a line was to run north to Harlem; on the West Side, north to Spuyten Duyvil, near Kingsbridge.

The East and West Side Associations joined forces in horror against it. On top of everything else, it was obvious that the expense of building it would require an exorbitant fare. It would be a railroad for the rich, who would ride upon it high above the city like Roman emperors. Pompously styled the Viaduct Railway, it was really a sort of parody of Roman aqueduct design. On March 11, 1871, the New York *Sun* remarked:

> The bill introduced at Albany on Thursday, proposing to construct a viaduct railroad on Manhattan Island, appears to have been intended simply to give the quietus *to all schemes of rapid transit*. The capital proposed for the Viaduct Company—enormous as it is—would probably not be more than a third of the sum required for so costly an enterprise . . . the idea of carrying the viaduct like *a huge* deformity across Broadway is of itself enough to indicate that the scheme is not meant to be taken in earnest.

This was almost exactly right. The mastermind of the Viaduct was none other than Tweed, and at bottom, of course, it was a rip-off scheme. To begin with, the city was committed to an initial subscription of $5 million for the first $1 million raised in private capital. Estimates are that Tweed stood to make about $60 million from it overall. Gustavus Myers, an urban historian, called it "an unparalleled steal."

When the Beach bill and the Viaduct bill came up for a vote in 1872, they both passed. The Beach bill was sent to Hoffman first, who vetoed it. A motion to override failed by just a single vote. The Viaduct bill was then dutifully signed into law.

But the Tweed Ring was falling apart. In July 1871 the New York *Times* had started looking into Tweed's affairs, and in a relentless series of articles had divulged enough scandal to electrify the nation. In December, an investigative committee of seventy citizens, headed by Samuel J. Tilden, had indicted

Tweed for forgery and grand larceny. Though he was able to delay the trial for another year through legal maneuvering, his hegemony was coming to an end. Eventually he was convicted and went to jail for life. But it is remarkable how long it took for the public to catch up with him. Meanwhile the Viaduct Railway scheme collapsed in disgrace, while the state's electorate, clamoring for reform, swept into office General John A. Dix as the new governor.

For the third time, Beach submitted his charter to the legislature. It passed the assembly unanimously and the senate with only three dissenting votes. The New York City Board of Aldermen immediately petitioned the governor to sign the charter into law. He did so two days later, on April 9, 1873.

But the wheel of fortune kept turning; it passed the zenith and dropped.

On September 18, the doors of Jay Cooke & Co., "the largest and most pious bank in the Western world," closed. A panic brought on by the vast oversale of American railroad bonds swept the investment markets of Europe like a tidal wave and then recoiled on American shores. One railroad after another failed—the Northern Pacific, the Canada Southern, the Chesapeake & Ohio. Five thousand commercial houses and national banks followed Jay Cooke & Co. into bankruptcy. Leading securities fell thirty to forty points in an hour. A few days later the stock market suspended trading. It was the Panic of 1873. All at once, railroads seemed the last thing in the world on which to make a safe speculation.

Beach was dismayed. Appealing to the city to help finance the line, he pointed out that funds from the city treasury were being used to help build the Brooklyn Bridge and to rebuild the Harlem Railroad. If any one project was in the public interest, he argued, it was his. "All the money can be had at thirty days' notice on condition that the City will guarantee the Company's bonds to the amount actually expended upon the first section of the road." A prestigious London firm, Sir Charles Fox & Sons, was prepared to back him but in the aftermath of the financial turmoil, the city refused to take the risk.

Beach was not one to languish in disappointment. He repaired his spirits by expanding his activities as a publisher. In 1872 he had started the *Science Record*, an illustrated octavo volume of 590 pages for republishing, in expanded form, significant material from *Scientific American* of the previous year. A few years later this was succeeded by the extremely influential *Scientific American Supplement*, a "review of reviews," or digest of current scientific opinion. At about the same time, he began to publish *Scientific American* in a Spanish edition with a view to uniting the scientific community of the Americas, north and south. Later, he started still another edition, one especially for *Architects and Builders*. This eventually became the best-selling periodical *American Homes and Gardens*.

Beach waited in vain. In 1870, four hundred thousand people had visited his model line. Some had come for the ride; others, to see the waiting room or to enjoy the brightly lit, whitewashed tunnel as a promenade in the evening when the car was not in use. But as time wore on, curiosity wore off. By the end of 1874 it was no longer being taken very seriously, and Beach had spent all he could afford out of pocket on lobbying fees. Increasingly he heard from self-styled experts in Albany that atmospheric power was limited, that it wasn't the answer. Proponents of locomotive subways weren't faring any better. New schemes had gained the limelight. The going thing now was the el.

Beach rented out his tunnel as a shooting gallery, later as a storage vault for wines. When at length proceeds could no longer even cover upkeep, he closed it down and had it sealed.

Beach's career was distinguished to the end. He remained as editor of *Scientific American* until his death in 1896; and six years before he died he saw a shield based on his own drive one of the more spectacular tunnels of the age—the great railroad tunnel between Port Huron, Michigan, and Sarnia, Canada, under the Saint Clair River.

His Broadway tunnel had an extraordinary fate. So thoroughly did oblivion befall it that when in February 1912 astounded BMT workers broke in upon it while building their own line—forty-two years after it was first revealed to the public—it was like an archaeological find. The station was still largely intact. The fountain, long dry, still stood; the car was on the tracks.

Even the shield was there, determinedly set against the forward tunnel wall. Though the wooden partitions of the shield had rotted, its rusted metal frame remained strong. The Public Service Commission offered it to Beach's son, Frederick (by then an elderly man in his last years as editor of *Scientific American*), as a relic; he presented it in turn to Cornell University, which exhibited it in the museum at Sibley College in Ithaca, New York.

The tunnel eventually became part of the BMT City Hall Station, where it is commemorated by a simple plaque.

CHAPTER 7

The Elevated Atmosphere in New York

I n Oliver Goldsmith's *The Deserted Village* there is a prophecy that goes:

> *Ill fares the land to hastening ills a prey,*
> *Where wealth accumulates and men decay.*

It is an eighteenth-century sort of prophecy, uninvolved with the Sibyl's voice. Unenigmatic, almost Newtonian, it could hardly be wide of its mark. Still, whatever the final destiny of a city (only God or the Sibyl could know that), it is an apt prophecy for the rapid transit story in New York, where humaneness of invention would be married to misfortune in almost every case.

To a large extent, as seems common in American corporate life, the same select group of men had a hand in many of the different companies, so that we encounter a sort of rotating directorate—either in succession, as in the revolutions of a carousel, or simultaneously, as in the double image of a stereopticon. The figures in the background never really go away; only occasionally through a sort of sorcery, they appear to disappear like the shipwrecking "rokkes" in Chaucer's "Franklin's Tale."

At one of the many rapid transit hearings held during the 1870's and 1880's, a certain "Old Judge Vanderpoel" was not overpatronizing when he gave some inventors this advice:

I admonish my friends—they are all young enough to be my children—that I have lived long enough to see that men who are always delving and working in this way are like a rolling stone that gathers no moss. They never accumulate wealth. Even if they hit on a good idea someone else seizes it and obtains the benefit of it. *Whitney, the inventor of the cotton gin, died a pauper; Fulton, under whose erection all your noble rivers are crowded with steamers, died a pauper; . . . and the same fate awaits all these schemes.* Now you gain nothing by it. You empty your pockets; they never will be replenished by the consummation of these schemes.

The schemes were many, and of an ingenuity and diversity that perhaps only a crisis could inspire: pneumatic els mounted on ornate Gothic arches; moving sidewalks; underground arcades; monorails; saddle elevateds; depressed railroads; "three tiers"; els propelled by screw shafts working in a large nut wheel; and every conceivable combination of these. There was even an elevated resembling a dirigible—a silk container with conical ends filled with hydrogen gas, which included a steam-operated lever that hoisted silk sails from within the car. As early as November 26, 1853, *Scientific American* could say: "It is difficult for us to remember all the plans which have been presented to us for elevated railroads on Broadway during the last eight years, and yet there seems to be no newer approach of seeing one erected now than when the first one was proposed . . . [Perhaps] there is no use in prosecuting the subject." The subject was prosecuted nevertheless, and not only by engineers. It was a topic as common as politics. In 1874, after a lapse of twenty years, the *Railroad Gazette* observed:

The number of people in New York who think they know how to build a rapid transit railroad is, we believe, quite as large as those who are sure they could edit a newspaper or keep a hotel. It is amusing to hear some of these assert, in the most dogmatic way, principles about which the most experienced engineer would hesitate to give an opinion. The whole subject has been up for discussion twenty years or more, and makes its appearance annually in the State Legislature. No systematic effort, so far as we know, has thus far been made to collect accurate information, and the public mind is in a state of chaos regarding the whole subject.

A number of ad hoc groups formed around the issue and held what today would be called teach-ins. One such group, organized in December 1872, called itself the New York Rapid Transit Association, and for over a year it met every Monday evening at 602 Sixth Avenue to listen to the speeches of engineers and concerned citizens, or to discuss the issues in the manner of a town meeting. Occasionally highlights from the proceedings would appear in the New York *Times* or *Scientific American*, and if a speech was felt to be particularly inspired it was published by the association itself as a pamphlet.

So honored was a speech given in 1873 by Simeon E. Church, a tireless proponent of rapid transit. It sums up as well as any the general feeling about the way things stood:

> Every year the legislature has been the unceasing battleground of rival interests. All manner of schemes have been pressed with all manner of pictures, plates, drawings, models, and designs, endorsed by imposing certificates, bearing imposing and illustrious names, and urged year by year upon the public and upon the legislature, with all the strength of earnest conviction, supplemented by vast material resources and interests, and yet we stand today, with absolutely nothing done . . .
>
> At the last session of the Legislature, no less than 27 bills were given the coup de grace, although each had persuaded itself and its supporters that it was just the thing, and was "sure to pass."

Church's lament was intemperate to a degree since by 1873 two elevated railway schemes had in fact become law—although they had gotten off to a shaky start. The first was Charles T. Harvey's West Side and Yonkers Patent Railway or, as it was sometimes called, the "long-legged railway" or the "railway on stilts." Approved by the legislature in 1867, it was the first elevated railway in the world, and was run cable-style: single-column wrought-iron supports were erected along the curbstones, with stationary steam engines ensconced at intervals out of sight in vaults beneath the sidewalk. These engines rotated drums, around each of which was wound a three-quarter-inch steel cable twined like a rope of hemp with hundreds of slender wires. It was as fine a cable as could then be made, and had come out of the iron works of Washington Roebling, who would use it with some variation for his monumental Brooklyn Bridge. The cable passed overhead at a continuous speed through a wooden box which ran the length of the track and had a slot along the top. A shank projected up through the slot and made contact with a grip mechanism in the car. Harvey found that his chief problem was "to attach and detach the car without slackening the rope and without producing a shock on the car or its passengers; it must slow up in stopping and gradually get headway in starting. It would hardly do to jump at once to full speed; it would rack everything to pieces." To enable the car to get underway before making fast, he devised a sort of shock absorber. He placed a barrel below the floor of the car, surrounded by a stiff spiral spring, with secondary springs of India rubber set at an angle from the spiral spring to the body of the car; these took up the initial shock of contact while storing up momentum. Slowing down was accomplished easily enough by brakes.

Harvey had made a winning presentation before the skeptical legislature. He prepared elaborate drawings and scale models in detail, and hooked up a tiny copper boiler to a diminutive drum that wound and rewound two little cables attached to toy cars on a circular track. As the surprised lawmakers huddled with childlike delight about the lively display, they flattered themselves that here at last was engineering they could understand. It appealed to them in other ways. The cables were noiseless and there would be no smoke, cinders, or oil. Moreover, streets would not have to be torn up, or sewer mains moved; the single-file construction would not obstruct the roadway, and in any case, Greenwich Street (which Harvey proposed for the experiment) was not a major thoroughfare. Tweed, whose candidate would soon be governor, voiced little opposition; he doubted the invention would come to very much, while in the meantime it kept more threatening ideas at bay.

Harvey's renown as an engineer combined in a convenient way with his political connections. Governor Fenton admired him, and Erastus Corning, the most influential legislator after Tweed, had been president of the Lake Superior Ship Canal Company in 1854 when Harvey was its chief engineer. Harvey had saved the company from disaster. With time on the contract running out, it was discovered that an underwater ledge thought to be a sandbar was composed of solid rock. He quickly improvised a drop hammer from the propellor shaft of an old steamer and broke the ledge into pieces small enough to be dredged. Corning swore everlasting gratitude.

Not all the legislators were won over at once. But Harvey clinched his case when he made them an offer they could hardly refuse. He would submit the first quarter-mile of his road to an impartial test, and tear it down at his own expense if it was deemed unsatisfactory. He put up $500,000 of his own money as security.

Work started on July 1, 1867. By December the first quarter-mile, from the Battery to Morris Street, was done. A photograph records the first ride, showing Harvey, in suit and bowler hat, in a handcar. We notice two things immediately: the absence of protective railings on either side of the track, making Harvey's perch look extremely precarious; and the cluster of apprehensive spectators on the sidewalk below. But Harvey did not fall; in fact, the ride went well. A "scientific adjustment" of the weight secured the car against derailment, and the commission appointed to inspect the road found it safe. By July 1868, the tracks had been extended to Cortlandt Street, the half-mile point. Governor Fenton, Mayor Hoffman, Alfred Craven, the governor of Minnesota, and the Common Council of Boston made the first official run on July 3. The next day the New York *Times* reported: "The car ran easily from the Battery to Cortlandt Street, starting at a rate of five miles an hour and increasing to a speed of ten miles." Harvey was authorized to proceed up Ninth Avenue to Spuyten Duyvil at the upper end of the island. Thus, after decades of theorizing, of scheme and counterscheme, an elevated railroad seemed at last at hand.

Company stock was at a premium in September 1869 when "Black Friday" cut at the knees of American finance with the broad impersonal swing of its gilded scythe. All through the summer Jay Gould, a secretive financier whose prodigious assets made him almost a "free-roving economic power" comparable to an industrial nation, though without its usual restraints, had been plotting to corner the gold market in a conspiracy that included the brother-in-law of President Grant. Friday, September

24 was to have marked the climax of his campaign. "The market opened in pandemonium," wrote one historian,

> after successive days of increasing tension ... Starting from 150 gold climbed spectacularly amid frenzied trading to 160 and 165, while concerns of all sorts hysterically directed their agents to buy gold at any price. The riotous scenes that developed in exchanges all over the country were like to engulf the whole nation in ruins. During the mad gyrations of the day, from Boston to San Francisco banks and brokerage houses closed their doors, while the streets of the financial centers were thronged by a milling mob. In Philadelphia, the clocklike indicator of the gold market could no longer keep up with the lightning fluctuations, and finally a black flag with a skull and cross-bones was flung over its face by some distracted humorist, and trading continued under the funereal emblem.

By noon the government had grasped the full dimensions of the plot. Millions of dollars worth of gold were at once "flung upon the market" and "within fifteen minutes the whole structure toppled and the price broke." Ruin was nearly universal—though it spared Jay Gould. He had been secretly selling for hours, betraying even his confederates. "There was a reminiscence," wrote Henry Adams, "of a spider in his nature."

Harvey, of course, was caught completely by surprise. "Black Friday" crippled the banking firm that had backed him, and he found himself (wealthy a few hours before) in difficult straits. A powerful clique of Wall Street stock operators gave him a loan—in return for control of his company until the loan was repaid. It was a Gould-like snare. As H. C. Stryker tells it in *Historical Sketches,* "they conceived the idea of having the railway appear for a time as a failure until they could acquire nearly its entire stock ownership at a low valuation and then 'boom' the same to high premium prices, make large issues of new stock and realize millions by the deal." When Harvey refused to go along, he was voted out.

The apparatus rusted for a year. When an effort was made to get it working again, it rattled and creaked and broke down. In a turn of poetic—or mechanical—justice, it had become quite as worthless as the clique had tried to make it seem. In May 1870 the New York *Herald*, which once fulsomely proclaimed its advent, dismissed it as a "crude contraption" and called for its demolition. On November 15, 1870, it was sold for $960 at sheriff's auction.

During the following year the company was reorganized and its name changed to the New York Elevated Railway. The new owners planned to do away with the cable apparatus and replace it with steam locomotives. In the meantime the company was harassed by litigation—from property owners, from the Ninth Avenue Horsecar Railway, but chiefly from Boss Tweed, because the road was now in competition with his own newly conceived Viaduct. At one point Tweed tried to incite a mob against it; and in March 1871 he asked the state senate to authorize him as commissioner of public works to tear it down in ninety days. The bill passed the Senate 29 to 9, but at the last moment Erastus Corning intervened (in response to an appeal from Harvey) and rallied the assembly to the railroad's cause. Tweed, already slipping under indictment, was defeated by a vote of 74 to 34.

The road was revitalized. By the summer of 1875 it was carrying passengers as far as Central Park, using "dummy locomotives"—engines camouflaged as cabins so as "not to frighten horses below." In May and June it carried 172,846 passengers; during the same period the following year, twice that. Such prosperity attracted tycoons, and in 1876 Cyrus Field ("Cyrus the Great" of Atlantic Cable fame) bought out the company. He doubled the fare to ten cents and rebuilt the line as a two-track road as far north as Sixty-first Street.

Meanwhile, another elevated road appeared.

Rufus Henry Gilbert's captivating proposal for a pneumatic el first appeared in the pages of Beach's *Scientific American* on April 13, 1872. Beach gave the design a fairly brief write-up, but assigned prominence to it by a flamboyant, three-quarter-page engraving. It showed Gothic arches, adorned with filigree-like open tracery, springing at intervals from Corinthian columns ranged along opposite curblines. The crown of the arch, soaring high over the center of the street, supported a double line of atmospheric tubes (each about 8 feet in diameter) with smaller tubes slung underneath for transport of the mails. Pneumatic elevators were indicated for the stations; as with Beach's underground, telegraph wires tripped by cars in passing would signal the traffic down the line. Beach gave encouraging news of the proposal's prospects in the legislature while noting opposition from property owners and tenants along the route. These would "consent to nothing" that roofs over the street and "cuts off their light and air." Beach added wryly, "everybody in New York wants rapid transit, but, strange to say, the moment that anybody gets to work with a definite plan for its realization, they are vigorously opposed and the work prevented."

Gilbert had thrust himself into the transit controversy with missionary zeal and had developed a portfolio of seven alternative designs. He was motivated, quite literally, by the Hippocratic Oath. Engineering had not been his first vocation.

Born on January 26, 1832, in Guilford, New York, Gilbert had spent a restless youth, working as a clerk in a drugstore and then in a machine factory, while studying mathematics and classical literature at night. After a year as apprentice to a physician, he decided that medicine was his real vocation, and went to the College of Physicians and Surgeons in New York. His precocious abilities quickly drew the attention of the dean, the eminent surgeon Willard Parker, who took Gilbert along on his rounds to the tenement poor. What he saw on those rounds stayed with him for the rest of his life.

Gilbert took his degree and settled in Corning, New York, where his fledgling practice thrived. Despite his comparative youth, he took on the most difficult surgical cases, and his fame spread throughout the East. But his new prosperity had its nether side: He worked himself to exhaustion. When his wife died he had a breakdown and went to Europe for a rest.

First in London, then in Paris, he sought distraction and renewal in long evening walks enriched by his antiquarian curiosity about the European past. He took trips into the countryside, to Chartres and Rouen, and breathed deeply of the pure light and air under the monumental cathedral spires.

His thoughts turned once again to the care of the sick. Taking up hospital management, he found in city after European city what he knew already to be true of New York: that 80 percent of the ailing came from slums. Poverty itself began to appear to him as a disease as much as cholera or typhus, and overcrowded cities as vast hospitals of patients languishing for a cure. In London, Sir Charles Pearson's optimistic rhetoric about the redemptive promise of rapid transit for the poor filled him with a new resolve.

When he returned to New York, the country was on the verge of civil war. He volunteered for the Union cause and was appointed surgeon of the Duryée Zouaves, one of the colorful volunteer regiments whose Oriental garb of turbans and short embroidered jackets paid homage to the French-Algerian legions of that name. During the battle of Big Bethel he performed the first surgical operation ever undertaken under fire.

He rose through the ranks: to medical inspector for the city of Baltimore, medical director for Fort Monroe, then medical director of the XIV Army Corps. By the end of the war he was a lieutenant colonel and the general director and superintendent of all U.S. Army hospitals.

He came home a hero, gave up medicine, and, to the amazement of his friends, went into railroads. As assistant superintendent of the New Jersey Central, he acquired a solid reputation through his remodeling of the road. When a journalist expressed astonishment at his quick success in his new field, he replied that he had a running start, since anatomy and engineering are "analogous." In 1867, he resigned from the Central to agitate full-time for rapid transit.

Gilbert designed and redesigned his el for six years. In 1872, with Tweed's fortunes on the wane, he was able to get a charter through the legislature. Initially, his plan was peculiar enough to discourage capital investment, although as a skillful fund raiser he began to make some headway until the Panic of 1873 cut his progress short. By 1875 interest began to revive—but with a twist. Unfortunately, the original charter contained a clause adopted as a concession to skeptical legislators: that his road *might be* operated by *other than* atmospheric power. Financial backers now came forward—to back that "other power." But a locomotive el was the last thing Gilbert wanted.

In his quest for financial support, he reorganized his company and took in William Foster, Jr., a wealthy businessman, as his partner.

Foster won Gilbert's confidence by assuring him privately he shared his ideals; at the same time he induced him to temporarily adapt his design to the use of conventional engines to make fund raising easier.

The partners created a board of directors and issued stock. Foster appropriated thousands of shares which he said he would undertake to sell "through personal persuasion." Instead, he kept them for himself. In the meantime he persuaded Gilbert to accept the backing of the New York Loan and Improvement Co., under Jose Navarro (one of the original incorporators of Tweed's Viaduct), who was willing to exchange stock in his own company for Gilbert's shares in the el. At the end of the period required for building the road, Gilbert would get his stock back. He never did. The gentleman's agreement turned out to be a devil's ransom. Gilbert's own stock was gone, his company in the hands of Foster and Navarro—who had been in league all along, and he had nothing but sorrow in return for it.

The two had been drawn to Gilbert after the passage in 1875 of the Husted Act, a momentous piece of legislation that decided the fate of rapid transit in New York for a quarter-century. This act created a special commission with broad powers to determine the type of transit any new road was to use, the route it was to follow, and any points of connection between it and existing lines. In September the commission recommended the elevated as the best system, and decided that the New York Elevated should run a loop through Battery Park at the southern end of the island and build another line up the East Side along Third Avenue. It also approved the Second and Sixth Avenue routes for the Gilbert El. Navarro was later to testify under oath that he and others had paid $650,000 into a "corruption fund" to secure the franchise.

The Rapid Transit Commission also did something remarkable for a public authority: it incorporated a private company for the benefit of private capitalists. Called the Manhattan Railway Company, it was to back up the other two, stepping in if necessary to complete their work. The same men sat on all three boards. No matter what happened, they had nothing to lose.

The sudden prospect of elevated railroads along four main avenues of the city aroused frantic resistance. For over a year a variety of injunctions poured forth to prevent the work. Shops displayed illustrations showing terrified horses plunging wildly in collision, or crashing through plate-glass windows as locomotives steamed overhead. In one, "a well-dressed lady weeps helplessly over her gown spoiled by a discharge of water; a dandy ruefully counts the drops of oil that have fallen on his silk hat." Red-hot cinders rain heavily down on rich and poor alike. To prove the el infringed upon its franchise rights, one horse-car railway built a double-decker car tall enough to bump against the overhead track. A manifesto by about one hundred and fifty doctors warned that riding on the el would induce mental and moral perversion, cerebral exhaustion, insomnia, mania, hysteria, paralysis, meningitis, and decay of nutrition. Assemblyman Robert H. Strahan predicted: "Such a structure will render ground floors mere basements. Upper floors will be transformed into railroad stations." Another opponent declared: "Our homes will present the same relative aspect that naked boughs and empty bird nests do." Not everyone saw this as bad: prostitutes began renting second-story apartments in anticipation of soliciting clientele from the passing trains.

In November 1877, the els had their way. The state Court of Appeals threw out the injunctions, and over the next ten months construction proceeded at a furious rate. By the summer of 1878 there were several miles of track on all four avenues.

Aesthetic controversy for a time diverted public opinion, since the two lines—the New York and the Gilbert Elevated—were architecturally distinct. The press devoted considerable space to their description. The Third and Ninth Avenue structures were graceful, with light latticework pillars braced and connected by a simple arch; their cars were painted on the outside a deep maroon picked out with gold. The Gilbert lines, on the other hand, spanned the center of the avenue on double columns with connecting girders. On the narrower downtown streets they occupied almost the entire roadway and completely blocked out the light. At the same time they were more lavishly appointed and picturesque, and a great deal was said in their praise. The New York *Herald* reported:

> The ladies were evidently charmed with its spacious and elegant coaches, decorated with all the taste and finish of a boudoir; its handsome young conductors in smart-fitting bright uniforms, the coat decorated with gold-scroll braid on the shoulders; its easy, delightful motion . . . its breezy ventilation so welcome on a sultry day, and above all its rapid transit so exhilarating to the spirits and gratifying to the mind.

Frank Leslie's *Illustrated Newspaper* gave its readers an advance view of the stations' design:

> . . . The exterior of each station is to be ornamented with iron pilasters and decorated panels of the same metal. The stations can be approached on either side of the line by covered stairs of easy ascent, the sides being protected and ornamented with appropriately designed panel-work. The depot pavilion has a depth of eight feet, and affords a pleasant promenade in front of the track for passengers. The general style of the exterior of the buildings with their many gables, ventilators, finials, etc., might be properly classed as a modification of the Renaissance and Gothic styles of architecture, presenting somewhat the appearance of a Swiss villa.

The charm of such Victorian Gothic structures notwithstanding, their overall appearance left many chagrined. One witness lamented: "South Fifth Avenue, one of the largest streets in the city, now presents the aspect of a gigantic tunnel." On June 15, 1878, *Scientific American* had this to say:

> When the elevated railways, now in progress of construction in this city, are completed, four great iron bridges, with numerous branches, will run the length of Manhattan Island. Perhaps in the future, after people become habituated to trains thundering over them, to thoroughfares blocked with great iron columns, to the impartial distribution of ashes, oil, and sparks upon the heads of pedestrians and upon awnings (a couple of the latter were set on

fire this way the other day), to the diffusion of dirt from upper windows, to the increased danger of life from runaway horses and the breaking of vehicles against the iron columns, to the darkening of lower stories and the shading of the streets, so that the same are kept damp long after wet weather has ceased, and to the numerous other accidents and annoyances inherent to this mode of transit, more such bridges will be erected, and we shall have two storied streets ... The business population on some thoroughfares will be troglodytes—dwellers in dark and shaded caverns—and the other portions will be aerial. There will thus be a differentiation, so to speak, the probable results of which students of evolution might profitably, perhaps, speculate over.

In effect, they turned the streets themselves into tunnels and bequeathed to the poor an even more airless, dark, and gloomy environment—a particularly sad irony in light of Gilbert's aim.

The Third Avenue El made its first, surprise run on the morning of August 26, 1878. "Even Asmodeus riding his two sticks," wrote one contemporary, "saw more than mere street throngs that morning ... Few [homes] had curtains. Men, belathered and betoweled, cut their faces and waved their razors in the windows, shouting curses at trainmen. Matrons tried to look dignified *en deshabillé.* If they had shades they yanked them down. Girls blushed and darted into closets."

Months before, on May 1, the Gilbert El had been inaugurated by a car full of dignitaries traveling from Trinity Church to Fifty-ninth Street on the Sixth Avenue line. On June 6, the line was opened to the public; the very next day, by a deft legal maneuver, the board of directors forced Gilbert out of his own company. Having used the prestige of his name, his engineering authority, and his fund-raising gifts, they cast him aside. His last official link with the company had been literally nominal: It had borne his name. The directors renamed it the "Metropolitan Railway"—so that it would not seem, they said, as if the great corporate fortunes of the road were too closely bound up with the fortunes of one man. Gilbert was thereby severed from its destiny.

To appease him they offered him token shares of stock and the title of Chief Inspecting Engineer. It was simply too humiliating for him to accept. Seven years of litigation failed to set things right. The road went on to gather copious profits, while Gilbert grew more impoverished and began to lose his mind. In July 1885 a friend found him unconscious in bed, his watch, money, and valuables strewn around the room. He had not eaten in six days. Two doctors and a nurse were summoned, but they could not save him. His death was attributed to "exhaustion brought on by chronic inflammation of the bowels—superinduced by neglect." He was fifty-three years old.

On September 1, 1879, the Metropolitan and New York Elevated lines were leased to the Manhattan Elevated under a single management headed by Jay Gould. Since the principals were substantially the same in all three companies, this involved primarily a lucrative exchange of stock.

Gould's hand in the railway mania in America had been large. The momentum had come after the Civil War, though in 1848 Andrew Carnegie (already cynical at sixteen) had rejoiced in letters to his family back home in Scotland that "this country is completely cut up with railroad tracks." It was especially the generation between 1865 and 1895 that was, in the words of Henry Adams, "mortgaged to the railroads." As the tracks moved rapidly westward after the Civil War, their progress was reported in the press like a series of military campaigns, while each new stretch of track prompted celebrations as though marking an army's victory.

Gould had emerged from Black Friday enhanced, for his reputation as a wizard among robber barons evoked nothing if not admiration from the powerful and rich. Within a few years he brought on the Erie Railroad scandal (Tweed, a director of the company, was also involved) when he had sold $5 million of worthless Erie stock. This debacle has been identified as the "first tremor of the financial quake" that shook international finance in 1873.

After two years as a major stockholder of the Manhattan Elevated, Gould plotted to take over the whole system. By that time he was perhaps the most powerful man in the United States. He was "buying and selling, building and tearing down

... great railway systems, over a territory between the Mississippi, Missouri, and Colorado Rivers. He operated in a country which exceeded in dimensions Germany, Italy, France and Spain combined; he employed directly every day more than one hundred thousand men." He controlled the Associated Press, owned the New York *World*, and, most important of all, owned Western Union Telegraph. He could toy with the stock market not only through his vast capacity for buying and selling, by paying into or withdrawing assets from banks, but through his manipulation of the press—orchestrating rumors of solvency or insolvency through their pages or sending out false or distorted information over the telegraph wires. (In 1884, a few years after he began to move on the els, he actually withheld the presidential election returns for half a day in order to give himself time to protect his stock market investments from the news.)

On May 18, 1881, Gould arranged for the state attorney general to seek annulment of the Manhattan Railway's charter. The New York *World* began publishing articles attesting that the road was insolvent and the directors corrupt, while rumors went out over the wire service that the company was near collapse. Its stock fell promptly from 57 to 29; by the end of July it was down to 15½. With Russell Sage and Cyrus Field, his co-conspirators, Gould began buying, but to keep the price from booming they got a New York Supreme Court judge to prepare a petition of bankruptcy for the company. As soon as Gould had enough shares to establish control, he let up. The petition was withdrawn, the stories and rumors reversed, and the company suddenly appeared to be in good health after all. The stock soared; by October 18 it was back to 48.

Gould, who began his career in New York as a boy with the invention of the mousetrap, now snapped it shut on the whole town.

The elevated railroads did not, after all, bring speed and comfort to the traveling public of New York. Nor did they open up the countryside to the poor. They spread the tenement housing northward, crowding the city toward Central Park and beyond, and darkening the vistas of a once pastoral scene as their lengthening shadows flattened against the doorways of country homes.

The theory of urban redemption by means of the railroads was based on an idea of asymmetrical growth, of a population growing more slowly than the means of diffusing it, while the relation between the two was actually developing in reverse. The situation would probably not have been changed much by an earlier deployment of rapid transit, despite the usual argument to the contrary, since railroads foster congestion—through rapid land development—even before their cross-ties are spiked. The fault lay, if it lay in any one place, in the idea of the big industrial town itself, not in the geometry of its ramification.

In 1855 the tenement population in New York was 500,000; 10,000 more lived in cellars; overall the population was about 700,000. Roughly 73 percent lived in some sort of slum. In 1890, after a full decade of the els, the population was 1,515,301, of which 1,250,000 could be said to be living in squalor—or 83 percent. This statistic does not include the indeterminate number inhabiting the windowless "inside" rooms of newer buildings which, despite their spruce facades, were slum-like in their privation of light and air. The annual death rate in New York was 28 per 1,000—almost the worst in the United States, exceeded only by cities in the Yellow Fever district in the South. The tenement quarters were said to "terrify and appall even the Salvation Army missionaries who know the worst of London."

The els helped transform the city into a larger version of its old self and were soon overcrowded in their own right. In 1885, after only a few years of operation, we read in the New York *Evening Post*: "As for comfortable city travel, we are back in the old days when the city had outgrown the streetcar system and as yet even the elevated roads were not. The daily journeys up and down have again become times of dread and seasons of anguish." On December 27, 1877, a "Feast of Thanksgiving" dinner had been held at Delmonico's for the Third Avenue El. Simeon E. Church (whose dream seemed about to come true) declared: "There will be seats enough for everybody. Hanging by a strap will pass into history." But in the spring of 1885, Lawson N. Fuller, a cable railway advocate, observed at a hearing: "The

THE ELEVATED ATMOSPHERE IN NEW YORK

Elevated Railroads carry so many that the people are huddled like sheep in a cattle train, and often are obliged to stand during the entire trip . . . The first rides I took in public conveyances in this city were in the Knickerbocker stages. I had to hold on to a strap and stand up all the way down town, and I have been holding on to a strap ever since."

In 1886 the New York *Times* reported: "It may be taken as a settled fact that the problem of rapid transit for this city has not been solved by the elevated railroads and that these structures cannot be permitted to remain permanently in the streets." The *Evening Post* pointed out that elevated travel was already "double the capacity of the cars," even though the trains were running "as frequently as possible consistent with safety." Yet the crowding grew worse. Between 1884 and 1889 traffic on both elevated and street railroads increased 46 percent, from 272,000,000 per annum to 398,000,000. In 1880, $32\frac{1}{2}$ miles of elevated road had carried 60,831,757; in 1890 the same mileage was carrying 188,203,877.

In the opinion of many, New York had ruined her broad, wide streets to no gain. All the original fears about the els, derided at the time by knowledgeable experts, returned in retrospect to condemn them. In 1890 John J. Derry, a Philadelphia engineer, summed up their impact on New York:

> The El system obstructs light, privacy, and air; is a nuisance from constant noise and drippings from the structure in inclement weather; the traffic is delayed by fogs, windstorms, snow, slippery rails and fires; it practically absorbs a street for structure and the cars and engines pass within 8 or 12 feet of house lines; it is a nuisance from cinders, smoke and dripping grease, produces injury to the eyes of pedestrians from constant falling of steel filings from the grinding of car-wheels on rails, obliterates each street section where stations are located; and the length of the train and capacity can never be extended beyond the limit of the strength of the structure.

For a brief spell, New York experimented with cable cars as a replacement for street railways. The first line opened in August 1885 and ran from Eighth Avenue and 125th Street north to Fort George. Their usefulness, however, was limited: cables run only in straight lines. The intersection of Fourteenth Street and Broadway, where the cars whipped almost out of control around a double curve, became known as Dead Man's Curve because of the many casualties. Stephen Crane, a journalist in New York during the 1890's, watched the cars with fascination. "They come down Broadway," he wrote, "as the waters come down at Lahore . . . long yellow monsters which prowl intently up and down, up and down, in a mystic search."

CHAPTER 8

A Jostle
of
Dante's Voices

In September of 1898, a long, lean, ramshackle sort of man, large-boned and stalwart with a Lincolnesque physique, disembarked amid some commotion at the city of Hankow in China bearing papers from an American syndicate for the survey of a large tract of land for a new railway. His eyes had a luminous, dark intensity at once unreadable and cold, and in a quiet voice he made a short speech to the local officials, delivering each sentence, reported an observer, "in a taut, energetic manner, reflecting a mind trained in logarithms and problems of strain." This was William Barclay Parsons, an American engineer and temporary fugitive from the rapid transit controversy in New York. Within a few years he would be called the Father of New York's Subway.

Parsons had come to China on a dare—to survey 1,000 miles of territory between Hankow and Canton under conditions believed to be so fraught with peril that almost no one expected him to survive. Between Hankow and Canton lay the "closed province" of Hunan, of the eighteen provinces then constituting the Chinese empire the only one not yet mapped or explored by a foreigner. Lord Beresford, the English traveler, had warned: "Foreigners who penetrate into Hunan, even by the help of the mandarins with a military escort, do so at the risk of their lives." In 1898, there were already open manifestations throughout China of the fierce nationalism that would culminate in 1900 in the bloody Boxer Rebellion. The inhabitants of Hunan were particularly xenophobic, hostile even toward other Chinese. From time to time a few geologists had managed to go a short distance up the Siang River, which branches out into the province from the Yangtze, but none had been permitted to disembark. Parsons' assignment was to go by land. He was not promised safe conduct—no one could promise that—but his party was assigned a company of soldiers, mainly to indicate its official character.

He set the tone for the expedition at once. When he arrived in Hankow, it was a Tuesday. He was supposed to set out on Friday but was told that the hundred men he had been promised would not be ready for at least another week. Parsons sent word to the officials that he would start on Friday nevertheless. Messages went back and forth, and then on Thursday evening he made it clear that if he had to he would start alone. When he awoke the next morning, his motley crew of one hundred were awaiting him outside. When he got to the first town, he was told by local officials that he would find nothing but "mountains and rivers," meaning difficulties and obstacles ahead. Parsons shrugged. When mountains and rivers were stressed again, a man who had accompanied the party from Hankow broke in, exclaiming, "No good to talk to this man of mountains and rivers. Talk to him only about 'plains.' "

Almost at once he was singled out as a "foreign devil" (yang-kwei-tze), but he overcame the stigma, "pushing ahead with indomitable will, making friends and admirers of men who were prepared to distrust and hate him." For one stretch of 500 miles, he remembered later, "I was the first foreigner ever seen." From town to town men or ragged boys carrying placards or wooden standards would announce the party and command the people to give place, while soldiers with spears, tridents, two-handed swords, and matchlock guns followed behind. Despite their primitive weaponry, these soldiers made a daunting sight, in their cloak-like coats with wide, loose sleeves, their dark blue trousers bound at the ankles, and their braids wrapped about the head enclosed in dark blue cotton turbans.

Parsons made it through. He recalled: "We had shown no fear, and consequently the people feared us; we neither molested nor interfered with anyone, therefore the people respected us; and we paid regular prices for our purchases, and would not permit our attendants to steal, therefore the people liked us." He entered Canton two days ahead of schedule, without having lost a single man.

Like so many other, lesser men whose belief in China's future was inseparable from their appetite for plunder, Parsons thought the new China would rear up like a giant from the mine. Her coal fields exceeded in quantity those of Europe, and contained all varieties, from soft bituminous to very hard anthracites. There were also beds of copper, iron, lead, and silver. Parsons foresaw

> future trains bearing their dark burden northward to furnish power for the furnaces and mills that will be built in central China to convert her ores into metals or work her raw produce of cotton and wool and hemp into articles of commerce; or other trains south-bound carrying a like burden to Canton and Hongkong to make steam for vessels of all nations, bringing goods from other lands to China, and taking back her teas and silks.

Parsons saw his mission as part of the completion of a cycle in history.

But his overall view was fatalistic: higher circles of development were problematical; the only certainty was that everything must run its course. He understood and appreciated the technology of the new age, yet regarded it as a phase, with a skeptical eye. He was not optimistic as to where it would lead.

> Perhaps the cause [of the fall of the Roman Empire] will be found not in critical historical analysis but in the working of a law of nature. The growth that had continued over many centuries had merely reached its full fruition, and in accordance with the laws of evolution and development the end had come. Natural forces are dynamic and the laws of nature are sometimes slow but they are inexorable. The Roman impulse had expended itself as prior impulses had done; and after that movement had come to a rest it was, in accordance with a law of nature, replaced by another impulse in the opposite direction.

As he crossed the perilous expanse of Hunan, Parsons must have had ample occasion to wonder what law of nature or impulse it was that was working itself out in New York. In 1885, he had begun in earnest to study the rapid transit situation, and hung out his shingle as consulting engineer. Prospects had looked good for a scheme called the Arcade Railway, and Parsons soon gained the confidence of its directors.

The Arcade was a Broadway subway scheme first suggested in 1866. Though defeated many times in the legislature, it became a perennial and outlasted all its rivals. It proposed "not merely to tunnel the street, but to remove the street itself, block by block, from wall to wall, and construct another street below supporting the present street on arches, turning what are now basements and sub-basements into stores." There would be four tracks—two for "way" or local traffic, two for express—flanked by sidewalks for an arcade promenade. Light would come down through clusters of "deadlights," circles of thick translucent glass set in the upper walk, which would also have open spaces covered with grates for ventilation. It was endorsed by the American Institute; by William J. McAlpine, the former state engineer who had managed to build Brooklyn's splendid Dry Dock on quicksand; and by many other luminaries. Its opponents said it would "disembowel Broadway."

In 1868 the Arcade was the subject of widely publicized hearings. The company claimed that below Seventeenth Street the excavation would be easy; above that point, where the island lies on the upturned edge of a vast primitive formation of gneiss, the difficulties would be arduous but not insuperable. Experts disagreed. Most of the testimony centered on the stability of downtown city monuments and important buildings, in particular Trinity Church with its lofty spire, the Saint Nicholas and Metropolitan hotels, and Astor House, all large buildings with extremely shallow foundations. The other major objection offered by realtors was that the plan would take over the underground basements or storage vaults used by stores.

Its advocates believed they were up against a coalition of interests, using these issues as a front, whose real desire was to drive people out of the city:

1) The first and least in influence are the owners of real estate in New Jersey and the suburbs of Brooklyn. These owners are many and do not act in concert. The population lost by New York enhances the value of their land . . .

2) The steam railways of Long Island and the horse railways of Brooklyn. If population increased along the line of their roads, their business would increase.

3) The Union Ferry Company and the Ferry Companies of North River. The number of people who cross by the ferries depends on the number who live out of the city.

4) The stages and horse railways in the City of New York, who do not want the competition.

5) A few rich and selfish men, who transact no business beyond receiving the rents of their property; who drive in their private carriages, or rather, are driven by their coachmen . . .

This hostile interest of railway corporations, stage, and ferry companies, possessed of great wealth and power, controlled and wielded by a dozen men, combined, active, vigilant, cover their conspiracy under the mantle of respectable millionaires and the war cry of vaults, and Trinity Church.

The Arcade's prospects seesawed back and forth; in time an insurgent faction became convinced that it was an untenable scheme. They charged that its plans were vague and changed daily. "All we have," testified Parsons, "are highly colored pictures or prints." The arrangements for ventilation in particular seemed inadequate. "It is not enough to make a hole in the roof; the result would be practically what was done in the London Underground, where the trains simply churn the air and a gradual fouling of the atmosphere develops." With others he broke away to form a rival company, the New York District Railway, in 1885.

Amid mounting dissatisfaction with the els, the District received a nearly unanimous welcome from the press. It emerged in a hail of slogans. It promised the "scientific street," designed to meet "all the demands which modern civilization has created." The foundation would be "adamantine and everlasting"; the excavation "minimum," capacity "maximum," ventilation "perfect," and the cars "impossible to derail." Moreover, these cars would be indestructible, thanks to a substance called Ferflax, personified in advertisements by the tragic profile of a woman—classical in cast—signifying victory over urban misery. This illustration enjoyed a prominence equal to the company title in promotional pamphlets. What was Ferflax? "Fer"+"flax," or "iron-fiber," a material "compounded of steel wire netting, vegetable fiber, and oxidized oil compressed into a solid panel by hydraulic power." It was tough, "not unlike horn," yet flexible, "like leather"; and a car made of it, "when receiving the force of the most severe collisions, side-thrusts, falling blows, and thumping when off the rails, cannot shatter." No passenger in a Ferflax car could be "transfixed with splinters," for in even "the worst overturning accidents it will not bend or twist out of shape." It had other virtues too: it was incombustible, and its lack of structural homogeneity made it nonresonant and non-conducting, ensuring a system that would be quiet and almost without vibration. This miracle material was to be ubiquitous: the roof, floor, and side panels of each car were to be covered with it, and it was to be used in the tunnel arching and the partitions between tracks.

"Perfect ventilation" would be on the "principle of the syringe." Derailment would be impossible because of a guard plate outside the rail and reflecting plates set into the walls of the tunnel at the cornice line. Unwilling to use the word "tunnel," the District described its plan as "an architectural structure replacing a superficial excavation."

Parsons had very little to do with all this hype. He had worked out the method of ventilation, which was sound (he never claimed it was "perfect"), after the fashion of the early London tubes. Otherwise, his job had been to map the route.

The Arcade and the District sought legitimacy through the courts, where eventually, after a series of adverse rulings, both met their end. Nevertheless, their dispute at least brought the discussion of subway engineering up to date and established, through a decision of the Court of Appeals, certain legal preconditions for such an undertaking; namely, consent of the city and of property owners along the route. However, if property owners refused to go along, the consent of the court could be had instead.

In 1891 the first precondition was answered by the formation of a new Rapid Transit Commission, committed to a subway. The commission adopted plans and offered the franchise for sale. During the next two years not a single bid was received. In the meantime, the Gould-controlled Manhattan Elevated Railway attempted to capitalize on the ensuing public despair. It applied for permission to build new lines and extend its old ones to a degree that would have crisscrossed the sky with trestles like a grid. With no other real hope in sight for expanded transit, the city actually tried to work out an agreement. It offered the company an extraordinary bargain—a tax of one-ninth of a cent per passenger, as compared to the one-quarter of a cent then paid by the street railroads and omnibus lines; and, even more tempting, *de facto* control of the whole rapid transit system in New York for years. But company greed overreached itself. Gould demanded a tax of just one-twenty-fourth, and the deal fell through.

In 1894 the Rapid Transit Commission re-formed and chose Parsons as Chief Engineer. At the time, he was only thirty-five years old and many veterans of the profession said openly that his appointment was a mistake. The gargantuan complexity of the challenge seemed too much for someone untried. The surface and elevated railways of New York City already carried more passengers annually than all the steam railroads in North and South America combined, including the suburban traffic of all the major cities. Overall they could count almost one billion paying passengers a year, with ridership increasing ineluctably at an annual rate of 6 or 7 percent. The commission, however, saw Parsons's youth as an asset. Once undertaken, the work would take a long time to complete. A man was needed who possessed vitality and stamina, who had many years ahead of him and could bear up under the long strain. Parsons would later recall that many of his friends spoke "pityingly" in those days of his "wasting his life" on an impossible dream.

In fact, the commissioners could not have chosen a better man. His credentials were impeccable. He had graduated from the Columbia University School of Mines (precursor of the School of Engineering) in 1882 with the highest average ever attained. The following year he published a little book on *Turnouts*—the arrangement by which one track leaves another— establishing exact formulae for their determination and providing accurate tables for use in the field. The book at once became a standard. Two years later he published *Track: A Complete Manual of Maintenance of Way*, also considered definitive. As engineer for the Arcade and the District he had "familiarized himself with every foot of land on Manhattan Island." This may have been only a slight exaggeration. At one court hearing on the District he was put on the witness stand and asked questions opposing lawyers were certain he would be unable to answer. But he answered each one quietly and without hesitation, describing the exact condition of particular localities all along the route, the number and character of the sewer pipes, the water drains, and so forth until the court began to murmur with amazement. He was already, wrote an admirer, "a thorough master of the thing he was to do."

As Chief Engineer of the commission, Parsons conducted a survey of rapid transit abroad. He went to England, France, Germany, and a half-dozen other countries, and by the end of the year had his recommendations for New York. His report contains a number of very striking observations, particularly for a man who was an ardent subway advocate. Of the London system he had this to say:

> No attempt was made to give the stations a pleasing appearance, in fact, any such attempt would have been rendered ineffective by the engine smoke and the hideous advertising signs with which the station walls in England are covered . . .
>
> Both (the Metropolitan and District) railways are operated by steam locomotives, discharging the products of combustion directly into the tunnel, which is without any system of artificial ventilation. The bad effect of this arrangement is minimized as much as possible by burning the best quality of coal, which is free from sulphur and makes but little smoke . . .

However, the air in the tunnel is extremely offensive ... The best condition of the atmosphere is just in advance of a locomotive, where there are no passengers, and the worst just behind the locomotive where the passengers are. None of the systems in use can save the travellers from the vitiation of the atmosphere by their own locomotive.

"It is not," he concluded, "generally understood how great is the consumption of air by a locomotive compared with which the other causes of foul air are small," which occasioned a look at the situation in New York:

One of the New York elevated railway engines burns about 10 lbs. of coal per minute, which forms approximately 250 cu. ft. of carbonic acid gas, or 15,000 cu. ft. per hour. In the same time a person produces 0.6 cu. ft. The deoxygenation of the atmosphere is equivalent to that of 25,000 people. In the ordinary railroad tunnel, such, for instance, as the Harlem Railroad tunnel in Park Avenue, the heavier locomotives burn about 35 lbs. of coal per minute, and therefore each engine destroys as much air as would 87,000 people. These figures do not include the production of sulphur fumes, or the increase of humidity by the escape of steam, which also very seriously increases the discomfort. The consumption of air by the passengers, allowing 300 to a train is, therefore, but slightly more than 3/1000 of one percent of that by a locomotive. The substitution of a motor other than an ordinary steam locomotive would at once remove 99.997% of the foul atmosphere from an ordinary railway tunnel.

In retrospect it can hardly be said that complaints about the air in the early locomotive tunnels were hysterical or neurotically extreme.

Once electric traction became feasible, it could not be long before it supplanted steam. But the superiority of electricity was not quite so obvious then as it now seems. Parsons made a concise comparison of their relative merits at the threshold of the change:

There is a widespread popular idea that electricity has some mysterious properties which render it vastly superior and more economical than steam as a motor power. Such an idea of course is fallacious in the extreme. Since electrical energy is developed by means of a steam engine, and as each transformation of power can be done only at a loss, or at the cost of coal, it is evident that all things being equal electricity must be less economical than steam. But as regards the two forms of power as applied to locomotion all things are not equal and therefore the relative economies vary according to the conditions. A locomotive is a very simple machine, and it is entirely self-contained, coal being burned under its own boiler, converting water into steam, which through the mechanism of the cylinder, piston rod and wheel propels. The only losses are in the boiler and internal friction of the moving parts of the machinery.

In the case of an electrical railroad steam is made under stationary boilers by which the main engines are run, whose losses correspond in kind to the losses above mentioned for the steam locomotive. The engines, however, drive dynamos which convert electricity. This electricity has to be conducted from the power house, some miles perhaps, to the trains upon the railway, and when it reaches the trains is, by means of motors, reconverted back into power, and turns the wheels of the electric locomotives. It is thus seen that while the steam locomotive has two sources of loss, boiler and engine mechanism, the electric locomotive has these two and three more, viz. dynamo, line, and motor. Fortunately for the economical aspect of electricity the boilers and machine parts of a locomotive are not and cannot be brought up to the highest efficiency, and it is possible to save enough in the first two losses to compensate for the other three.

Parsons' report, like so much that he was to say and do, became the standard against which the work of other men would be measured. Entirely on the basis of it, the Rapid Transit Commission of 1894 established the major guidelines for the subway that would be built in New York.

The commission had the power either to sell a franchise to a private corporation (as the 1891 commission had hoped to do) or to involve the city itself in rapid transit construction and ownership. The choice was put to the people in the November election; public ownership was favored by three to one. The commission then mapped out a route, drew up plans and specifications, and called for contract bids, according to the following terms: the city would pay the contractor the amount of his bid out of funds provided by city bonds; he in turn would pay as rental the interest on the bonds, plus 1 percent per annum as a sinking fund sufficient for their payment at or before maturity. At his own expense, he would also provide rolling stock, powerhouses, and other equipment—the infrastructure—so as to indemnify the city against loss in case he should fail to build and operate the road. At the conclusion of the lease, the city was to purchase this investment at a price to be determined by arbitration. Thus, the city would get the benefit of the immediate construction of the railway without a burden to the taxpayer, while the contractor could finance his work by what was tantamount to a low-interest long-term city loan. While the city would eventually come into outright ownership of the road, the contractor would earn income from it for the duration of his fifty-year lease. He could also renew the lease if he wished.

This ingenious formula, in some respects analogous to the Paris arrangement but considerably more subtle, depended on the loan of the city's credit—and here an obstacle arose. The extent of credit rested on the city's debt limit, as determined by law, and in 1894 it was clear that the credit needed to match the probable cost of subway construction far exceeded the amount the city could command. This one hitch, which had to be overcome before private capital could be enticed into the undertaking, held up the process for years. Eventually it was resolved by two actions: a constitutional amendment raising the debt limit and the increased valuation of taxable properties owned by the city against which it could borrow as security. This solution, worked out by Abram S. Hewitt who also devised the overall contract formula, was not achieved until 1899.

Meanwhile, New York began to appear oddly laggard. Glasgow had opened a little cable-car subway in 1886, and Budapest a trolley tunnel in 1896—the first underground on the continent of Europe. In 1897 Boston cut through the old colonial burial grounds between Park Street and the Public Gardens and in September of that year inaugurated the first subway in North America. The motorman, reported the *Boston Globe*, "compelled the pent-up lightning [electricity] to do his bidding," and the trolley "hissed along like a brood of vipers." Paris meanwhile was ironing out the last legal kinks for its Métro.

Parsons, who had labored on the commission plans for four years only to see them gathering dust, began to fear that he might become just one more casualty of New York's rapid transit debacle. With a keen sense of his own destiny, he had gone off to China to measure himself against a challenge more commensurate with his worth.

When he returned in 1899 the Rapid Transit Commission at once recalled him as Chief Engineer. The Gordian knot had been cut, the path to a subway cleared. So grateful was the city to Abram S. Hewitt that the New York Chamber of Commerce presented him with a medal and in a flowery oration predicted his immortality.

John B. McDonald, a contractor identified with large undertakings, snared the contract with a bid of $35 million. He had only one competitor, the Onderdonck Construction Company, which bid high. Perhaps McDonald bid too low, for he had trouble raising the security: $1 million for construction, a bond with surety for $4 million, and an additional bond of $1 million to secure performance of the contract. At length he had to turn his contract over to August Belmont, Jr., the financier and American representative of the Rothschilds, whose father had been a director of Tweed's Viaduct. Belmont organized two companies, one within the other, to take charge of different parts of the contract's obligations: a construction company with a capitalization of $6 million to furnish the security and the Interborough Rapid Transit Company, or IRT, for the lease and operation of the road. McDonald was retained as contractor for the work.

Unhappy as McDonald was at this turn of events, it was the only way he could preserve for himself a substantial piece of a very substantial pie. His other consolation lay in the fact that the task left to him was the very thing he knew best how to do.

In 1900 McDonald was fifty-six years old. Born in County Cork, Ireland, he had come to the United States as a boy with his father, an independent contractor, from whom he learned his trade. He was a sort of prodigy, and at the age of twenty was made general superintendent of the Croton Dam, with six hundred men under him. A few years later he took charge of the masonry work in the reconstruction of the Fourth Avenue stretch of the New York Central Railroad, and supervised the company's work at Ninety-sixth Street, where four tracks converged from different tunnels under one arch. Thereafter, contracts came on a more ambitious scale: the West Shore Railroad in the Potomac Valley, the extension of the Illinois Central to Wisconsin, the Akron Junction in Ohio, and many others. But it was his work on the Baltimore Belt Line—"an enormously difficult project which put him in the front rank of his profession"—that ultimately secured his national reputation.

McDonald was a colorful figure. A short, square, iron-gray man with broad sloping shoulders and a deep chest, his "whole appearance," wrote a contemporary, was "one of strength," his every movement "cat-like," "supple," and "intense with purpose." His large, hard, muscular hands told much about his laboring background, but what seems to have struck journalists most was the powerful configuration of his head: bald and "almost flat" on top with a "marked broadness just above the ears." Shrewd hazel eyes looked out from under bristling brows of sandy gray.

A jovial demeanor somewhat offset this imposing impression, and in the company of friends he divulged a hearty appetite for drink and good cigars. He owned a yacht, was a good amateur golfer, and belonged to a number of clubs, among them the Apawanis, the New York Yacht Club, the Friendly Sons of St. Patrick, the Chamber of Commerce, and Tammany Hall. Many regarded him as a "silent power" in Democratic politics. His Tammany connection in fact proved highly convenient for the subway undertaking, for smooth progress depended on the cooperation and stability of the hired crews.

The route finally decided upon began with a loop near City Hall, proceeded with four tracks up to Grand Central Station, then westward to Broadway and along Broadway to 104th Street. From there one double track line continued along Broadway to Kingsbridge, and another eastward under the Harlem River through the Bronx to the Zoological Gardens. The total length of the system would be about 21 miles, including 5 miles of el. The work was to take four and a half years.

As Parsons went over the final blueprints with his staff, the excitement in New York reached fever pitch. Almost no one seemed to doubt that deliverance was at hand. McDonald and Parsons were hailed as heroes in the press, and Belmont as the most selfless of philanthropists. Extravagant predictions were made about the speed of travel that would soon be commonplace, and the New York *World* (whipping up the jubilation) pushed the slogan "To Harlem in Fifteen Minutes," which other papers soon took up like a chant.

For the ground-breaking ceremonies on March 24, 1900, the *World* hired the Pain Fireworks Co. of New Jersey to explode 100,000 pounds of dynamite. It was a bright spring day and John Philip Sousa, "The March King," set the mood with his famous band. Twenty-five thousand people swarmed across the little park in front of City Hall.

Mayor Robert A. Van Wyck hoisted a silver spade created especially for the occasion by Tiffany & Co. Its handle was made of wood taken from one of the thirteen gum trees planted in Washington Heights in 1803 by Alexander Hamilton to symbolize the thirteen original states; its grip was from a piece of oak from the flagship *Lawrence*, part of Commodore Perry's victorious fleet on Lake Erie during the War of 1812. Van Wyck carried it gingerly like the artifact it was. Slowly, with his right foot, he forced the blade level with the ground, then tossed out the first shovelful of earth.

From atop the Pulitzer Building, the *World*'s pyrotechnic display now began. The "men at the mortars"—observing the ceremonies from afar through powerful field glasses—lit the fuses of twenty-one cannons in the national salute. With each thundering detonation "that woke echoes in the New Jersey Hills," the crowd let out a cheer. To Harlem in Fifteen Minutes "ran from lip to lip and swelled into a splendid chorus." Steam craft in the harbor blew their whistles, church bells chimed, and at the ferry slips the fog bells were rung. All along the waterfront factory whistles joined in. At the large pier the sirens of the revenue cutters *Hudson, Calumet,* and *Manhattan* and the immigration cutter *Chamberlain* wailed away in unison.

Now came the second phase, meant to imitate the siege of a town. "Over the heads of the cheering multitude swept the fire of aerial guns, discharged in heavy volleys, blotting the sky with tiny puffs of white smoke. Japanese 'daylight shells' sent their echoes flying among the tall office buildings, mingling with the roar of voices and the blare of trumpets." Twenty great "flag bombs" blasted into flight, each holding in its core 144 tiny American flags of silk. As the bombs exploded high above the crowd "the little flags released and carried by the wind fell broadcast in patriotic showers." "In thousands of New York homes," concluded one account, "the silken souvenirs of the birth of real rapid transit for New York will be cherished throughout the coming years."

At the end of this tumultuous fanfare a somewhat subdued McDonald stepped forward, took a very small quantity of earth with the spade, and "instead of throwing it out boldly, turned the shovel over on it beside the hole." Parsons, nearby, looked at him in astonishment. "If your laborers shirk work like that," he ventured, "there will be trouble." McDonald laughed.

Van Wyck then made a speech: "No Roman citizen ever entertained a keener pride in the glory of that imperial city than does the New Yorker in the fame of New York. The foundation of her structure is too solid to be shaken by the unjust attacks of the misinformed stranger or the misguided son." He then went on to say that the project would be second in importance only to the Erie Canal.

Parsons' dedication to the work was absolute. But he was not jubilant. In May 1900, just two months after the opening ceremonies, he wrote:

For New York there is no such thing as a solution to the Rapid Transit problem ... By the time this railway is completed, the normal city growth will, in itself, be enough to provide a lucrative business without decreasing at all the burdens on existing lines. In addition to this, however, plans have already been drawn by every property owner for the undeveloped real estate at the northern confines of the city which the Rapid Transit Railway is projected to reach. By the time the railway is completed, areas that are now given over to rocks and goats will be covered with houses, and there will be created for each new line, just as there had been created for each new line constructed in the past, a special traffic of its own, independent of the normal growth of the city. The instant that this line is finished there will arise a demand for other lines.

Parsons did not confine these thoughts to a diary, but willingly and often expressed them in public. "The great cities of the Old World," he observed in one interview, "show no signs of standing still. London, twice the size of New York, is still growing. We have no means of foretelling the ultimate fate of a modern city or assigning a limit to its growth. We know only that the great cities of ancient times—Babylon, Carthage, Athens, Rome—grew to the point of decay."

Ceremonies aside, real work began on the subway at the corner of Bleecker and Greene streets. Parsons lowered a pick between two cobblestones, paused for photographers, then raised it and swung it down with force. A huge crowd had gathered, mostly the unemployed, and as the appointed crew began to tear up the street, they surged forward past a phalanx of police and suddenly a great melee erupted as they fought one another for the first stones dislodged. These men were not souvenir hunters. A rumor had gone around that anyone lucky enough to come up with a cobblestone would get a job. The next day the press reported that policemen had to work "like football rushers" to drive the men back.

Times were hard. The IRT work force consisted of 12,000 men, paid twenty cents an hour for a ten-hour day. A large proportion were Irish, Italian, and Polish immigrants, some just off the boats, many with numbers for names. When a blasting accident occurred and bodies had to be identified, the report sometimes had the most pathetic of statistical rings—a dark Pythagorean sound of embodied number. But there were others too, from more privileged backgrounds, such as Edwin Arlington Robinson, the poet, just out of Harvard and "hired to check stone weighting during the removal of rock and debris." Another poet, John Masefield, "tended bar and filled the growler [or beer can] for the thirsty workers."

The workers answered to McDonald; he answered in turn to Parsons. That was the essential chain of command. For the most part the two men got along.

At Bleecker and Greene the first order of business was to build 900 feet of new 4-foot-diameter brick sewers at a depth of from 1 to 30 feet. Over the years the old pipes and sewers had been laid in a mass without plan, as tangled as fern roots in a wood. Water pipes, thickly encrusted with filth, were discovered running through sewers; great tubes were dug up whose presence was wholly unexplained.

In all, 45 miles of conduits would eventually have to be relaid. At Murray Hill, where the subway plunged below the Park Avenue trolley tunnel, the intersecting pipes were hung by chains to a wooden framework of supports while blasting went on below and huge cranes swung about above as men scrambled back and forth on wooden gangways with wheelbarrows full of earth, mortar, stones, and bricks. One major new sewer was built for about a mile from the East River to Canal Street to link up with the old channel that had emptied into the Hudson. At the Harlem River, tubes constructed on land and sealed watertight were sunk to the river bottom enclosed in a rectangular structure of iron and concrete, and then bolted to the advancing tunnel at either side.

Beyond 120th Street on the West Side, the subway became a viaduct spanning the Manhattanville Valley—once known as the Hollow Way—then dipped into a tunnel deep below Washington Heights, emerging from the northern side of the cliff at Fort George. In this section the burrowing became real mining. Vertical shafts were started at 157th and 195th streets and at two intermediate points. The tunnel between, 2 miles long and 125 feet down, was then the longest two-track tunnel in the United States.

Workers came upon all sorts of subterranean springs, brooks, and ponds. Many had once beautified the island in the open air—a "sunfish" pond at Madison Avenue and Thirty-second Street; at Cedar Street a pond once popular for skating; at the intersection of Mulberry and Baxter streets a spring prized in former years for its therapeutic properties—all casualties of pollution. Up in Harlem engineers met up with a long-forgotten subterranean lake.

Huge mastodon bones were unearthed at the Dyckman Street Station; and near the Battery, while working through "made ground," there emerged the charred hull of the Dutch merchant ship *The Tiger*, which had caught fire and sank in 1613. Other discoveries included chests of coins and colonial weapons and tools, and Aaron Burr's hollowed-out pine logs along Elm Street—the city's first rudimentary water supply system.

The engineering problems were often immense. Building foundations thrust out into the line of the route, elevated roads thundered overhead, the streets swarmed with traffic. There were quicksands to contend with and steep hills to pierce. Sometimes, as along Centre Street, Fourth Avenue, Forty-second Street, and especially Broadway, whole streets had to be propped up on stilts as men worked in the trenches.

Inevitably, there were accidents. The first victim, Nicola Sacks, was crushed beneath a steam boiler at Sixty-fourth Street and Broadway in December 1900. In the deep tunnel at 164th Street a rockfall killed five. In January 1902, at Forty-second Street and Park Avenue, Moses Epps broke for lunch in a shed packed with dynamite and lit a candle to warm his hands. He stepped out for a moment, and the candle fell over. In the resulting explosion, seven died and 180 were injured. Perhaps the costliest mishap occurred in 1903, near the spot where the deep tunnel emerges from the side of the hill at Fort George, at 145th Street and St. Nicholas Avenue. A delayed blast caught a whole crew of men coming back into the heading. Overall, at least 50 men lost their lives in the building of the first IRT line, although one paper, the *Evening Telegram*, put the figure at 120, with thousands more injured or maimed.

Tunneling was done by cut and cover, except. of course, where the subway passed beneath the Harlem river, where Parsons used cast-iron tubes. With his usual thoroughness he had analyzed all the options:

> When it came to decide on the construction details, there were two distinct and opposite principles that presented themselves: ei-

ther to drive tunnels of circular tubes, as was being done in London, and at such depth as to pass beneath all pipes, mains, sewers, and other sub-surface structures; or else to make an open excavation, remove or otherwise rearrange the water and gas mains, the sewers and similar structures encountered, to build the railway as close to the surface as variations in topography and other local conditions permitted, and then to restore the surface of the street. The first plan involved no interference with existing street traffic, and would have probably been cheaper in first construction, but it also entailed the use of elevators at all stations, the expense of operating which, at a sensible cost per passenger, would have more than offset the savings in initial cost. At certain important stations, where in rush hours a congestion of traffic can be looked for exceeding that to be found in any other city of the world, it is probable that no system of elevators that could be installed at reasonable expense would be sufficient to handle the crowd. London experience in this line is not comparable, because the concentration of travel in New York is so much greater. Furthermore, the deep tunnel is necessarily precluded from receiving any natural light.

The second plan offers the objection of interference with street travel, and of discommoding those residing or doing business near the route, but such inconvenience is confined solely to the period of construction. When that is finished there will be the maximum of convenience. The structure will be close to the surface, with a distance (according to the plans in question, of less than fourteen feet) from the street level to the platform of but little more than one-half the distance from street level to the average elevated railway platform, or about the same as that from one floor to another in an ordinary dwelling . . . By roofing over such portions of the stations as lie beneath the sidewalks with glass, it will be possible to illuminate the stations not only with daylight but with sunlight, and use artificial means only as evening approaches, and to destroy the popular antipathy to a "hole in the ground."

The antipathy was to increase, however, as the holes spread, consuming much of the original enthusiasm. Streets were slow to be restored, even in a temporary way with planks, and stretches of the route looked like the aftermath of a bombing. Along Forty-second Street from Park Avenue to Broadway, where the structure curved uptown, it intermingled with the foundations of new skyscrapers and the conditions were particularly bad. "The whole place was a great chasm," reported one journalist. "Business in the neighborhood went to ruin. Crowds hurrying to the Grand Central Terminal passed rows of empty houses, from which storekeepers and other occupants had fled as from the plague. The neighborhood of City Hall, too, resembled a cross between a mining camp and a mound dwellers' colony." About 3½ million cubic yards of earth and rock were removed over the course of four and a half years.

Parsons brought the work in almost on time and within cost, despite a strike at the main powerhouse and substations in March 1903, and a general strike in May of the same year. Imperturbably calm, self-possessed, and diplomatic, he kept morale high among his staff, and his eye on even minor engineering details. He had, as the *Times* put it, an "infinite capacity for taking pains." No one had a word to say against him. The men who worked under him "all believed in him thoroughly as an engineer and a man."

McDonald came in for more criticism, but most of it was unjust. As the man in charge of the actual execution of the work, he presented an obvious target for public dissatisfactions. But he faced the importunities of the press and occasional political harassment with a stolid professional chill. He always said he "had nothing to say," except that the "work was being done and would be complete from the contractor's end of it, in advance of the contract time." Which it was.

City officials took a trial run in handcars through the finished portion on New Year's Day, 1904. In a separate tour, August Belmont rode through with a group of fellow financiers, said to have a combined worth of about $400 million. He showed off the work as though it were his own.

Opening day was set for October 27. All through the summer and early fall doubts persisted about the quality of the ventilation, the perennial question about traveling underground. In early October Commissioner of Public Health Thomas Darlington sought to reassure the public in an essay published in the Sunday *World*. But his presentation had just the opposite effect. In-

NEW YORK

A PICTURE PORTFOLIO

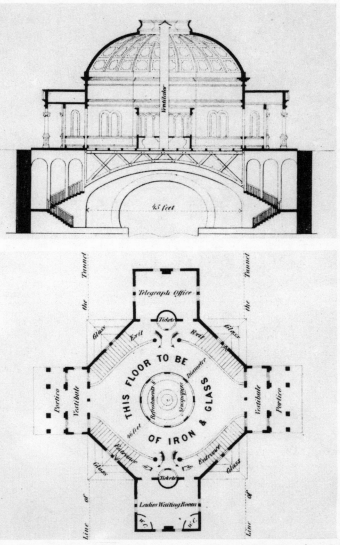

The first known design for a New York City subway station, by
A.P. Robinson, 1864. Today undeservedly forgotten, Robinson
was an extraordinarily brilliant and far-sighted engineer.

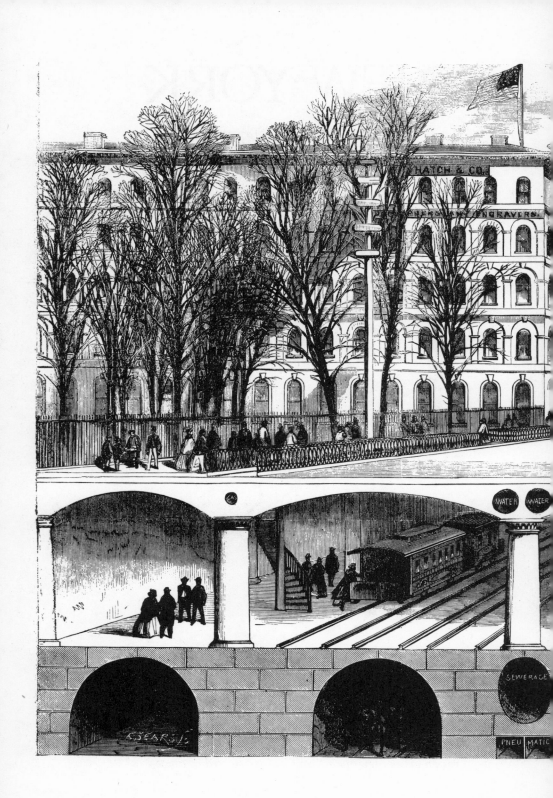

One of the many conjectural drawings of what a New York subway might look like. This one was issued in the late 1860's by the Arcade Railway Company.

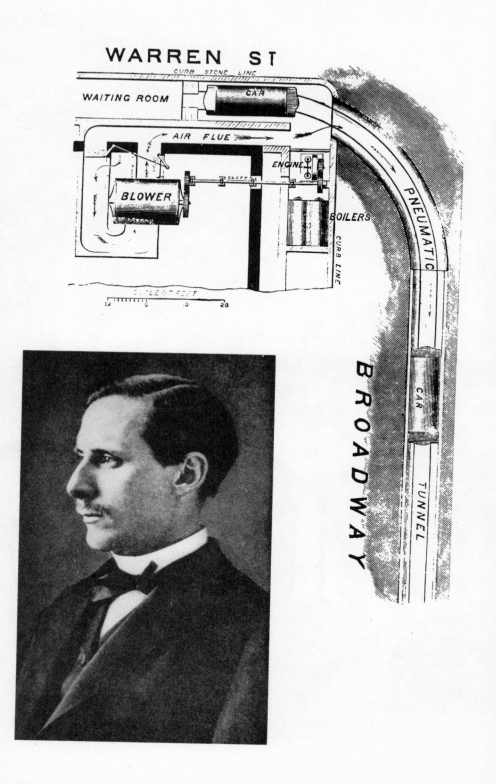

Left, Alfred Ely Beach, the publisher
and inventor whose secret pneumatic
subway was New York's first; and
the general plan of its operation,
showing the arrangement of the
machinery, the air flue, the tunnel,
and the mode of operating the
passenger car. Above, an elevated
"pneumatic passenger railway"
designed by Beach in 1867. Below, two
views of Beach's subway under lower
Broadway, in 1868. The motive power
was a giant helix fan driven by a
stationary steam engine.

Left, William March ("Boss") Tweed, the "Briareus of plunderers," who ruled New York during the 1860's. He implacably opposed Beach at every turn. Below, a rare view of the pneumatic subway car in motion. Right, a stereoscopic photograph of the line's Warren Street end, and a photograph recording the tunnel's "rediscovery" in 1912, when BMT workers broke in upon it while building their own subway line.

Above, the allurements of traveling by streetcar. Below, the notoriously corrupt financier, Jay Gould, depicted as a spider maneuvering across the web of telegraph lines he controlled. He eventually owned all of the city's els.

*Above, the locomotive envisioned as a demon. Below, the "iron horse" of the el
driving decent citizens and property owners to virtual insanity and ruin. Almost
all the many misgivings about the els turned out to be more than justified.*

Left, a street railroad strike in March of 1886 degenerated into a riot when management personnel attempted to run one of the cars on their own. Working conditions for drivers in those days were exceptionally cruel: this strike was for sixteen cents an hour and a 12-hour day. Right, Charles Harvey, who designed and built the first elevated line in New York in 1867. It ran along Greenwich Street and was powered by cables hauled by stationary steam engines. Below, Harvey is testing the first half-mile section of the line in a handcar, as apprehensive bystanders look on.

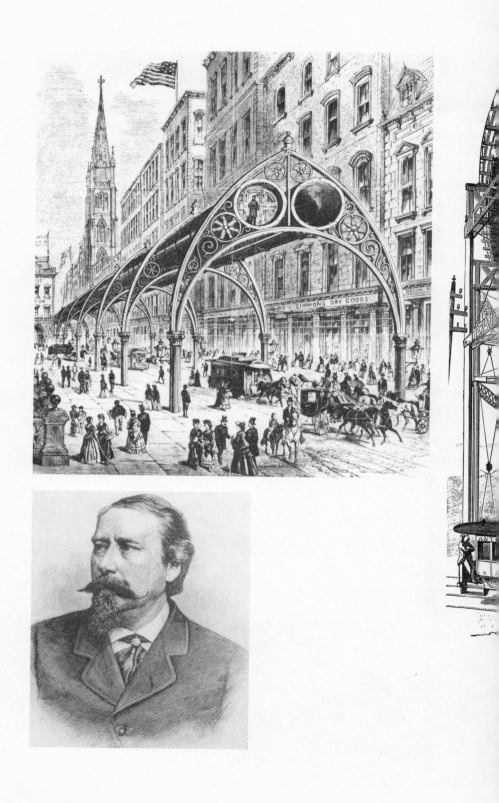

Rufus Gilbert, the distinguished surgeon and Civil War hero, who took up railroad engineering to relieve the plight of New York's tenement poor. He believed that a rapid transit line running from the inner city out to the suburbs was the best hope the disadvantaged had of escaping their blighted environment. Upper left, Gilbert's ornate Gothic arch design for a pneumatic el. Above, the snake-like curve of the Manhattan Elevated at 110th Street and Eighth Avenue.

Left, William Barclay Parsons, Chief Engineer of New York's IRT, at work on subway plans in his office. Below, signing of the IRT contract, March 24, 1900. Alexander E. Orr, head of the Public Service Commission, is at center. Both Parsons (standing, fourth from left) and contractor John B. MacDonald (the farthest to the right of those seated) gaze directly into the camera for posterity.

The groundbreaking ceremony at Bleecker and Greene Streets. Parsons methodically lowers the pick.

The first formal subway inspection, at City Hall Station in February 1904.

Views of the City Hall Station, the pride of the first line, and an architectural drawing of the once-standard New York kiosk design. Across right, an IRT kiosk; across below, its Budapest counterpart—both roughly modeled on Turkish summer houses of the Near East.

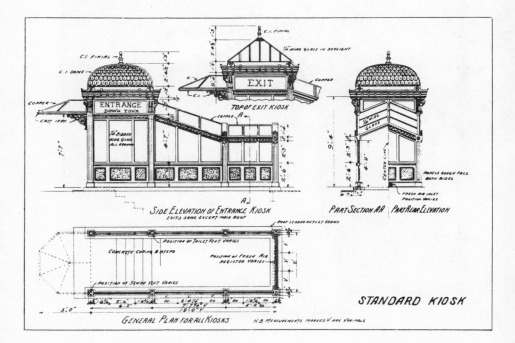

SIDE ELEVATION OF ENTRANCE KIOSK
EXITS SAME EXCEPT MAIN ROOF

PART SECTION AA   PART REAR ELEVATION

GENERAL PLAN FOR ALL KIOSKS   N.B. MEASUREMENTS MARKED V ARE VARIABLE

STANDARD KIOSK

Left, August Belmont, financier of the IRT. He invested nearly as much money in his own private subway car as in all the art for the entire IRT line. Below and right, three decorative plaques: at the Fulton Station, the steamship Clermont; *at 116th Street, the Columbia University seal; at Canal Street (BMT station), a ceramic mosaic landscape in stained-glass style.*

Major William Barclay Parsons of the First Reserve Engineers, who has already arrived in Europe to take up the difficult task of reconstructing French railroads damaged by the retreating Germans. Photo by Press Illustrating Service, Inc.

tending to demonstrate that the subway would improve public health by doing away with overcrowded cars—where the air was "toxic"—he managed almost to condemn respiration itself:

Foul air is a factor in the causation of many of those diseases which we have epidemic with us at the present time. The bad air has always been one of the most important factors in the production of certain diseases such as consumption, pneumonia and typhus fever.

The exhalation of people contains not only water, which we see on a frosty day in winter, but also carbonic acid gas, and certain other organic materials, and forms of albuminous ammonia. The moisture which comes from the breath in an overcrowded car helps to spread disease because it increases the growth of bacteria already in the car. The action of carbonic acid is another factor. The analysis of air in theaters, schools, cars and berths of ships which are not thoroughly ventilated by modern methods shows a great difference from the normal amount after a short time . . . But the principal danger from exhaled air is not in the moisture in itself nor the carbonic acid gas, but in the toxins which it contains. The exhalations of persons in a crowded car or room when condensed on cold glass, with the vapor of the atmosphere, forms when allowed to stand a glutinous matter which has the odor of perspiration. This organic matter from the lungs is nitrogenous in character, but is oxydizable. It is absorbed by wool, feathers, paper &c., but least by straw and horse hair. It is very noticeable on damp days in school rooms, particularly on the blackboard, when the blackboard, chairs, tables, etc. become sticky with this material.

These toxins, which are manufactured in our bodies by the action of the living protoplasms, or by energy and vital force expended, are called leucomaines. So far they have not been obtained in sufficient quantity to determine their composition, but their deleterious effect in the human system is certain. Condensed vapors of this kind have been injected into animals, and death produced within twenty-four hours. Not only does this predispose toward disease, but the constant breathing of foul air produces paleness, restlessness, increase of the heart beat, dilation of the pupils, anaemia, and various other symptoms.

Fortunately, these products of decay become harmless when sufficiently diluted with fresh air.

Unfortunately for Darlington even the new electric underground railroads of Paris and London were not famous for air that was "sufficiently diluted." There was little reason to suppose that the tunnels of the IRT would somehow be freer from the "products of decay."

October 27 arrived. Protestant Bishop Greer gave the subway his blessing, praying earnestly that it "might minister to the happiness and welfare of the people and tend to the peace, contentment, priority and upbuilding of homes." Archbishop Farley delivered the benediction.

McDonald was not among the dignitaries originally invited to speak. When he found this out, he was furious and called in a reporter, complaining bitterly, "When the dirt is off your shovel Wall Street doesn't give a damn for you." Later, when he was added to the speakers' list, he was gracious and paid a compliment to everyone on the roster.

Parsons' speech was the shortest of the day: "Mr. Mayor and Mr. Orr, I have the honor and very great pleasure to report that the Rapid Transit Railroad is completed for operation from the City Hall Station to the station of 145th Street, on the west side line."

Several speakers revived the slogan To Harlem in Fifteen Minutes, but according to the New York *American*, the police commissioner saw the new technology in a rather special light. " 'Do you know,' he said to Mrs. McDonald—as he squared about in his seat to emphasize his words—'that this subway is going to absolutely preclude the possibility of riots in New York. If a riot should break out at any time now we could clear the road and send out a trainload of a thousand men, dropping as many of them off at every station as necessary, and have an armed force in Harlem in fifteen minutes.' "

A silver key turned the electric current on. The new mayor, George McClellan, son of the Civil War general, took the silver-handled controls, and the eight-car train with its load of dignitaries set off from the City Hall Station to 145th Street. Under the mayor's unpracticed hand, however, the going was rough and a standby motorman quickly intervened. McClellan waved him aside. The train lurched on, overshooting stations, falling behind schedule, jerking people off their seats. At 103rd Street a frazzled, piqued, and embarrassed McClellan finally gave way.

That evening the subway was opened to the general public. As New Yorkers descended into the stations, they were handed a timetable and a little booklet reassuring them that the subterranean air was as pure as the air in their own homes. Written by Charles F. Chandler, a Columbia University professor, the booklet was transparently an attack on Darlington, though Chandler would not deign even to mention his name. "The air," he advised, "is not poisoned by peculiar organic substances which some investigators think they have discovered in human breath."

Seventy thousand people took the plunge. From most eyewitness accounts the experience must have been appalling, although it is hard not to suspect much striving for effect. The account in the New York *Tribune* is typical:

> Indescribable scenes of crowding and confusion, never before paralleled in this city, marked the throwing open of the subway to the general public last night . . .
>
> Men fought, kicked and pummeled one another in their mad desire to reach the subway ticket offices or to ride on the trains. Women were dragged out, either screaming in hysterics or in a swooning condition; gray haired men pleaded for mercy; boys were knocked down, and only escaped by a miracle being trampled underfoot. The presence of the police alone averted what would undoubtedly have been panic after panic, with wholesale loss of life.
>
> Hardly had the passengers on the first express train reached the One-hundred-and-forty-fifth-St. terminal, climbed the stairway and crossed the road to return to the downtown entrance when one of the worst crushes of the evening began. Two thousand people, composed of Washington Heights residents, who wished to go downtown, and those who had ridden uptown and wished to return, then surged and swarmed madly at the downtown entrance, frantic to descend . . .
>
> For fully half an hour with revolving and flying wedge formations, charges and counter charges and cane rushes, the mad stampede continued, the crowds increasing every moment as fresh incoming trains disgorged their human freight.

Only after police reserves were called in could order be restored—promptly putting to the test the police commissioner's coarse fantasy about riot control.

Still, the unruly debut showed at least that New Yorkers were thrilled to have the subway. As they stared out of the fast-moving trains with momentarily newborn eyes, "the novelty of the whirlwind rush through the long tunnel, the thunder of grinding wheels and the mad dance of flying shadows past the car windows all had their effect." Some complained that the fluttering sensation of the eyes caused pain, and worried about a new eye disease. But there was little feeling in the following days that the subway had been a mistake. Only the *Evening Telegram*, in a cryptic little paragraph buried amid exuberant commentary, sounded an ominous note: "Original sponsors of a subway had planned for the employment of pneumatic pressure, the cars to fit in the tube like the piston in a locomotive cylinder. A section of the tube, extending from Murray Street to Warren, was built and is still standing. Bricked up and useless, it is a tomb for the crumbling timbers and rusted metal frame of the first subway car."

Parsons' design was original, "quite unlike the ordinarily accepted picture of an underground railroad." Instead of an arched roof with masonry sidewalls suggesting a tunnel, he built a rectangular structure that suggested a covered way. It had a flat roof and "I" beams supporting the roof and sides, with bulb-angle columns between the tracks. The shallowness of the excavation allowed sunlight to come in through deadlights in the sidewalks whence it was reflected by bright white and decorated tiles. "Underground railways," Parsons wrote, "have always been associated in the public mind with dark, damp, dank, smoke-laden tunnels—veritable approaches to lower regions." He hoped his own work would not be regarded in the same way.

The IRT subway was supposed to be handsome; the contract had contained a promising clause: "The railway and equipment constitute a great public work. All parts of the subway where exposed to public sight shall therefore be designed with a view to the beauty of their appearance, as well as to their efficiency." When the work was done, the IRT claimed that "no effort or expense was spared in living up to the spirit of this provision. All parts of the road and equipment display dignified and consistent effects of the highest order . . . such as may uplift and refine the public taste."

This was hardly so. The decoration was simple, consistent, but essentially perfunctory. Most stations had faience or terra-cotta cornices, white or glazed tile ceiling panels, wide ornamental moldings, and a scattering of rosettes, friezes, and pilasters. Each station had its own color scheme and a different combination of vault and artificial lighting. Of more genuine interest were a series of individual panels, all quite small, depicting some symbol or event associated with the district of each stop. Not without some charm, most of the panels were ceramic mosaic bas-reliefs done in simple, naturalistic style. Their subject was usually obvious: at Columbus Circle, the navigator's caravel *Santa Maria*; at the 116th Street Station, across from the campus of Columbia University, the university seal; at Fulton Street, the inventor's steamboat *Clermont*; and so forth. A less readily decipherable icon is the beaver at Astor Place, commemorating the fact that John Jacob Astor made his killing in furs.

The most picturesque features of the original IRT had a sort of Arabian cast to them, putting one in mind of O. Henry's remark that New York was like "Baghdad on the subway." The tops of the cars were painted a bright poppy red, and the wired-glass, cast-iron kiosks that enclosed the entrances were modeled on summerhouses of the Near East. (The word kiosk is derived from the Turkish *kiushk*, meaning pavilion, and the Persian *küsch*, meaning palace or portico.) Their appearance in New York was not their Western debut. Striking Art Nouveau versions with arabesque wrought-iron blossoms had already been built for the Paris Métro; and the subway in Budapest had adopted a variation featuring a more intricate lattice work design. For half a century replicas in traditional styles had been popular in parks and gardens throughout Western Europe, and in both France and Belgium they were used widely as newspaper stands. Yet though their lineage had already somewhat fallen from the exotic to the everyday, in New York they elegantly served a most courteous purpose, to shelter, as one writer put it, "descending passengers from wind and emerging ones from rain." One hundred and thirty-three of them were built, all forged at the Hecla

Iron Works, the foremost manufacturer of architectural metal-work in the world.

For a long time the kiosks were among the last reminders, with the old Pennsylvania Station, of an extinguished era. One by one the city inexplicably tore them down until, in 1967, the last one was removed. Nothing but dark, damp, dank stairwells mark their place.

The original City Hall Station was unquestionably the pride of the line; of the five hundred thousand dollars specifically allocated to decor, it received the lion's share. The architects were Heins and La Farge, who designed the arches of the Cathedral Church of St. John the Divine; Rafael Guastavino, a Spanish-born architect, assumed chief responsibility. His accomplishments included the vaults for St. Paul's Chapel at Columbia University, and indeed the station he designed has something of the feeling of a chapel about it. There are no straight lines, and its continuous succession of low projecting terra-cotta arches has a rhythmical semicircular sweep. The roof is inlaid with three great stained-glass skylights, and braid-like patterns of earthenware tile adorn the vault. Later, Guastavino reworked the same design for the interior of Grand Central Station's Oyster Bar. In this he may have been inspired by a thirsty journalist who in 1904 described the City Hall Station at first sight as a "cool little vaulted city of cream and green earthenware, like a German beer stein." Unfortunately, the station is now seldom seen by the public. Trains use it solely as a turnaround loop.

The stations were supposed to be free of advertising, according to the contract. The New York *Commercial* had rejoiced: "The beauty of the interior will never be defaced ... The stations have been so constructed that they leave no room for the introduction of advertisement without marring the effect of the whole." But when McDonald had turned his contract over to Belmont, advertising privileges were part of the deal. This was withheld from the public and when it became known a few days after the subway opened, there was an outcry, but nothing could be done. The New York *Press* declared:

> We congratulate Mr. August Belmont on his magnificent daring in the seizure of this splendid prize from the people. We salute

Mr. William Barclay Parsons, the genius of the scheme which official neglect, or worse, has perverted. We hail Mr. John B. McDonald, the Hercules of the huge physical conception, so massively well executed.

Thinking of the present we join in the thoughtless hurrah, out of gratitude for the gifts the car lords have been pleased to give us. Thinking of the future, we drop a tear.

The night the subway opened, even as the public was thronging madly through its halls, seventy men of great wealth representing the country's major railroads and including some of its most prominent financiers held a testimonial banquet in the ballroom of Sherry's in honor of August Belmont. At the room's western end, in the center of a gigantic oval table, stood a perfect facsimile of the Seventy-second Street Station, 10 feet wide and 40 feet long, complete with platforms, stairways, ticket booths, tracks, artificial illumination, tiles, ornamentation, and even colored signal lights. The tracks were electrified and two miniature IRT cars, each about 4 feet long with toy motormen in tiny cages, ran over them back and forth. On either side American beauty roses and chrysanthemums were heaped across a carpet of reddened oak leaves interspersed with masses of ferns. About the room were tropical plants in profusion, and palms and garlands of smilax embellished the halls.

Most of the guests had been connected with the subway in some way; all were enthusiastic over the reception given it, and eager to tell one another of the possibilities for new underground railroads and tubes. When sherbet was served each diner received a souvenir—a silver medal with portraits of Belmont, the mayor, and the president of the Board of Rapid Transit Commissioners and an inscription commemorating the beginning and end of the work.

The mayor made a cliquish sort of speech and at its conclusion two men came into the room bearing an immense silver loving cup with three large handles and the letters *A.B.* embossed on it in gold. The IRT was, after all, Belmont's road. If he had spent five hundred thousand dollars on "art" for the whole line, he had spent almost that much on his own private conveniences for its use. His own car, *"The Mineola,"* was quite unlike any other

IRT car built. It had a fully furnished office, a lounge with leather chairs at either end, a lavatory, linen closet, bar, pantry, refrigerator, and oven, a steward's galley with hot and cold running water, and a kitchen with nickel-plated coffee urns. The ceiling, in "arched Empire" style, was tinted "pistachio green"; the windows—some of them stained glass—were hung with green velvet drapes. Throughout, the wood inlay was natural mahogany with brass trim. Of course, the car had its own motorman. At Forty-second Street and Park Avenue, where the financier had built the Belmont Hotel, a special set of tracks connected Grand Central Station with the hotel's basement. The tracks went all the way to Belmont Park, and occasionally Belmont would slip away with guests through a secret exit for a tour of the tunnels or to see the horses run.

The subway ran at a profit for awhile, $6 million a year, incremental to Belmont's already prodigious hoard.

McDonald looked into the future. "Having shoveled and blasted this four-track highway 54 feet wide under the most crowded part of New York," he boasted, "we have demonstrated that the rapid transit problems of the metropolis can be completely solved. It is now simply a question of more tunnels." He was wrong, but he was also right: "There is not a street in the city that cannot be tunneled ... I think we have made a beginning of an underground city."

Shortly after the subway opened, Parsons resigned. Before the year was out he was appointed to the Panama Canal Commission and to an advisory board of the Royal Commission on London Traffic, where one of his colleagues was Sir Benjamin Baker. In 1905 he completed the Steinway Tunnel under the East River by improvising an artificial island and working from four separate headings at once. In the same year he undertook the Cape Cod Canal, which demonstrated that a canal without locks could be built between two bodies of water where considerable tidal differences existed, thus proving established opinion wrong. In the spring of 1917, the United States entered World War I and as a first contribution to the Allied cause raised nine regiments of engineers. By then almost sixty years old, Parsons volunteered and assumed command of the Eleventh Engineers Regiment of the First Army. On June 14 they sailed on the *Carpathia* for England. From Plymouth Harbor the regiment traveled by rail to Folkestone, crossed the Channel to Boulogne, and then moved on to Audricq. On August 18 they arrived at the front on the Somme near Peronne—the very first American forces in France.

Under Parsons, the regiment demonstrated its ability to tackle any variety of work, from building ice plants to railroads. It was said of the Eleventh that "given a few steel rails, a few ties, a case of tin cans and four waste planks they would guarantee to build a barracks fit for anybody to live in." Their work was often so exposed to enemy fire that it had to be done at night or on days obscured by fog.

Sometimes they had to fight. Southeast of Arras, northeast of Peronne, and 8 miles from the British lines lay Cambrai, an important railway junction held by the Germans since September 1914. When the British offensive reached the city outskirts, the Eleventh was sent forward to Gouzeaucourt with orders to establish a railway yard.

All was quiet. The engineers left their arms at camp, so as not to be encumbered, and carried only tools. As they began their work, heavy shelling started to the east; then a few shells burst on the top of a nearby ridge where the British batteries were posted. The firing became a barrage. It advanced over the ridge, pounded down the slope, and finally focused across the tracks from where the men were working. British soldiers appeared, falling back through the open fields. It was suddenly clear that the enemy was attacking in force. The engineers tried to retreat by train, but were cut off by the intensity of the fire. They turned, improvised a company, and together with a scattering of British and Canadian troops made a stand. Fighting back with picks and shovels, they actually delayed the enemy advance until reserve forces could mount a counterattack.

These "Fighting Engineers" became a legend. From the Atlantic to the Vosges, from the Mediterranean to Flanders, they built roads, railroads, bridges, docks, and warehouses, and dug and held trenches. In the Meuse-Argonne offensive, which closed the war, they constructed an entirely new railway from Aubreville up into the Argonne, to connect with an existing line at Apremont. On one occasion, under the astonished eyes of the enemy, they laid $1\frac{1}{4}$ miles of track in seven and a half hours. All in all, the Eleventh took part in five major engagements, for which they received five silver bars on the staff of the regimental colors. Parsons himself was awarded the Distinguished Service Medal, the Victory Medal and five clasps, the Distinguished Service Order of Britain, the Office of the Legion of Honor of France, and the Order of the Crown of Belgium.

In his dedication to perfection Parsons took his motto from St. Paul—"This one thing I do"—and believed, as he told the graduating class of Trinity College in Hartford one Sunday afternoon in June 1921, that "every act we commit, no matter how trifling, and every word we speak has some effect for good or evil, and what we do or say is done or said for all time." He found corroboration for this in natural law (the law of the conservation of energy, according to which nothing is ever lost or destroyed), and in philosophy in the observation of Marcus Aurelius that "nothing can come out of nothing or go back to nothing." It followed that "no one effort of a single individual is ever lost without leaving behind its effect . . . There rests on men as individuals an inescapable responsibility for all their acts."

When Parsons returned from the front in 1918 he had other things than subways on his mind. He gave lectures on the affinity of psychology to physics and concluded that Einstein's theory of relativity had "application in human thought"; he pondered the relation between orbits in atomic structure and celestial bodies and wondered whether they might have something to teach us about the relationships between individuals and nation states. To better understand what it was to be an engineer, he undertook a history of his profession, and his account of engineering in the Renaissance remains unsurpassed. In his last years the decay of civilizations and great cities haunted him, and it became almost his obsession to cast some light on the "unexplained Maya ruins of Yucatán."

In the meantime, New York was digging away. "Dual contracts" with the IRT and the BRT (Brooklyn Rapid Transit Co.)

had been signed by the city in 1913, and in 1918 the first of the new expansion lines began to open. They brought the subway up the East Side of Manhattan and into Brooklyn and Queens. At Forty-second Street the cross line of the old IRT "Z" formation became the crosstown Grand Central Shuttle in a configuration resembling an "H." When the shuttle opened on August 1, 1918, the vastly elaborated Times Square and Grand Central stations, with their network of corridors, made it difficult for travelers to find their way around. As crowds milled about looking for the shuttle going in the right direction, many "became confused, then frightened, and mauled one another in attempts to fight their way to the street." Appalled at the rioting, the chairman of the Public Service Commission closed the shuttle down. That evening, the son of one of the transit engineers was reading a book on ancient mythology when he came upon the legend of the Minotaur. He suggested to his father that continuous lines of different colors be painted on the walls to provide clues to the right train, just as Theseus had unraveled Ariadne's linen skein as he made his way through the Minotaur's maze. This was subsequently done.

The Minotaur, however, roamed a larger lair. Three months after the shuttle opened—on November 1, All Saints Day, the day after Halloween—a BRT dispatcher, pressed into service as a motorman during a wildcat strike, took a treacherous downhill S-curve at high speed on the approach to Malbone Street in Brooklyn and lost control of the train. The rear wheels of the first car left the tracks; the second car flew up into the tunnel's ceiling; the third and fourth cars followed in collision, as bursts of shattered wood and glass compounded the destruction. The fifth and last car of the train somehow escaped unharmed.

The crash caused a short circuit, cutting off power to the third rail—an event that might have proved lucky, except that BRT electricians some distance away in the powerhouse thought it was the result of union sabotage. Just as some of the disoriented survivors were groping their way across the tracks, current was restored.

In all, nearly a hundred people died, and another two hundred were injured. To this day the disaster remains the worst in subway history. No subway map will tell you where Malbone Street is. Shortly after the accident, the name of the street and the station was changed to Empire Boulevard; the BRT, whose motto had been Safety First, plunged toward bankruptcy. A few years later the company was reorganized as the Brooklyn-Manhattan Transit Company, or the BMT.

In the 1920's and 1930's the subway—and the el—became favorite symbols in the writings of social poets and critics for proletarian degradation under capitalism. Most of this literature is top-heavy with argument or rhetorically banal. But here and there a striking passage stands out, such as this stream-of-consciousness soliloquy from Elmer Rice's play *The Subway*, admittedly more notable for its threading together of popular apprehensions than for literary grace:

> It's called the Subway ... it's an epic ... an epic of industrialism ... It fills me ... obsesses me ... the city ... the city ... steel and concrete ... industrialism, rearing its towers arrogantly to the skies ... Higher and higher ... deeper and deeper ... "Their foundations are bound into the chambered rock. Their pinnacles pierce the clouds." ... Up and up ... fists of steel shaking defiance at the skies ... still higher and higher ... All mankind joining the mad mechanistic dance ... bondsmen to the monsters they have created ... slaves to steel and concrete ...
>
> And under the earth ... miles and miles of burrows ... hundreds of miles ... walls of concrete ... rails of steel ... winding and winding ... the subway ... the entrails of the city ... speed ... speed ... Faster and faster ... a labyrinth ... an inferno ... a great roaring and the clatter of steel upon steel ... A subway train ... a monster of steel with flaming eyes and gaping jaws ... Moloch devouring his worshippers ... Juggernaut crushing his tens of thousands ... A subway train ... Down there under the ground ... under the steel towers that scrape the skies ... A subway train ... roaring ... roaring ... the beast of the new Apocalypse ...

In his 1922 novel *The Beautiful and Damned*, F. Scott Fitzgerald found the el a "roaring cave" and the subway a "crowded terror" and "an echo of hell." Of far more imaginative significance, "The Tunnel" section of Hart Crane's epic 1930 poem *The Bridge* transforms a subway ride from Times Square to Brooklyn Heights into a journey through hell itself, the ninth circle or nadir of despair symbolized by the dive of the train beneath the river. Pieced together, as Crane remarked in a letter, "almost all from notes and stitches I have written while swinging on the strap at late midnights going home," "The Tunnel"—with its juxtapositions of past and present, horror and sublimity, commercial trashiness and spiritual aspiration—looks back through T. S. Eliot's *The Wasteland* to Dante's *Inferno*. Though the poem ends on a promise of deliverance as the train climbs upward from the river, it is in passages like the unforgettable apparition of Edgar Allan Poe

> *And why do I often meet your visage here,*
> *Your eyes like agate lanterns—on and on*
> *Below the toothpaste and the dandruff ads*

that Crane discovers living equivalents for the jostle of Dante's voices.

By 1927, the city's jilted romance with the subway had embittered even the establishment. The City Club, a group of civic-minded citizens without any political ax to grind, made an emotional appeal to the Board of Estimate and Apportionment to abandon subway expansion plans, "in the name of New York's two million children." In an open letter, the club called the subway a "bottomless hole" into which funds urgently needed for parks, playgrounds, schools, hospitals, beaches, and other necessities were being cast. Describing subway conditions as "intolerable" and "inhuman," it went on:

> We do not get a civilized ride for a nickel today. We get instead a chance to hang on, like a chimpanzee, to a flying ring suspended from the roof of the car while we are crushed to a point of indecency by our fellow sufferers. [That] rare plum known as a "seat on the subway" is plucked by a very few; the trains are like cattle-cars ... subways create manufacturing—by the time they are built they will be followed with new workers ... Without in-

dustrial decentralization, we shall never catch up with our rapid transit congestion, no matter how many new subway systems are built.

In the years following their inauguration, the major subway systems of London, Paris, and New York ramified into increasingly complex networks. Meanwhile, two other major systems were built: in Tokyo in 1927 and Moscow in 1935. By 1935, there were also a number of other systems operating on a smaller scale: in Glasgow, Budapest, Boston, Philadelphia, Madrid, Barcelona, Buenos Aires, Sydney, Osaka, and Berlin. Subways had become an international phenomenon.

The distinctive features of the Tokyo system, which converted the main stations into vast concourses like underground cities, developed much later. But the Moscow story was significant from the start. At about the time Hart Crane was bringing his epic to an end, had he put his ear to the ground he might indeed have heard, far to the East, faint echoes of Dante's jostle of voices—not living equivalents imaginatively joined, but something like the thing itself, welling up in Chaos from the ninth circle of despair.

CHAPTER 9

Labor Saturdays
and a
Czar's Ransom

On July 16, 1934, Lazar M. Kaganovich, Minister of Transport, Commissar of Railways, and First Party Secretary for the Moscow Region, delivered a "criticism" of the progress of work on the Moscow subway before a large assembly of "shock brigadiers of Metrostroi and the factories of Moscow." Ground had been broken in November 1931, three years before. Since that time there had been problems.

The work force, he acknowledged, was inexperienced. They were unfamiliar with methods of excavation, even with simple modern building techniques such as pouring and reinforcing concrete. But no one, he said, should have found this surprising. Volunteers had come to the project from all walks of life: there were textile workers, workers from chemical plants, municipal employees, metal workers from the Urals, miners from Donbas, laborers from the collective farms. Few of them had ever been involved in work of this kind. Even the professionals, the engineers, had at first been indecisive. They had not firmly directed the work.

The crowd shifted noticeably in the front rows, their starched garments rustling like leaves in a stray wind. It was not forgotten by anyone that Kaganovich was Stalin's purging right arm.

"You, comrades, know, of course," he went on, "that we are not engineers, and that we don't know much about the movements of subsoils. Until now we knew different movements: the workers' revolutionary movement, and the counter-revolutionary movement. But we did not know what to do about this movement of the ground." There was laughter and exaggerated applause. Everyone wanted to take this joke at face value, to believe that no one would be blamed. Apparently it was possible to make technological mistakes and still be a good Communist.

The subsoil of Moscow had indeed been a Protean adversary. The tunnels had to be driven through a fissured limestone that was palpably soft with water, like a sponge. Just above the limestone lay a bed of Jurassic clay, and above that a crust of glacial drift. In some cases the limestone had "deteriorated into a form of red marl destructive to cast iron," while pockets of swelling clay had been known to "crumple twenty-inch thick timber beams like matchsticks." There had also been a number of fatal, surprise encounters with underground rivers "which cut the route of excavation like so many seams."

Although Russian engineers had proposed a subway as early as 1902, it was not seriously considered until 1931, when Stalin complained about tramcars "overburdening the streets, retarding traffic and creating an incredible noise." On June 15, 1931, the Plenum of the Central Committee of the Communist Party had decided on a subway as part of an overall plan for the modernization of Moscow. At that time, the city was still largely medieval in character, a maze of some twenty-five hundred streets and lanes with fifty-one thousand dwellings, mostly one- and two-story wooden-frame houses. Twenty-five thousand tramcars carried almost seven million people to and fro. Thus the usual incentives for a subway were acute enough, but after a year of trying to cope with the subsoil, the experts recommended that the project be dropped.

This was injudicious. Stalin's interest in the "Metro" was personal: he wanted Moscow to be the new industrial capital of Russia, to outshine Leningrad. Moreover, a date had already been set for the celebration of the Seventeenth Anniversary of the Revolution—November 7, 1934. Stalin was so determined that a Metro would adorn it that the effort took priority over the consumer needs of the entire nation. Half a billion rubles were allotted to the first line—almost twice the average yearly investment in consumer goods industries.

The engineers, under pressure, were willing to try anything, and in fact experimented with every method of tunneling known: the open tunnel method, the French caisson system, artificial freezing, the Belgian double-passage method, the British shield system, the American flying-arch. But real progress did not become possible until the discovery late in 1932 of "grouting," a chemical process for hardening the subsoil so that a tunnel could be driven through it and lined with cement.

Using force pumps connected to 15- to 30-foot-long one-inch-diameter perforated pipes, silicate of soda, or "water glass," was injected into the ground, followed by calcium chloride or sodium chloride (common salt) in solution. Sometimes the solution was mixed with cement. Within minutes these chemicals would congeal, and "in some cases they rendered the soil almost as hard as common building brick."

The original Metrostroi work force consisted of six thousand coal miners. At their head, as Chief of Construction, was R. R. Rottert, widely respected for his work on the Dnieprostroi Dam. P. P. Zarembo was the Chief Engineer.

Equipment and materiel were drawn for the undertaking from every part of Russia. "The metallurgical plants in Dniepropetrovsk and Kolomna supplied cast-iron segments; Kiev, Cheboksary, Tashkent and other cities sent complex signalling and communications apparatus, cable, escalators, rails, ties and cement . . . while the Soviets built for themselves installations for freezing floating earth, and compressors for caisson work." In addition, an international staff of technical advisors was also on hand to contribute their expertise. Several came from New York, after plans for the Second Avenue subway were abandoned during the Depression. But the most important were from the London Transport Office, in particular Lord Ashfield.

None of these specialists, however, not even Zarembo or Rottert, commanded the power usually implied by their titles. Real authority lay with Kaganovich's chief assistant, Nikita Khrushchev, "at that time hardly more than a burly Ukrainian peasant who had shown some promise by his tough tactics as a foreman in projects in the Ukraine." The most significant had been the Moscow-Volga Canal, a gigantic slave-labor undertaking only slightly less important to the nation's prestige than the stupendous Dnieper hydroelectric power plant project which Kaganovich had helped organize. Kaganovich's harshness in building what was to become the largest power center of its kind in the world rivaled his infamous term in Tashkent, in 1920–1925, when he enforced Soviet rule in Turkestan. In fact, what the two officials had most in common was experience in the use of slave labor on a large scale.

Khrushchev was forty years old when he took effective control of the building of the Moscow Metro. His only engineering qualifications derived from his experience in the mines, though apparently he felt that was qualification enough. As an ideologue, however, he knew how the work should be done—according to party principles. Every day he would go down to the construction sites to "check, criticize, and advise" the different foremen "on all specific and urgent problems." His field office eventually vied in authority with the offices of the project manager and the chief engineer. Shaft overseers, party organizers, individual brigade leaders, and engineers came to congregate there as a matter of course before reaching decisions.

He was vigilant. "Self-seekers," he cautioned at one point, "have wormed themselves into our construction sites . . . It is necessary to fight in a Bolshevik way, so that every bricklayer, plasterer, [and] painter fulfills his output norm." That norm was mercurial, hard to pin down. As often as not it was set by whatever could be done during stretches of maximum toil, or by what a special team could do under special conditions.

The usual conditions were very hard. Although the avowed purpose of the subway project was to establish the superiority of Communist labor, in every respect it merely demonstrated that the Soviet system could surpass industrial capitalism in its most savagely exploitative form. The wages were low, the hours extraordinarily long, and the conditions hazardous. The worst sort of sweatshop factory labor was more humane.

Even official accounts concede "errors in judgment." For example, proper care was not taken to shore up many of the buildings along the route. "We knew, of course," wrote an engineer, "that we were tunneling under a great city, that every disturbance of existing foundations might lead to disaster." And often it did. Yet such negligence was sometimes perversely portrayed as heroic. Hence the story was told, as though to Khrushchev's credit, that once when a building threatened to topple into an excavation and a commission of experts asked Khrushchev for a delay, he waved them aside contemptuously. "What's the matter with you?" he demanded cleverly of the engineer in charge. "Are you frightened of buildings?"

Khrushchev was especially passionate about tunneling shields. Russia had two, one imported from England, the other a Soviet copy. The surveyor had tacked up a chart in Khrushchev's office on which he marked the daily progress of each shield. At the slightest sign that either was slowing down, Khrushchev would get agitated. He insisted on an average advance of one full meter per shift, four times the speed compatible with minimum safety. The consequences of this rule can hardly be measured. We know only that whole shifts were sometimes crushed to death in cave-ins or drowned by inundations in the shafts.

Sometimes the workers were caught in a situation where inaction was hardly less fatal than any action they could possibly take. According to one account:

> The shield approached the silt—a brown fluid mass. The caisson worked under an air pressure of 2.3 atmospheres. With every hour the conditions became more difficult. Sometimes the silt resisted and unprecedented efforts were necessary to stop it, to save the tunnel, the machine, and, chiefly, the people. Once a fire broke out in the caisson. In order to avoid rapid spreading of the fire in compressed air rich in oxygen it became necessary to lower the air pressure, but this opened the way for the silt that poured in torrents into the shaft.

The incidence of "caisson's disease" was out of all proportion to any work of its kind ever undertaken, before or since. At times the air pressure in the chambers would reach 30 pounds to the square inch, twice the norm, yet the men were forced to work underground for two or three days on end. As the bubbles of nitrogen built up in their blood, they developed stomach cramps, painful joints, difficulty in breathing, and convulsive fits. The "bends," as they are called, left many men paralyzed for life; others, perhaps luckier, simply died.

Khrushchev was not the only one responsible for all this. Kaganovich had set the tone. In one of his edicts, on December 29, 1933, he said: "The main task is to speed up the construction tempo . . . In the shortest possible time we must increase the speed of excavating five times and the speed of the tunnel building eight to nine times." Khrushchev applied these statistical goals literally, which is undoubtedly how they were meant. Chief Engineer Zarembo later wrote: "The time schedule grabbed us by the throat."

By 1934 it had become clear that the Metro wasn't going to be ready in time, so the government appealed to the Komsomol, the Young Communist League, to become "guardians" of the work. The league began organizing *"subotniks"*—Labor Saturdays—when everyone was supposed to donate his or her labor to the state. As many as eighty thousand "volunteers" took part at the program's height. For the next year and a half the progress was unprecedented—three to five times as fast as comparable work had ever before been done.

Kaganovich's joke about "movements" was the only point of humor in his speech. He soon got down to what was on his mind:

> We must detect the unconscientious workers and catch them red-handed . . . The unconscientious worker must not think that if he puts plaster on, covers up bad work, adds the waterproofing, and then puts a layer of concrete over it, that no one will see the bad work . . . Don't let the subway builders think that we are "Ivans who forget their relations" . . . We will check up from day to day . . . The organs of authority will take all measures necessary. I hope we will not have to take these measures.

Any experienced worker in his audience would have known what measures he was talking about. Six months before, Kaganovich had appointed I. N. Kuznetsov, "whose past experience was 'the battlefront and the Cheka, and nothing else,' " to the post of Assistant Chief of Construction. The title was a front; his real assignment was to "find out" and "move away" unsatisfactory workers.

Everyone was potentially unsatisfactory. One of Khrushchev's own assistants frankly recalled that "it was a difficult time. People, even Communists, came and asked to be released from work." When someone showed up with a certificate from the doctors' commission stating that he was unfit to work, the assistant admitted he did not release him. Why not? "It is necessary to get used to the work. When you start working, fatigue occurs immediately, but you should not leave your working place: fatigue passes, and working inspiration begins. The doctors' commission does not know it, but we—the party organization—do know it." Kuznetsov moved a great many men away— usually to labor camps or the Siberian mines. To escape their fate, workers sometimes sought refuge in the remotest recesses of the underground tunnels. Kuznetsov went after them. "My men descended into the shafts to hunt them out. Sometimes it was necessary literally to drag them up into the daylight."

No one was immune from such treatment, particularly in the building of the later lines. After 1935, as Stalin's terror spread to almost every segment of Soviet society, the unskilled personnel supplied by Komsomol to supplement the miners were replaced by forced labor. Valentín Gonzalez, a Communist hero of the Spanish Civil War who went to Moscow in the 1930's for "special political training," fell from grace and was put to work on the Metro so that he could prove his loyalty. The conditions were harrowing.

Lack of modern machinery and equipment made our work very difficult. Human muscles and effort had to replace the missing tools. I often worked in water up to my knees . . .
. . . I was a forced laborer. I had to stay in the job into which I was put, without a possibility of leaving, or even of being transferred to another gang of workers in the underground. There was no promotion of any sort open to me. The N.K.V.D. [secret police] had listed me as a worker capable of maximum output. In my first job, which was placing great nuts and bolts with the help of

enormous spanners, this classification meant that I had to place 265 a day, while the normal rate was 165 a day. My pride drove me to exceed even that maximum norm, as often as not. The same happened when I was put on work with concrete or when I had to shift soil with a wheel barrow. But however hard I worked, my pay was always the same: 300 rubles a month, the basic wage of workers in Moscow—a starvation wage. In practice, however, I hardly ever got as much as 200 rubles, when all the deductions had been made.

He was not alone.

Almost 90 per cent of the construction workers were in a position similar to mine. Many of them were old fighters, former military leaders, or even N.K.V.D. men. They had fallen into disgrace and had been allotted this sort of work which offered them the faint— the very faint—hope that their efforts would in time restore them to their former position in the ruling class.

This was early in 1941. When the Nazis invaded Russia in June, the ordeal intensified. Lenin's embalmed body was concealed in one of the Metro stations near Red Square and the underground began to be prepared for use as an air-raid shelter and hideaway. According to Gonzalez:

It sometimes happened that we stayed underground for six days on end, working without a break except for a short nap now and then when we could not go on. At the same time the network of spies and *agents provocateurs* in the labor gangs was intensified. For the mildest word of criticism anyone was likely to be arrested as a "defeatist" within a few hours, and with him all those who had been within earshot but failed to report the remark.

When the war at last brought the subway work to a halt, Gonzalez was sent to the coal mines in Vorkuta, north of the Arctic Circle. "Vorkuta" means "people of the Underworld," and it is said that the first settlers of the region—which lies in a zone of permafrost—were deported convicts. On the day Gonzalez arrived, it was 53° below zero.

The Metro was often a way station en route to the mines, a sort of purgatory on the way down to hell. As we know from Aleksandr Solzhenitsyn's revelations of the Gulag Archipelago, millions before him and since have suffered a similarly bleak fate. The constant threat of deportation hung over the workers like a sword—"The alternative," wrote Gonzalez, "was Siberia"—and this did much to reconcile them to their toil. For in Vorkuta

> the soil thaws for only a brief spell in summer, and then only on the surface. Underneath the crust is the solid depth of everlastingly ice-bound earth. In July and August the climate is bearable, but soon the ground freezes again. And when the polar night begins, the Vorkuta is a black, icy hell. Only the doomed prisoners work on, night or day, ice or thaw.

Kaganovich seems not to have been troubled by his role in bringing about such miseries. Once he even admitted casually that purges were indiscriminate: "When a forest is cut down, the chips fly." All that mattered to him was to be a loyal Bolshevik. "A Bolshevik," he said, "should be willing not only to sacrifice his life for the party, but also his self-respect and sensitivity." In 1957, when the party no longer regarded him as a good Bolshevik, it sacrificed him too, expelling him and then blotting out his name.

One day, as the first line neared completion, subway diggers came upon some white sand below the foundations of a razed building. Baffled by the unexpected strata, they diverged somewhat from plan and dug deeper, and over the next several days gradually uncovered an extraordinary find: first a courtyard, pentangular in shape, then a perfect maze of passages flanked by dungeons, storehouses, cemeteries, and sundry rooms that had once been connected with the Palace of the Czars. According to legend, Ivan the Terrible brought his enemies to that courtyard to watch them tortured with elaborate devices, or torn to pieces by savage bears. One passage, indeed, extended out some distance to where a dense forest populated with wild animals once stood. This maze, laid out so as to accommodate large quantities of provisions, served also as a hiding place from invaders.

Ivan had built this labyrinth, or underground city, as it was called, in the 1560's, but historians had long ago dismissed its existence as folklore. To the persecuted Metro workers in Moscow, however, there could have been little unbelievable or shocking in the discovery.

The first line opened on May 15, 1935, six months late. The Seventeenth Anniversary of the Russian Revolution had come and gone, but it did not matter. The world was duly impressed. Everyone admired the phenomenal speed with which the subway had been built, and the international reputation of communism was enhanced because so many workers had been "volunteers." Moreover, the construction had a beauty unmatched in the subways of the West. Khrushchev, promoted to First Secretary of the Moscow City Committee, was awarded the Order of Lenin.

The Moscow Metro was a many-spendored thing. In the stations' spacious vestibules and along their lofty vaulted halls, light flashed and coruscated from carved crystal chandeliers of a magnificence not likely to be encountered in the capitalist world outside the mansions of the Vanderbilts and Astors. Each station was designed as a monument to a historic event or significant figure. Mosaics and frescoes, enameled bas-reliefs and stained-glass murals exalted scenes of military and nationalistic glory from the past—a fourteenth-century battle with the Tartars, Russian knights in a cavalry charge against Swedish aggressors, struggles with the Poles, Field Marshal Kutuzov's campaigns against Napoleon. Nor were more recent and peaceful events, like the festivals celebrating the opening of the Dnieper hydroelectric power plant and the tercentenary of the reunion of the Ukraine with Russia, neglected. In the best tradition of Socialist Realism, the latter shows lovely Ukrainian girls dancing to the sound of lutes while children throng around them bearing great bouquets of flowers as several heavily decorated Soviet heroes look proudly on.

In each detail the decor seemed to manifest a loving care. Facings and columns, for example, exhibited an abundance of decorative variety; there were porphyry, feldspar, granite, enamel, and bronze as well as more exotic materials like labradorite, of a dark gray color impregnated with sparkling ultramarine; above all, there was marble of every description—pink and light gray from the Urals, dark red and white from the Georgian Caucasus, and from the veins in the Crimea marble of a ruddy gold "like the hue of sunrise over snow-capped mountains." By January 1, 1943, 70,000 square meters of marble had gone into the Metro's first twenty-two stations—more than had embellished all the palaces of the Czar in the fifty years before the Revolution.

Such extravagance was meant, of course, to show that Soviet wealth was now at the disposal of the people. The stations were like secular cathedrals, pseudoreligious monuments of a nationalistic kind. Even more than bridges or power plants, subways stood for the miraculous in technological achievement. As Khrushchev remarked in recalling his Metro years: "We thought of a subway as something almost supernatural."

The Moscow subway and the subway built beneath the marshy tidelands of old St. Petersburg (now Leningrad) after World War II are, in a way, "Potemkin Villages," showcases of Soviet life to the world. But they are not just that, after all. Millions of people use them every day. The service is exceptionally humane: fast, comfortable, relatively quiet, glamorous, and reliable. Almost without fail, bright yellow, blue, and green trains slide into the stations every ninety seconds, on schedule. The Metro staff of red-capped women are always on hand to give helpful directions to strangers and to see that things go smoothly with the crowds. Sometimes the crush is heavy, and the people are packed in like "fish in a bottle," as Moscovites say, but there is none of the degrading struggle for space normal in the rush hours of New York.

The air in the stations is changed four times an hour; and from one to six in the morning, when the system is closed, the stations are scrubbed clean. Once a month the tunnels are washed down with pressure hoses. To reduce vibration, rubber pads have been mounted between the rails and ties, and rubber gaskets are fitted between the axles and the wheels. The vaulted ceilings with their coffered recesses absorb noise. Moscow has a number of deep-level stations with about a mile of escalator shaft for every 4 miles of tunnel. Some of these escalators are over 200 feet long and travel at a remarkable speed, a meter a second.

The people are proud of their system, and justly so. And they treat it with respect. There is virtually no crime. It is a model of how a subway ought to be. Everyone should see it if he can. But no one should forget.

CHAPTER 10

The New Cimmerians

In one of his essays Thomas Babington Macaulay conjures up the pessimistic image of a New Zealander, in the distant future, sitting on the remains of London Bridge and "contemplating in solitude the ruins of what had once been the metropolis of the world." It is an interesting image, particularly from Macaulay, who found so much to hope for in the "improvements of the nineteenth century"; and it shows he was of two minds about the doctrine of progress, after all. As it happens, William Barclay Parsons found this image unusually provocative and in accord with his own ambivalent feelings about the profession of engineer. Both men intuitively foresaw progress ending in calamity.

Parsons worried a great deal about specialization. "A world of scientific specialists," he wrote, "would be the death of civilization." He felt an engineer should have broad training in the humanities, but saw this tradition vanishing in the increasing subdivision of once unified disciplines. The art of construction, he pointed out, is the "oldest art there is," and the architect and engineer were originally one. The word "engineer" meant "the man of character" or "the man of genius"; but the word "engine" was first applied (in Latin) to "an instrument of war." Over a period of time the architect, or "chief builder," became the maker of churches, bridges, houses, and so forth, as distinguished from the engineer, who became "the master of the works of war." At the time of the Industrial Revolution, Parsons wrote, "when canals, harbors, lighthouses, roads and other works, disassociated from any military connection, began to assume a more ambitious character, so as to approach in magnitude the works of national defense," the term "civil engineer" was adopted to distinguish certain builders and designers from their "military confreres." The profession was formally split, while it was also split off from the profession of the architect. Parsons saw the "application of steam as a source of power" as the main force behind this development. During World War I, however, military engineering underwent a revolutionary expansion. War machines and fortifications were no longer its peculiar province, but all the activities of civil engineering and more: "Railroads and roads, their construction and maintenance, bridges, locomotives, cars, engines of all types, buildings, tunnels, accurate mapping and range finding, water supply and its purification, photography, the laws and practical application of electricity, and the chemistry of gases and liquids"—all of these became part of the everyday work. Military engineering became "advanced civil engineering," and war repossessed aspects of architecture in a new one-sided unity under the sign of Mars. The latter part of Parsons' own career is a dramatic illustration of this development.

Parsons, who was prescient in many matters—in 1920 he predicted an energy crisis by the end of the century and recourse to solar power—foresaw that just as all the activities of peace had been appropriated for use in war, so would the purposes of war be worked into the works of peace. In the 1950's President Eisenhower caught a glimpse of this with a shock when he warned of the "military-industrial complex" in the domination of American life.

There are many ways to read the subway story, but surely one way is as a sometimes unconscious working out of this perilous course. Let this be a tentative theory for the whole, not for application in every case, for in their astonishing variety subways seem almost to have taken on a life of their own.

Where they are leading is perhaps not entirely obscure; the foreshadowings of myth may hold a clue. Is this strange? It has been said that the longbow, a landmark military invention, was first revealed in the Greek tale of Philoctetes before any archer shaped it from a tree. And of myths themselves, William Blake surmised: "The Authors are in eternity." We might well turn back to Macaulay, and before him to Homer and Vergil (remembering the humanities) for an image: of the ancient tunnel-bound Cimmerians, who first appeared as a historical people toward the end of the eighth century B.C., near the Sea of Azov, one hundred years after Homer imagined them and gave them a name.

On September 1, 1938, the London Underground was mobilized for war. The British government took control of the system under the Emergency Powers Defense Act and over the next several years its tunnels and stations served England and the Allied cause in a remarkable number of ways. Every night nearly two hundred thousand people found sanctuary in deep-level shelters and tubes; the Elgin Marbles and other treasures of the British Museum were safely sequestered near Piccadilly in the tunnels of the Aldwych branch; while from underground factories emerged the component parts of Halifax bombers, tanks, and even bridges for the war. Winston Churchill's War Cabinet had its command center in one station; another housed the headquarters of Anti-Aircraft Control. General Eisenhower plotted the D-Day landing on the beaches of Normandy from a London Underground shelter 110 feet down.

From August 25 to late December 1940, London was under relentless assault from the German air force; on September 7 the tube stations were used as shelters for the first time. Three-tiered bunks, furnished with chicken wire springs, were set against the walls; and the platforms were marked out into narrow corridors by white lines. Electrically operated 10-ton flood gates, controlled from a station at Leicester Square, could seal off the tunnels in seconds against gas attack and flooding, where the lines connected to the Thames. Hydroplanes scanned the river for mines or unexploded bombs. Most trains continued to run during the day; at night they used reduced lighting on open track. Hurricane lanterns were stockpiled in case electric power stations were hit.

The shelter commandeered by General Eisenhower was one of eight built especially for the war, all placed where they might form part of new Underground lines or extensions at a later date. Four were dug north of the Thames, four south. Each consisted of tunnels, 1,400 feet long and 16½ feet across, divided into two stories by a concrete slab, with alternate entrances through spiral staircases and shafts. Pneumatic lavatories emptied into the sewers above by compressed air.

Sleeping spaces in the stations were reserved; this customary use fostered miniature underground communities. Some enclaves, such as the Swiss Cottage Station on the Bakerloo line, published regular newsletters and bulletins. "Greetings," began the first issue of the *Swiss Cottager*, published in September 1940, "to all our nightly companions, snorers, chatterers, and all who inhabit the station from dusk to dawn."

In such profound sanctuaries, where neither the screech of sirens nor explosions could be heard, many passed the war in gratitude. But the missiles' hurtling terror would not always be denied. One bomb "broke through the pavement at the foot of the Duke of Wellington's statue outside the Royal Exchange, passed through the wide booking hall of the station below, shot along the course of the escalator shaft, and burst only when it reached the platform itself where hundreds had gathered for the night."

In Paris, where most stations were too shallow to provide refuge from aerial bombardment, the system was requisitioned by the German Occupation Forces for their own use. After the Allied invasion of Normandy, some forty were converted into repair shops and factories for small airplane parts; but the French Resistance fought back with sabotage, using the tunnels for swift assaults all over the city. At the same time, an independent telephone system was strung through the sewers, and command posts were established in the old gypsum quarries of the Place Denfert-Rochereau. On August 12, 1944, Métro personnel staged an insurrectional strike that shut the system down—thereby helping to pave the way for the liberation of Paris by the Allies twelve days later.

On the eve of World War II the New York els began to come down. Years before three hundred and thirty-seven of the old locomotives were sold for use abroad—some to Africa and India, to replace elephants hauling teak and logs, most to the mines of China, Chile, and Peru. When the Sixth Avenue El was dismantled in 1938, it yielded 17,000 tons of structural steel and 2,800 tons of rails. The Japanese government was able to purchase this material through an intermediary and converted it into weaponry against the Allies. The Second Avenue El was torn down as if in vengeance. Its latent potential as an arsenal was large: 29,400 tons of steel and 95 tons of copper—scrap enough, it was said, for 117,600 bombs, 58,800 16-inch shells, or three battleships. The New York *Tribune* reported on August 29, 1942:

> Second Avenue shopkeepers, duly grateful for the newly discovered sunlight and unimpeded view of the sky brought to them by the progressing demolition of the avenue's elevated structure, appeared concerned yesterday with more unselfish benefits to be derived.
>
> Eng Wing, Chinese laundry proprietor at 756 Second Avenue, expressed the feelings of the merchants and householders as well in three words. He said: "Good for Jap." He was gazing up past Forty-second Street, where huge iron girders were to be loaded onto trucks en route to be made into weapons of war. Mr. Wing said it was good to have the sunlight and fresh air.
>
> Samuel Price, proprietor of a grocery and delicatessan at 760 Second Avenue, a few doors from Mr. Wing's shop between Fortieth and Forty-first Streets, said he would rather see the El's iron and steel structure over Tokio than astraddle Second Avenue.

Such a weird destiny for the els—one pitted against the other in war—had been foreseen by F. Scott Fitzgerald in *The Beautiful and Damned.*

> The elevated, half a block away, sounded a rumble of drums—and should he lean from his window he would see the train, like an angry eagle, breasting the dark curve at the corner. He was reminded of a fantastic romance he had lately read in which cities had been bombed from aerial trains, and for a moment he fancied that Washington Square had declared war on Central Park and that this was a north-bound menace loaded with battle and sudden death.

The widespread bombing of cities—but above all the use of the atomic bomb—changed the world. This has been said often; one should never tire of saying it; it was a watershed. Extinction had but one precedent—the deluge—and one analogy—the Apocalypse: both were miraculous catastrophes as unimaginably placed in the power of man as the creation of the world itself or the resurrection of the flesh. One morning the world awoke to discover destiny turned upside down. Reality acquired an unreal dimension, absolute in a mythological way, materially abstract and yet so palpably real that history itself could already point to Hiroshima and Nagasaki, to a prefiguration of the end of time, an actual heap of ashes.

If nuclear war was deemed unthinkable, global strategists at least urged that everybody think about it, which meant not to come to grips with reality's unthinkable side, but to cut off its mystical head. Sufficient unto the day is the evil thereof, in this as in no other case.

The problem of urban congestion in such a context may not seem to count for very much. In fact, its role is large. The old reasons for going underground remained, and a new and overriding one appeared: the apparent necessity for underground shelters—subways, basements, vaults—for security and continuance of life. In every subway built since World War II, this has been a consideration, along with rapid transit and refuge from vehicular exhaust. It was obvious that in any future war cities would be on the front lines, if there were any lines at all. Such is "realism" in our technocratic age, in which "myth" is commonly used as a pejorative synonym for fiction. As Sir Kenneth Clark once summed it up, nuclear power watches over us like an "inverted archangel."

In recent years, subways have undergone a great boom. In Germany (the most conspicuous example) there has, since the late 1960's, been a laying down of track not seen in any one country since the English Railway Mania of the Industrial Revolution. With the government financing up to 50 percent of the cost of coordinated local urban transport systems, highways and other surface road projects have been shouldered aside.

The keystone of the new development plan is a regional strat-

SUBWAYS WORLDWIDE

A PICTURE PORTFOLIO

Rhythmic archwork on a grand scale in a Moscow station.
More marble went into the stations of the first line than into all
the palaces of the Czar in the fifty years before the Revolution.

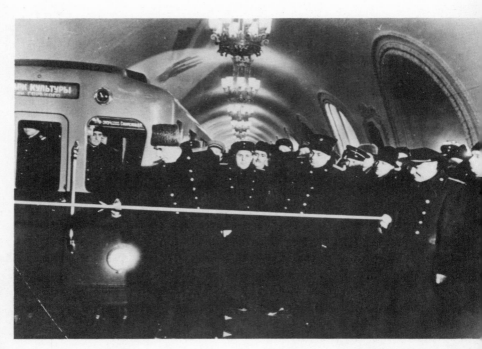

Above, the official opening of the Moscow Metro, with Lazar M. Kaganovich, Minister of Transport, solemnly snipping the ribbon at Krasnoya Presnya Station. NKVD agents peer suspiciously at the camera through the car windows. Below, a mosaic panel in the Kiev-Belt Station vestibule commemorates the opening in 1932 of the gigantic Dnieper hydroelectric power plant. Right, one of Moscow's famous deep-level high-speed escalators.

Left, Walker-Schreiberplatz Station at rush hour, and Munich's new Marienplatz Station. Right, a magazine cover inspired by the fact that Mexico City recovered many buried archaeological treasures during the excavation of its Métro. Below, a modern Mexican station reminiscent of Aztec architecture. Mexico City has perhaps the most beautiful subway in the world.

MARCH 9 1968/VOLUME 93/No. 10 P. 225-248

SCIENCE NEWS

Archaeology
in the
Subway

A ceiling fresco of swirling forms, in Station République in Paris.

POWER

THE
NERVE CENTRE
OF LONDON'S

UNDERGROUND

Left, one of many decorative posters issued by London Transport—this one from 1930. The posters, with their revolutionary use of sans-serif type designs, changed the whole field of modern typography. Above, one of the 350-foot-long black-and-white murals of the new Charing Cross Station on the Northern Line which depict the building of the old Eleanor Cross, in Trafalgar Square, nearly 700 years ago.

Some Stockholm stations, blasted out of granite, were adorned by paintings and carvings that emphasize their cave-like character.

Intersecting vaults in the ceiling of Washington, D.C.'s Metro Center Station. The station has often been compared to a cathedral.

Above, George Tooker's haunting portrayal of lost souls in a New York City subway station. The central figure, a woman, looks out with terrified eyes, her face set like a tragic mask.

Left, a futuristic maze of corridors in a BART (Bay Area Rapid Transit) station in San Francisco. BART was the first fully automated and computerized subway system in the world.

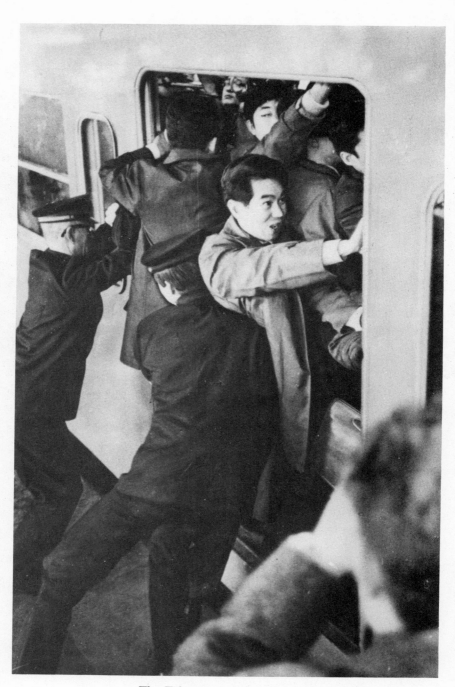

The Tokyo morning rush hour, called "tsukin jigoku,"
or "passengers' hell." Here, specially-hired "shiroshi-
san," or pushers, try to pack in two more office workers.

egy for the important Ruhr Valley, Germany's industrial heartland and Europe's most populous area. Commuter trains, deep-
level subways, and independent underground streetcar lines are
now consolidated into a single network administered by a central authority. City after city has set jackhammers to its pave-
ments in a project reminiscent of the reconstruction boom of the
postwar Marshall Plan. Bielefeld, Bochum, Bonn, Bremen, Co-
logne, Dortmund, Duisberg, Düsseldorf, Essen, Frankfurt, Han-
over, Munich, Nuremberg, Recklinghausen, and Stuttgart all
now have subway systems either completed or in progress, not
to mention the older systems of Hamburg and Berlin.

Frankfurt, whose medieval center was ravaged by wartime
bombing, has become a modern city with a far-reaching "U-
Bahn." Its tunnels, spacious enough to accommodate conventional trains, make it the first city in recent times to consider the
possibility of their eventual use by commuter lines. Frankfurt
also has an "S-Bahn," or suburban railway, with independent
tunnels that link up with the city's main overland railway
termini. The systems come together at the three-level
Hauptewache Station: the U-Bahn, deepest down, the S-Bahn
above, and just under the street, a large concourse with restaurants and shops.

The Munich arrangement is even more complex, with a U-
Bahn, a Metropolitan Railway or S-Bahn, trains, and buses all
traveling in tandem, with coordinated schedules. Much of the
city's historic center has been reclaimed. Once clogged thoroughfares have metamorphosed into pedestrian malls, arcades
and covered ways adorned with gardens, fountains, kiosks,
shops, restaurants, theaters, cafes, museums, and churches. The
delicate tunneling techniques that skirted historic monuments
such as the Rathaus (City Hall) and the famed twin-towered
Frauenkirche were perfected in Ruhr Valley coal mines. Four
unexploded bombs were unearthed during excavation, and
thereafter mine detectors became standard equipment at the
worksites along with cranes and drills. One old air-raid shelter
also turned up, for which Hitler had thrown out the first shovelful of dirt in 1938. Wide spaces have been left between pairs
of U-Bahn tracks, for use as roads in fleeing advancing armies.

Berlin has the oldest subway system in Germany, begun shortly after the Paris Métro. At the time, the city had one through route, the Stadtbahn, which opened in February 1882 primarily as a military road for the deployment of troops. The *Elektrische Hoch und Untergrund Bahn* opened in March 1902 and ran for 8½ miles east-west from Potsdamer Plaza to the Zoological Gardens. Its construction included a unique variant called "house tunnels"—a strange combination of underground and elevated ways whereby trains actually passed *through* rows of houses at the middle level, leaving top floors intact. The Untergrund Bahn was first extended westward to Knie; then the Potsdamer Line was opened by way of Friedrichstrasse as far as the Spittelmarkt. Additional lines were inaugurated in 1910 and 1913.

By 1939, Berlin had some 40 miles of subway, not counting elevated or open-cut portions. Most of the system centered around the mile-long Unter den Linden and the Friedrichstrasse—an area that contains many of the city's magnificent old houses and public buildings. The oldest stations recall London's Earl's Court or King's Cross stations, though on a smaller scale, with iron-and-glass roofs that vault above the tracks.

Toward the end of World War II, the German capital took on the character of a fortress, and many of the deepest U-Bahn stations were converted into hospitals. When the city was eventually partitioned, the U-Bahn was divided too. Today, trains run back and forth "in exchange": at the border, East Germans hold up a westbound train until its eastbound counterpart comes rumbling through.

Not every community, of course, has welcomed the subway with open arms. In Amsterdam, when the government announced plans in 1975 to clear the Nieumarket, an old working-class district in the center of town, for subway construction, squatters moved into the condemned houses and police armed with tear gas, water cannons, and bulldozers had to push through barricades and fend off rock-throwing crowds to drive them out. When the government at length backed off, workers and bohemians "in the stuffy, dark-paneled bars in Jordaan, the soul of old Amsterdam," touched glasses and cheered.

In other cities, subway hopes have gone repeatedly unsatisfied. Italians, for example, have some good jokes about their subways. Mussolini started a line for Rome in 1938, in preparation for the 1942 World's Fair; the fair never took place and the project languished; then in 1955 a tunnel was completed along the original route—from the main railroad station to the undeveloped fair site 7 miles away. When it opened, everyone said it went "from nowhere to nowhere," since it ended in an open field.

The second line was nothing more than a railway spur that ended in a suburban cemetery. A few years later, it was extended to Ostia, arousing hopes that a network might be ready in time for the 1960 Olympic Games. The games came and went, along with the better part of a decade, causing some to jest that a man would walk on the moon before a real subway was built. That came true in 1969.

A subway was considered in Milan as early as 1864 when an Italian army engineer drew up plans based on what he had seen in London. Actual digging, however, did not start for almost a century. Since 1957 the progress has been minute. According to the Milanese, "building the Metropolitana takes as long as building the Duomo"—the city's many-spired Gothic cathedral begun in 1385 and not yet complete.

Overall, the reasons for slow going have been good ones in both Rome and Milan. Aside from the usual impediments—such as just-under-the-surface cables, pipes, and wires twisted together like snakes on the Gorgon head, and a subsoil copiously veined with rivers and voids—there has been a prodigious treasure trove of archaelogical finds.

In Milan, for example, the remnants of an early Christian baptistery turned up beneath the Piazza Duomo. In Rome, in an area that was once a pagan necropolis and is now a workers' suburb, a huge stone sarcophagus was found dating from the first century A.D., along with perfectly preserved ancient Roman roadwork smoothly paved with flagstones and flanked by terra-cotta drains. Near the Trevi Fountain some second century B.C. dwellings and shops were unearthed, and at ancient Ostia, near Rome's Intercontinental Airport, richly colored frescoes in the

Pompeiian style were found, together with an ancient apartment complex from the Republican Age that may have included a shopping center. One line failed three times to find an acceptable site for a station under the Piazza Della Repubblica. The workers descended about 15 feet and struck the walls of the Diocletian baths, which in 298 A.D. were the largest in Rome. Other probings came up against the Diocletian Villas, which the baths once luxuriantly served. Erotic murals that had enlivened an ancient house of prostitution were disclosed near the Colosseum, along with Latin graffiti deemed by reporters "unprintably obscene." Between the Via Cavour and San Pietro in Vincolo, secret galleries and underground chapels—among the earliest Christian sanctuaries—regularly interrupted the route.

As befits a subway cut through such hallowed ground, many of the stations bear evocative names: the Colosseum and Capitoline Hill, for example; the Circus Maximus, the Via Veneto, and the Spanish Steps. More recent tunneling has been directed below the "archaelogical table," and this is probably all to the good. Power machinery is a peril to the past, and not everyone operating the levers is tempered by a sense of history. The New York *Times* quoted a workman from Naples as saying, "with a grin": "If I see any old stones, I cut right through them with a jack-hammer. Isn't the Colosseum enough of a ruin for Rome?" One is reminded of the vignette of transience in Federico Fellini's film *Roma* that portrays subway workers uncovering priceless frescoes which disintegrate before their very eyes.

Peking undertook its subway "in accordance with Mao's policy of self-reliance." "There may be twists and turns," he said, "but we will overcome and correct them." The first line (5 miles long and completed in October 1969) followed the site of one of the old city walls, under Chang-an Boulevard, from an industrial suburb on the western outskirts to Peking's main railway terminus.

Each station is finished in marble of a different color—cream, red, green, black, and pink—all quarried in Yunan province some 2,000 miles away. Lacquered posters of a political rather than commercial kind are plastered along the walls, though a few salute historic landmarks such as the Gate of Heavenly

Peace in Peking. There are also ceramic wastebaskets and spittoons. Originally all the lighting was red, to signify that the East is red. But the ruddy glimmer it cast was dark, which sent passengers groping. At length it was agreed that clear white light was best. The stations are immaculate and about as quiet as the London Underground.

To the south, Hong Kong opened its "lump of underground iron" (as the people call it) on February 12, 1980. "Robed oriental clerics lighted joss sticks and chanted incantations to drive away evil spirits," while newspaper ads announced encouragingly: "Hong Kong's underground iron is built for you."

In the midst of this refurbishment and growth, some systems, particularly in the United States, have declined. The Chicago subway, begun during World War II, soon fell into disrepair. In Philadelphia, policemen in pairs now patrol the stations with dogs. But New York is the most repellent example.

In the mid-1950's Colonel Sidney H. Bingham, head of New York's Transit Authority, recommended that the subway be turned into a "people conveyor belt." "Conveyor belts," he pointed out in a publicity pamphlet, "have provided highly efficient and reliable mass transportation for bulk materials over a long period of years." The "humanity" of this proposal is just what New Yorkers have come to expect from custodians of their subway system. In 1966 the Mayor's Task Force on Urban Design called the subway "the most squalid public environment in the United States: dank, dingily lit, fetid, and with screeching clatter." There is no doubt as to how the "bulk" of the people feel about it. In November 1958 the head of the Transit Authority was actually afraid to identify himself to other passengers on a stalled train.

Daily revelations of new perils and alarms humble any attempt to describe what the system is like today. The New York *Post* recently called it a "torture pit." The *Daily News* has asserted that a regular passenger is subject to lung cancer and emphysema from breathing the air. Rats dart about the tracks, stuffing themselves on a cornucopia of rotting trash (70 tons a day); the corridors are used openly as urinals; the trains arrive, almost always late, "with a black blast of iron"—in William Burroughs' phrase—forcing a column of unspeakable air ahead. As they grind to a halt, they spray the atmosphere with metallic dust particulates and bits of asbestos deposited on the rails by an archaic braking system. Poor ventilation traps and concentrates exhaust fumes from automobile traffic overhead, while the noise level approaches the threshold of pain, as certified by the Public Health Department. In the station at 86th Street and Central Park West the decibel level exceeds that of the SST. Not surprisingly, the effect of all this on passengers has provoked much clinical curiosity. In a recent experiment that recreated typical conditions, "once every morning and once every afternoon, about a dozen rats were put in plastic cages about the size of a breadbox. The cages were mounted on a mechanical shaker, which jerked them one hundred and fifty times a minute from side to side. At the same time the rats heard tape-recorded subway noises blaring away at from sixty-eight to one hundred and twelve decibels." All the rats became sick; some died.

But passengers also have to contend with FEAR (writ large): of assault, of violation, of being pushed onto the tracks. Two facts go a long way toward revealing how things stand: the New York subway has fewer riders today than it did in 1918; and the Transit Authority police force is one of the largest para-military units of any kind in the nation.

In such an environment graffiti is truly the handwriting on the wall, the last signature of contempt for a system that shows such contempt for its patrons. Yet as the sculptor Claes Oldenburg has memorably remarked, these scrawlings somehow testify to an unconquerable gaiety: "You're standing there in the station, everything is grey and gloomy and all of a sudden one of those graffiti trains slides in and brightens the place like a big bouquet from Latin America."

A painting by George Tooker in the Whitney Museum depicts lost souls in a New York subway station: within a recessive blank passageway of alternative routes and culs-de-sac, figures make desperate or surreptitious phone calls from exposed booths. The central figure is a woman, her eyes bright with fright or welling tears, her face a mask, like a player in a Greek drama.

New York's deteriorating system is certainly an aberration; worldwide, the momentum has been the other way. Mexico City, for example, opened a subway in September 1969 that is perhaps the most dignified and beautiful in the world. Tens of thousands of archaeological artifacts covering six centuries of history, from delicately worked jewelry in ceramic, leather, and clay to a 22-ton Aztec calendar stone, were uncovered in its building, and many of these have been incorporated into the station designs. The subway's long concourses and vaulted stations form a continuous historical and cultural display, a contemporary monument that at once edifies and soothes as it brings into harmonious relation the bustling functions of a late twentieth-century metropolis and ancestral homage, so vital to the psychological well-being of a people. In a nation beset by social unrest, it is remarkable that the system is untouched by crime. Only collective pride can account for this. The director is a sort of curator, whose staff prominently includes anthropologists, archaeologists, and art historians. During construction these men were posted block by block to make sure that everything possible was preserved.

Each stop marks a historic event or celebrates some aspect of Mexican life. Zocalo Station occupies the site of Montezuma's Palace, later the headquarters of the conquistadores of New Spain. Insurgentes Station, named after the rebels who rallied to Padre Migues Hidalgo in 1810 in the first attempt to free Mexico from Spanish rule, is laid out like a pre-Columbian temple in the form of a caracol or snail. A sculptured sandstone panel recounts the revolt, and motifs of angels, in Spanish-Colonial style, are brightly mirrored in plinths of polished marble. There is no apparent effort, as in Moscow, to edit or rewrite history; Mexicans honor their mingled past. Yet the Metro (so called because French engineers acted as advisors) does not have an anachronistic cast. Some stations are embellished by contemporary murals, and all the cars are bright orange with red and blue seats. Platforms and walls are bathed in diverse combinations of pale greens and blues, muted reds and browns, yellows, and creams, while the sun's rays stream down through ceilings of glass or translucent alabaster domes. Each station also has an avant-garde logo rendered in simple silhouette. Chopoltepec is represented by a grasshopper (the word means "grasshopper hill" in Aztec); Sevilla, by the remnant of a colonial aqueduct that once passed nearby; Insurgentes, by a freedom bell; Zaragoza, by a soldier on horseback in honor of Ignacio Zaragoza, the revolutionary hero; Observatorio, by a planetarium dome; and Cuartenoc, named for Montezuma's son, the last Aztec emperor, is symbolized by the head of an eagle, Cuartenoc's image in Mexican folklore.

From an engineering point of view, the subway itself is almost a technological miracle. Seven thousand three hundred and fifty feet above sea level, the city lies in the basin of an old volcanic lake, in subsoil that is 80 percent water. Earthquakes shake it; each year it sinks about an inch. To keep the excavation dry, polarized electromagnets were used to draw the water to one side, while flexible tunnels of iron and concrete were devised to "float" in the mud. To archaelogists hereafter, the subway, though now underground, may well prove the nearest remains.

In Stockholm, where by law all public buildings, including subways, must exhibit some decoration, a more than legalistic beauty has sometimes been realized. Stations blasted out of two-billion-year-old granite have occasionally been left unfinished, their rugged formations, rough ledges, and wrinkled aspect the most dramatic innovation yet in subway design. Artists have reveled in the freedom of such a setting. Some have created cult-like sites; others have done their best "to neutralize the cave atmosphere by murals of pastoral scenes." Still others have carved sculptures into the walls. In one station in an immigrant district, children were allowed to do the painting in a natural diversity of styles; in another, a prize-winning artist rendered portraits of her heroes—Simone de Beauvoir, Sartre, Sappho, Rachel Carson—in a mural dedicated to Peace.

The transformation of subway stations into art galleries is in keeping with recent efforts to modify the underground with new comforts and distracting decor. Perhaps this may be traced in a general way to 1951, when the Paris Métro first introduced quiet pneumatic tires. In any case, Paris has pointed the way. In the mid-1960's the Louvre Station began exhibiting in recessed niches and glass cases reproductions from the museum's collection: the Venus de Milo, Colombe's Virgin and Child, medieval gargoyles, and the Babylonian Legal Code of Hammurabi carved in diorite. Shortly thereafter, the F.D.R. Station displayed works by Van Gogh and Modigliani in colored glass, and the circular entrance hall at Saint Lazare was decked out in swirling Art Nouveau. The Varennes Station, beneath the Rodin Museum, now contains photo reproductions and plaster casts of the master's sculptures, and the Gobelins Station has a tapestry exhibit, in honor of the seventeenth-century tapestry works once located nearby. Elsewhere, abstract painters and French poets have been celebrated with biographies and huge mounted blow-ups of their work. The redecorated Nation stop sports orange-and-yellow Pop Art designs.

Even the London Underground shows evidence of aesthetic revival after a forty-year lapse. In 1895 William Barclay Parsons observed after a visit to the Underground: "No attempt was made to give the stations a pleasing appearance, in fact, any such attempt would have been rendered ineffective by the engine smoke and hideous advertising signs." Then in 1916, Edward Johnston was commissioned to draw a new and unique alphabet for London Transport's exclusive use; his sans serif design—which spurned the "kitsch historical Gothic of the Edwardians"—was the first pure sans serif since Roman times. It revolutionized the whole field of modern typography. Johnston's lettering became the hallmark of an outstanding series of publicity posters issued between 1916 and 1939, which aimed at "evocative enticement," making use of iconography that was "selective and deeply patriotic: the beefeater and the guardsman, the cockney and the bargee, the lover and the child, set within an idealized view of past and present in town and country." Some incorporated Cubist, Vorticist, and other modern abstract idioms, and dealt imaginatively with sobering themes—like the flight of time, portrayed by a black-cloaked, airborne figure carrying a scythe.

In the last few years Underground art has reappeared. At the new Charing Cross tube stop, long murals in black and white—showing carpenters, thatchers, scaffolders, hodmen, and other artisans at their crafts—honor the building of the old Eleanor Cross seven hundred years ago in Trafalgar Square. Erected by

Edward I between 1291 and 1294, the cross marked one of the Twelve Stations past which the body of his wife, Eleanor of Castile, was carried on its long journey from Lincoln to Westminster Abbey. At the new Baker Street Station, sepia designs recreate scenes from seven of Sir Arthur Conan Doyle's tales of Sherlock Holmes.

Some new subways celebrate the space age by flaunting its technology. The most conspicuous example is the San Francisco Bay Area Rapid Transit network, or BART. Aboard each train is an attendant outfitted in an astronaut-like uniform of blue slacks and blue tunic with diagonal stripes across one shoulder; his purpose is to make the station announcements. Station agents wear blue blazers; service line supervisors wear double-breasted navy suits.

The cars are air conditioned, carpeted in wool across wide aisles, with fully upholstered cantilevered seats and large gray-tinted picture windows. They are sleek, silver, 70 feet long, and fabricated like aircraft out of lightweight stressed aluminum with integrally structured bodies and frames welded together in a rigid bond. Like rockets or missiles, they are remote-controlled from a "situation room" furnished with computers and consoles that monitor display boards flickering with colored lights. Central computers control pace and scheduling; wayside electronic gear control stopping, starting, and speed. Powerful electric motors accelerate the trains up to 80 m.p.h. in less than thirty seconds, and stop them just as fast.

The stations (designed by sixteen different architects) are all executed in snappy red-and-blue brick and cream-colored stone with bright fluorescent lights. They "glow in a dazzling, multicolored array of huge graphics, enamel murals, mosaic columns, and fiberglass reliefs" while the "soaring structural forms, steel and concrete manifest an infinite variety of textures." Instead of tokens, magnetically coded cards about credit-card size provide admission.

Such is BART, the largest locally financed public works project in American history. It includes the world's longest, deepest underwater tunnel, and is the world's first fully computerized and automated rapid transit system.

It also doesn't work, or not very well anyway.

It began on June 19, 1964, near Walnut Creek 9 miles west of the Berkeley Hills when President Lyndon Johnson touched off a charge of dynamite in an abandoned onion field, inaugurating the Diablo Test Track.

BART is the latest in a long line of unusually diverse transit facilities that have served the San Francisco Bay Area over the years, including commuter bus, conventional bus, trolley, trolley coach, commuter rail, and the cable car. These operate over a wide terrain, since the bay and its tributaries break up and disperse the residential and industrial districts across 571 square miles, from the hilly peninsula on which San Francisco rests to Oakland 7 miles across the bay.

Shortly after World War II, regional thinking about civil defense and military logistics had led to a recommendation on the part of a joint Army-Navy board for an underwater transit tube across the bay. Eventually, it was decided to integrate the tube into an overall rapid transit subway-elevated system laid out in the form of an "X," with Oakland at the fulcrum. The legs of the "X" would run southwest to Daly City through San Francisco, northwest to Richmond, northeast to Concord, and southeast to Fremont with thirty-three stations along the way.

Of the system's 71 miles, 23 are underground, including the 3.7-mile tube beneath the bay. Some of the most difficult tunneling took place under San Francisco's crowded Market Street, 75 feet down in saturated soil. The water table was lowered by sinking wells; even so, compressed air was required to aid boring by shields and "mechanical moles." Three of the stations lie practically submerged, their massive structures contending against hydrostatic pressure that would otherwise cause them to float. Immovability was perhaps not the wisest engineering objective in an area that is deeply seamed with earthquake faults, "where seismic movement through the ages has tilted, fractured, and in some places ground the rock to fine powder." When twin-bore tunnels were cut through the Berkeley Hills, they were braced with horseshoe-shaped ribs of steel and lined with 18-inch-thick concrete. Elsewhere solid steel rings anchored 12 miles of tunnel in sand, mud, and silt. The underwater tube was constructed by laying prefabricated sections (aligned with laser beams) in a gigantic trench dredged in the bottom of the bay.

There were mistakes. Signal cables along 8 miles of track were sheathed in plastic rather than metal or concrete. Bay area gophers, who apparently had "demonstrated a taste for wiring in the past," ate right through them. "Any gardener around here," remarked one critic in disgust, "knows gophers eat plastic."

Once launched, BART behaved like a neurotic machine. Doors of speeding cars flew open; trains stopped inexplicably between stations, speeded up instead of slowing down, slowed down instead of speeding up, glided past stations where passengers were waiting to board, and stopped at stations without opening their doors. On one occasion, a train pulled into Fremont Street, "barrelled on, lurched severely as it crossed a track switch, overshot the station, plowed through a thirty-foot long sand barrier at the end of the track, smashed through a chainlink fence, and ended up at a forty-five degree angle with its nose resting in a parking lot." A tiny speed control crystal in the train's circuitry had failed.

The system was also supposed to provide "automatic and continuous detection of the presence of trains." However, "ghost trains" soon began to show up on the control boards, while trains that were actually on the tracks disappeared. In the end, nineteenth-century practice was revived, with manually operated red and green signals at each station. Dispatchers refused to wave a train on before a telephone call from the station ahead confirmed that the track was clear.

The computerized Washington Metro has shown more promise. When Washington, D.C., embarked on its subway in December 1969, its conscious purpose was to create a system as different as possible from New York's. "To Washingtonians," wrote one journalist at the time, "the New York subway means crowds and hassles, straphanging, vandalism, creeps and criminals lurking in dark corners. It means 'Jojo 138' spray-painted across the windows of cars so that riders can't see out. It means gloomy, noisy stinking stations too cold in winter, too hot in summer." To discourage crime, every Metro nook and cranny is monitored by closed-circuit TV. Each car has an emergency call box for passenger use, and plainclothes police ride every train. The concave station walls (all station platforms are islands) curve beyond the reach of desecratory hands. Vending machines and advertising, which foster loitering, are banned.

In other respects, the Metro manifests a higher aim. The stations command a feeling of grandeur and architectural power that would be enviable in any public monument. Above the open, columnless platforms, coffered ceilings soar to a magnificent height. At the Metro Center Station, where two lines cross, intersecting vaults suggest the transepts of a cathedral. After the performance of a Handel oratorio at the station's debut, the director of the Washington Choral Society compared its acoustics to those of a fine concert hall.

The system is comfortable and quiet, with continuous welded rails—no clickety-clack over joints—and a roadbed laid over neoprene synthetic rubber pads. Inside the cars sound is muffled by rubber mountings and air-cushioned springs; "pinpoint" air conditioning adjusts automatically to the number of passengers.

The first line opened in March 1976 with "cross-bearing priests from the Episcopal Church of the Epiphany marching down a station escalator, followed by a blue-robed choir from the New York Avenue Presbyterian Church." The ceremony was sponsored by the Downtown Cluster of Churches, an ecumenical organization which described itself as "deeply interested in transportation." One minister said: "Nothing can separate us from the love of God, not fifty feet of soil or these vaults."

Even so, the vaults had in fact come perilously close to severing them all from one object of more immediate celestial ambition. As the gigantic laser-guided mechanical moles chewed through Washington soil, they just missed cutting through wires that linked space technicians on earth with astronauts exploring the moon. Other wiring turned up which no one wished to acknowledge, along with a strip of the "hot line" connecting the White House with the Kremlin. Less sensational perhaps, but no less worthy of note, the workers met up with Old Tiber Creek, a long-forgotten stream turned sewer that in colonial days refreshed the city below Capitol Hill.

As the Washington Metro made headway, the embarrassing

lessons of BART proved useful in determining the engineering for a comparably automated system in Atlanta, Georgia, called MARTA, which from the start required a certain degree of manual operation of the trains. In MARTA's subway construction, cut-and-cover was the rule, with the notable exception of deep-level Peachtree Center Station, mined from below through a geologic ridge of granite that forms part of the watershed divide between the Atlantic Ocean and the Gulf of Mexico. Peachtree Street is, of course, Atlanta's most famous thoroughfare, known to millions from *Gone With the Wind*. More exciting to the engineers, its underlying strata proved able to support three huge intersecting caverns without help from the customary lining of reinforced concrete. Stockholm's exposed-rock stations furnished the precedent.

Curiously enough, new geologic theories postulate that before the advent of continental separation and drift (when the land mass of the earth was one), the two rock zones were actually linked: at opposite ends of a single mountain range extending from Stockholm through Norway, Scotland, Iceland, Newfoundland and Labrador, all the way down to Atlanta by way of the Appalachian chain.

Perhaps Alfred Ely Beach was just ahead of his time. In 1967, Lawrence K. Edwards, a former Lockheed engineer and designer of the Polaris missile, suggested a "gravity vacuum" train for BART. In his conception, the underground line, in the form of a pneumatic tube, would follow an undulating course, with stations placed on summits. In between the stations would be vacuum tunnels. The train would be drawn into the tunnel by atmospheric pressure, accelerate by gravity down an incline, then be slowed by gravity on the rise as it approached the station ahead. Normal air pressure in the station, along with small mechanical brakes, would bring it to a halt. In other words, natural forces would do the work of engine and fuel. The hypothetical ride is smooth, noiseless, energy efficient, and fast. Such a subway is reputedly now under construction in the Soviet Union.

Far more ambitious is a scheme reported in the New York *Times* in February 1978:

Dr. Robert M. Salter, senior scientist of the Rand Corporation in Santa Monica, Calif., described a coast-to-coast subway transportation system on which his company has done a detailed study.

He said that the trains would be supported electro-magnetically to reduce friction and would travel in underground tubes with air pressure reduced to the equivalent of about 170,000 feet of altitude. Speeds of several thousand miles an hour could be attained, allowing a coast-to-coast trip in about 54 minutes, even including a brief stop at a midway point. The study by Rand is of an initial network of about 10,000 miles of subway linking such cities as Los Angeles, Dallas and New York.

The enterprise would be too big and expensive for any organization to attempt at one time, but might be achieved over several decades, with the underground tubes built first for the military for communications and transportation use and portions later consigned to private organizations for a civilian subway, Dr. Salter said.

Such a vast, far-reaching development as a continental underground reflects a clear and present trend. Its initial impetus can perhaps be traced to the French-designed Métro in Montreal, which was rushed to completion for Expo '67, the most celebrated of recent World's Fairs. The Métro's fast, quiet, pneumatic-tired trains and bright, spotless, and creatively designed stations startled visitors from all over the world and did much to accelerate the international subway boom and assure the preeminence of the French in the process. But its role as a catalyst was parmount in another respect, which now looms large:

Montrealers say they can shop or dine or be entertained in their subterranean metropolis for a week or month without visiting the same place twice. Or setting foot outside.

Under Place Ville Marie (a skyscraper complex dominated by a 42-story cross shaped office building, built in 1962), there are 73 business establishments, including a restaurant, theatres and shops ranging from a classic bookstore to toy emporiums and jewelry boutiques . . .

Without going outside, Montrealers can walk below ground along nearly five miles of intersecting promenades, corridors, concourses and plazas.

This complex gave fresh currency to an old idea, stamped in a new and beguiling way: the underground city. Its evolution can be seen in the new RER, or Reseau Express Regional, in Paris, a commuter underground that interconnects with the Métro as it cuts through the city to the suburbs. Many of the stations function as transfer junctions and resemble junction towns. Chatelet-les-Halles, underneath the former central marketplace of Paris, is a huge five-level complex with moving sidewalks and shopping arcades; at the Auber Station, there are seven levels with 3 miles of corridors and seventy-three escalators. "As above, so below," wrote one correspondent. At La Defence, "you can get a herring sandwich, shop for an oriental rug, stroke the trunk of an elephant, get a quick urine analysis, make a bank deposit, dine in a restaurant, get your hair done, buy a dress, a pet or a motorcycle, get your blood tested, and have a beer." Such an environment is not just a commercial district recapitulated below, but the semblance of an entire city with all its functions concentrated in one place.

The most dramatic examples are in Japan. In Tokyo, the half-mile-long Ginza Sugo Eki (Ginza Consolidated Station) has forty-eight black marble entrances and extends three stories beneath what is perhaps the largest shopping district in the world—from the Imperial Moat to the Kabuki Theatre. Six different underground lines converge under its roof and some platforms are larger than two football fields. When it opened on August 26, 1964, it took a white-robed, white-hatted Shinto priest the better part of a day to traverse its myriad corridors of chrome and imitation marble while shaking *sakaki,* the sacred branch, to chase away evil spirits.

In 1972 Ginza was linked by a U-shaped passage to an even larger station at Otemachi, under the busines district. Thus, a traveler could tour an area comparable in size to midtown Manhattan, without once venturing out of doors. In hot or inclement weather he can go from one department store or supermarket to another in the corridors, many of which are shopping centers in themselves. Shinjuku, an underground station in western Tokyo that handles over two million people a day,

> . . . is so dense and so complicated, both in terms of people and transportation lines, [that] the result is a "megastructure" which is practically an underground city in itself. Its three-dimensional arrangement of mechanical systems, train tunnels and pedestrian passageways is interlocked with its comercial facilities which fill every available space, no matter how small. No separation is made between the transportation function and those of sales or recreation . . .
>
> In addition to public facilities like lockers, restrooms and endless rows of telephones, there are hotels, travel agents, game shops, bars, restaurants, department stores, specialty shops, bakers, shoe stores and supermarkets. In Shinjuku over 3,000 different underground shops compete with one another for the attention of the passers-by . . . The underground arcades create hundreds of tiny, artificial environments designed to lure the people from their path between trains and stores.

The manager of one subterranean marketplace at Shibuya (a mixed residential and commercial neighborhood) said his complex "had come into being when surface parking problems drove cars underground." A jewelry store owner in another Tokyo complex observed: "Living underground like this, people lose the idea of time and season. And sometimes when you go out, you may be surprised to find it's raining."

As in Tokyo, so in Osaka, which has still larger *"chikagi"* or underground streets. Beneath the main railroad station there are one hundred eighty stores averaging 700,000 visitors a day. "It is much easier," remarked one merchant, "for commuters and visitors to go through the underground passages than to walk on surface roads."

Even so, the crush of humanity below can be phenomenal. During the evening rush hours (known popularly as *"tsukin jigoku,"* or "passengers' hell") specially hired husky young *"oshiya,"* or "pushers," pack passengers into cars up to three

times their capacity. "In a single day," according to one correspondent, "more than 100 windows were broken in Tokyo's
subway trains—not by hooligans, but by passengers whose
arms, legs, and heads got violently banged against them.
Eighty-five passengers were hospitalized or given emergency
treatment for sprains or cuts, and it was a comon sight to see
half a dozen people stretched out on the station master's
floor, recovering from fainting spells." Transport executives
didn't think this was all bad. On the contrary, they claimed:
"The physical exercise involved in a passenger's resistance to
the pushing of other passengers, and the physical effort of
hanging on to a strap in order to remain upright, stimulates
the cerebrum, dispels morning drowsiness . . and is a good
pre-work warm-up." One opportunistic firm marketed a
"rush-hour coat" with a "slippery surface for slithering
through crowds."

The trend toward underground cities has been accelerated
in Japan by their oblique conformity to a native tradition.
"Travel in Japan has always been extremely difficult," wrote a
student of Japanese history a few years ago:

> In addition to geographic barriers, there were government
> restrictions for reasons of political control. There were a
> number of circuits along which travel was permitted, and these
> were punctuated at prescribed intervals by post towns, which
> functioned as rest and entertainment centers and also as market
> towns for the travellers . . .
>
> As public transportation developed and traveling became a
> daily necessity instead of a special opportunity, the traditional
> relationship between travel, market and entertainment func-
> tions was maintained, so that the major transfer points in the
> transit system became the modern counterparts of the old post
> towns.

Such developments are part of a pattern. In the United
States, for example, since the early 1950's, the mining of limestone beneath Kansas City has created some 24 million square
feet of underground space. The huge caverns, 50 to 300 feet

down, are being developed with the same sort of industrial variety usually associated with a vast new tract of land. Honeycombed with warehouses, light industries, and offices, furnished with railroad spurs, track docks, and parking areas, hundreds of people now regularly go to work in their depths.

Much of the research for underground construction is being done in Minnesota. A new maximum-security prison for four hundred inmates will be carved into the side of a hill east of the Twin Cities. At the University of Minnesota, Williamson Hall, a two-story underground building, houses a bookstore, offices, admissions, and records.

In Lake Worth, Texas, a junior high school is located underground, and at Fort Worth, Texas, a library beneath two city blocks. One architect admitted: "We studiously avoided using the word basement in association with the building. We always refer to it as the main level, with the ground level called the plaza level." More than two dozen subterranean houses are under construction in Oklahoma, where a consulting engineer suggested one reason for the growing appeal of the underground: "Crime has driven some people into subterranean structures because earth-covered buildings are more secure." They are also insulated from crowding and noise and preserve some measure of privacy. Another reason is that they are energy efficient: 50 to 85 percent. A few years ago, the Federal Housing Administration began approving loans for underground dwellings.

One of the pioneers and ardent advocates of this trend, who designed the underground house displayed seventeen years ago at the New York World's Fair, believes that murals will eventually replace windows.

A subway is not necessarily a public works project anymore. Department store owners in downtown Fort Worth built their own double-track mile-long line between a parking lot (for five thousand cars on the banks of the Trinity River) and their commercial complex. In Houston, over 3 miles of air-conditioned, carpeted pedestrian tunnels link more than fifty skyscrapers and parking garages—the most extensive underground concourse in the country. Dallas has a similar tunnel system on a smaller scale.

Even in New York, where rather less attention has been paid to underground commerce than elsewhere, "you can get anything from pretzels to pants. There are snack bars, bakeries, men's and women's clothing stores, nut shops, jewelry and watch-repair shops, card shops, florists, luncheonettes, hosiery stores, record shops, barber shops, shoeshine stands, and bank branches. At Times Square alone, you can pick up a dozen donuts, retrieve the pictures you left to be developed, grab a hotdog, purchase a new record album, and buy a bouquet of flowers."

This is all very convenient; but is it good? Much would seem to argue for it: what impressive advances we have made! How far we have come from the smoke-laden tunnels of the early London Underground. How captivating the landscape of the Métro in Montreal. Now, especially, since the underground has shown itself to be energy efficient—and coal mining is coming back into fashion—we have new incentives for cultivating the nether realm. Subways are the crossroads of the new underground cities. Commerce has grown up alongside them; in time, as in the caverns of Kansas City, no doubt industry will too. Dwellings would seem to be the next phase. Is this really what we want? Can any artificial setting, however convenient and attractive, ever make up for our natural and familiar world? The question is possibly urgent. Even allowing for a just admiration of what some underground systems have achieved, the wide-spread naturalization of an inorganic environment is historically strange, and stirs more than ossuary unease in one's bones.

The subway was the harbinger, and is the fulfillment, of the Industrial Revolution. It was, and is, its quintessence. It made general, even more than the surface railroad, the climate of the mine that had once been the fate of an unfortunate minority. Though much of the obvious degradation of the early tunnels (which led people to "ask only to be treated on a par with water, drainage, and gas") no longer applies, the essentially unnatural environment remains. Artificial lighting and ventilation, which make subways possible, both came out of the mine, as did the subway itself. The word "subway" was first applied to underground conduits for carrying eletrical wires;

subway workers are still called "miners." The genius of the great Marc Brunel notwithstanding, it was with some intuitive sagacity of their own that the Thames watermen, fearful for the preservation of their open-air trade, ran up a black flag at the inauguration of his tunnel in 1843.

The Industrial Revolution, which has given us so much—who would deny it?—is quite capable of taking it all away. We cannot "turn back the clock," but we ought at least to be keeping track of the time.

We ought at least to be reminding ourselves that what began with a desecration of the environment thrives in a world where the environment itself, from pole to pole, is studied for sacrifice in war. In Peking today, in addition to the subway, there are tunnels that in complexity rival the catacombs of Rome: hundreds of miles of tunnels, furnished with dormitories, kitchens, theaters, and shops—capable, apparently, of supporting eight million inhabitants! Begun in 1965 in preparation for "inevitable" war with the Soviet Union, the project may be compared to the Great Wall itself in ambitious grandeur. Mao said: "Dig tunnels deep. Store grain everywhere." And the people did. In the last few years the network has been "beautified," and some dormitories now double as hotels. May the day indeed not come, as the last in a series of kindred developments, when the underground of the world is so extensive—and the land above so stricken with chemical waste—that nuclear war will no longer seem the unnatural calamity it once did, and prolonged sanctuary underground a premature grave? Conceivably, we will then regard our surrogate, sepulchral comforts as the epitome of life itself, and grow as elaborate in our mortuary splendors as Egyptian kings.

In copper mines once worked by the Etruscans, coins have been found bearing the effigy of *Janus bifrons*, or Hermes, the patron of Pelasgian miners. The god of roads and gates and the guardian of travelers, Hermes also conducted the shades of the dead from the upper to the lower world. "He summons wan ghosts from Orcus," wrote Vergil, "and consigns others to dreary Tartarus, gives sleep and takes it away, seals up the eyes of dead men." As the double-headed Janus, he was equally conversant with the secrets of geology and of the future.

Aeneas, before his descent, set forth "with a prayer from the bottom of his heart" to pluck the golden bough sacred to Proserpine and impervious to water and fire. He sacrificed to Night, mother of the Furies, and to Earth. Perhaps in our scientific pride we have profanely propitiated in reverse—sacrificing Earth herself and making the Furies our lords. Lewis Mumford, one of our most profound and accurate students of urban civilization, has suggested the bleakest result. "The Victorian industrialist," he wrote:

> exposing his fellow citizens to soot and smog, to vile sanitation and environmentally promoted disease, still nourished the belief that his work was contributing, ultimately, to "peace and plenty." But his heirs in the underground city have no such illusions—they are the prey of compulsive fears and corrupt fantasies whose ultimate outcome may be universal annihilation and extermination; and the more they devote themselves to adapting the urban environment to this possibility, the more surely they will bring on the unrestricted collective genocide many of them have justified in their minds . . .

So Aeneas, on the way to Avernus, encountered the dreadful images of war—the "iron cells of the Furies" and "lunatic strife," "guilty Joys" and "unsolid Dreams." What Sibyl guides us now? What Thesean clew of thread unwinding wound back up may lead us out?

> . . . The way to Avernus is easy;
> Night and day lie open the gates of death's dark kingdom;
> But to retrace your steps, to find your way back to daylight,
> That is the task, the hard thing.

NOTES

CHAPTER 1

14 "Mythology is the study": Graves, *Larousse Encyclopedia of Mythology*, p. 1.
15 "Next to the air we breathe": Church, *The Great Need, A City Railroad As A City Work*, p. 2.
16 "We must determine": Coleman, *The Railway Navvies*, p. 21.
17 "all the gay, gallant, and polite world": Burney, *Music, Men and Manners in France and Italy*. 1770, p. 173.
19 "so furiously hot": *Ibid.*, p. 167.
20 "Twixt Naples and Dicarchian Fields": Petronius, *Satyricon*, p. 290.
21 "images and pictures of saints": Günther, *Pausilypon*, p. 10.
21 "desolate except": *Ibid.*, p. 20.
23 "destiny takes pleasure": *Dream Tigers*, "The Plot."
24 "a little above Lake Moeris . . . and it is beyond my power": Herodotus *The Histories*, p. 161.
27 "had suddenly risen up": Godwin, *Athanasius Kircher*, p. 46.
28 "a number of *cuniculi*": Sandstrom, *The History of Tunnelling*, p. 33.
28 "Hail Caesar, we salute you . . . mechanical silver": Suetonius, *The Twelve Caesars*, p. 195.
28 "They fought like brave men": Tacitus, *The Annals of Imperial Rome*, p. 268.
28 "this time to witness": *Ibid.*, p. 268.
29 "the water came rushing out": Suetonius, *op.cit.*, p. 201.
30 "In the Dark Ages": Gies, *Adventure Underground*, p. 44.
31 " 'Water is a giant' ": Quoted in Sandstrom, *op. cit.*, p. 22.
31 "refused to a man": Sandstrom, *op. cit.*, p. 81.
31 "In no other branch": Vogel, *Tunnel Engineering*, p. 1.

CHAPTER 2

49 "when it is remembered": Beamish, *Memoir of Brunel*, p. 13.

49 "alphabet of the engineer": Quoted in Beamish, *op. cit.*, p. 323.

51 "measured the length": Beamish, *op. cit.*, p. 44.

52 "without requiring dexterity": *Ibid.*, p. 59.

53 " 'Is anybody hurt?' ": Quoted in Beamish, *op. cit.*, p. 333.

53 " 'It was a most extraordinary jumble' ": Quoted in Garnett, *Master Engineers*, p. 168.

53 " 'My affectionate wife and myself' ": Quoted in Rolt, *Isambard Kingdom Brunel*, p. 15.

53 "to imitate (by some mechanical means)": Beamish, *op. cit.*, p. 207.

54 "In five years": *Ibid.*, p. 206.

54 " 'We consider that an underground tunnel' ": Quoted in Beamish, *op. cit.*, p. 206.

54 "augur-like cells": Beamish, *op. cit.*, p. 208.

55 Wellington's interest in the tunnel: cf. preamble to the Thames Tunnel Archway Co. of 1808, which declared that the tunnel would be of "great national advantage as a military road or pass."

55 " 'We have neither' ": Quoted in Garnett, *op. cit.*, p. 24.

55 " 'A man who can do something' ": Quoted in Rolt, *op. cit.*, p. 4.

56 " '. . . thirty-nine borings": Quoted in Beamish, *op. cit.*, p. 210.

56 "making accurate experiments": Beamish, *op. cit.*, p. 211.

56 "rang out their joyful acclamations": *Ibid.*, p. 211.

58 "as to have become absolutely fluid": *Ibid.*, p. 225.

58 " 'the variety of the strata' ": Quoted in Beamish, *op. cit.*, p. 250.

59 "the feed pump": *Ibid.*, p. 227.

59 " 'It is a widespread belief' ": Frazer, *The Golden Bough*, p. 334.

60 "tipped and skewed . . . buckled and broke": Garnett, *op. cit.*, p. 33.

61 "a trained engineer whose father": *Ibid.*, p. 36.

62 "A strong feeling of apprehension . . . the tide was now rising": Beamish, *op. cit.*, p. 245.

64 "but the just judgement": Quoted in Lee, *The East London Line and the Thames Tunnel*, p. 8.

65 "mounted on decorative urns": Klingender, *Art and the Industrial Revolution*, p. 211.

66 "The water is in—the tunnel is full": Beamish, *op. cit.*, p. 261.

67 " 'We have completed and secured' ": Quoted in Beamish, *op. cit.*, p. 276.

68. " 'piece-work on a large scale' ": Quoted in Beamish, *op. cit.*, p. 278.

68 " 'An extraordinary stiffness' ": *Ibid.*, p. 281.

69 "The water came from the springs": Beamish, *op. cit.*, p. 298.

70 "at two-hour intervals": Garnett, *op. cit.*, p. 120.

71 "greeted with an outburst of popular prints": Rolt, *op. cit.*, p. 144.

72 "in a remote Calabrian monastery": Garnett, *op. cit.*, p. 29.

72 "an arched corridor": Quoted in Lampe, *The Tunnel*, p. 209–210

72 "By day the tunnel was filled": Clements, *Marc Isambard Brunel*, p. 251.

73   " 'Neanmoins, si je l'avais' ": Quoted in Beamish, *op. cit.*, p. 333.

CHAPTER 3

76   "like a giant with one idea": Quoted in Klingender, *op. cit.*, p. 88.
77   " 'In the confines of Egypt' ": Quoted in Sandstrom, *op. cit.*, p. 8.
77   " 'The mine is more terrifying' ": Quoted in *Ibid.*, p. 13.
78   "The price of maintaining a culture": *Ibid.*, p. 35.
78   "when the woods and groves are felled": Quoted in Mumford, *Technics and Civilization*, p. 71.
79   "raise water from Lowe Pitts by fire": David Ramsaye, quoted in Klingender, *op. cit.*, p. 5.
80   "Fire menaces him in blasting": Simonin, *Underground Life*, p. 132.
80   "bursts out with a gurgling sound": *Ibid.*, p. 134.
80   "in a covering of wool or leather": *Ibid.*, p. 134.
80   "everything concurs to vitiate the air": *Ibid.*, p. 134.
80   "the soil above a burning coal mine": *Ibid.*, p. 133.
81   "in all directions like the streets": *Ibid.*, p. 132–133.
81   "a very romantic spot . . . variety of horrors . . . winding glen": Young, *Annals of Agriculture and other useful Arts*, Vol. 4, pp. 166–168.
82   "a region of smoke and fire": Britton, *Autobiography*, Vol. 1, pp. 128–129.
82   "The Black Country is anything but picturesque": Nasmyth, *Autobiography*, p. 88.
83   "dark hives, busily puffing": Mumford, *The City in History*, p. 446.
83   "It was a town of red brick": Dickens, *Hard Times*, p. 65.
83   "killing airs and gases bricked in . . . labyrinth of courts": *Ibid.*, p. 65.
83   "lay shrouded in a haze": *Ibid.*, pp. 145–146.
84   "In a greater or lesser degree": Mumford, *The City in History*, p. 447.
85   "Wherever the iron rails went": *Ibid.*, p. 451.
85   "The strength of England": Quoted in Coleman, *Men and Coal*, p. 27.
85   "Here the whole world is railway mad": Quoted in Rolt, *Victorian Engineering*, p. 23.

CHAPTER 4

88   "During the years which immediately followed the Restoration": Macaulay, *History of England*, p. 336–137.
90   "before the names of Wellington and Peel": Pearson, *An Address delivered at a Public Meeting on the 11th, 12, and 18th of December*, 1843, p. 84.
90   "having to be present": Pearson, *op. cit.*, p. 176.
91   "Looking at it in the mass": Pearson, *op. cit.*, p. 75.
91   "except upon the personal guarantee": Pearson, *op. cit.*, p. 24.
91   " 'A poor man is chained to the spot . . . desire to get out of town' ": Quoted in Barker and Robbins, *A History of London Transport*, Vol. 1, p. 55.
92   "many of the brethren . . . overwhelmed even the incense": Douglas, *The Underground Story*, p. 45.

92   "had descended to one of filth": *Ibid.*, p. 45.
93   " 'one day there would be an underground railway' ": Quoted in Lee, *The Metropolitan Line*, p. 8.
94   " 'What we propose to do' ": Quoted in Barker and Robbins, *op. cit.*, p. 109.
94   " 'If you are going a very short journey' ": *Ibid.*, p. 59.
94   " 'the line could be worked by ordinary locomotives . . . Generally speaking' ": *Ibid.*, p. 59.
95   "the taste of cheap port . . . a nightmare": Ellis, *British Railway History*, Vol. 1, p. 118.
95   "a train was attached": Klingender, *op. cit.*, p. 160.
95   "would be as sweet": Douglas, *op. cit.*, p. 31.
96   "to accelerate the mails": Quoted in Mackay, *Life of Sir John Fowler*, p. 153.
96   "omnibus character": *Ibid.*, p. 151.
96   " 'It must be obvious' ": Quoted in Barker and Robbins, *op. cit.*, p. 106.
97   "dwell bitterly . . . paper with bank notes": Harrison, *London Beneath the Pavement*, p. 141.
98   "a large mass of fire brick": Day, *The Story of London's Underground*, p. 10.
98   "The condensing apparatus": *Ibid.*, p. 10.
98   "flap valves, worked by rods": Barker and Robbins, *op. cit.*, pp. 119–120.
98   "the fumes were thus left": *Ibid.*, p. 120.
99   " 'It was not known' ": Quoted in Mackay, *op. cit.*, pp. 167–169.
99   " 'A few wooden houses on wheels' ": Quoted in Day, *op. cit.*, p. 6 (Douglas, *op. cit.*, p. 43 has a variant and gives a different source).
100 "In some places": Mackay, *op. cit.*, p. 165.
101 "drink a bumper": *Ibid.*, p. 172.
102 " 'The men all came into the station' ": Quoted in Barker and Robbins, *op. cit.*, p. 118.
103 " 'Ventilation has always been an objection' ": Quoted in Mackay, *op. cit.*, p. 178.
104 "It is not enough": Parsons, "Argument of Parsons at governor's Hearing on Arcade Railway Bill, Albany, 23rd, April, 1886."
104 "painted dark green": Barker and Robbins, *op. cit.*, p. 124.
104 "giant onslaught": *Ibid.*, p. 148.
104 "every resident": *Ibid.*, p. 148.
104 " 'Next year' ": Quoted in Barker and Robbins, *op. cit.*, p. 148.
105 "When constructing the District at Blackfriars": Mackay, *op. cit.*, p. 162.
106 " 'It's convenience' ": Quoted in Day, *op. cit.*, p. 21.
106 "device for splitting": *Ibid.*, p. 20.
107 "acted as a disinfectant": Quoted in Barker and Robbins, *op. cit.*, p. 238.
107 "The sensation altogether": *English Illustrated Magazine*, August, 1893.
108 "In London the trains": *Engineer's Report on the New York City Central Underground Railway Co.*, Appendix B.
109 shield description: see Barker and Robbins, *op. cit.*, p. 302.
110 "The water encountered": Vogel, *Tunneling*, p. 224.
111 "glided with an ease": Quoted in Day, *op. cit.*, p. 66.

112 "purchasing the scattered": Hendrick, *The Age of Big Business*, p. 121.
129 "Straphangers pay the dividends. . . . The secret of success": Quoted in the *Encyclopaedia of American Biography*, p. 610.
130 "the bend in the river made famous by Turner": Douglas, *op. cit.*, p. 152.
131 " 'Northampton and Birmingham' ": Quoted in Lee, *The Metropolitan Line*, p. 22.
131 " 'I do not intend' ": *Ibid.*, p. 23.
131 "a great trunk railway": *Ibid.*, p. 24.

CHAPTER 5

136 " 'Since the city and its suburbs' ": Quoted in Parsons, *Engineers and Engineering in the Renaissance*, p. 20.
138 "They looked down": de Maupassant, *Bel-Ami*, p. 242.
140 "one day at St.-Cloud": Benevolo, *The Origins of Modern Town Planning*, pp. 132–133.
142 "used to the fogs of London . . . Necropolitan": Heuze, *Chemin de fer transversal à air libre dans une rue spéciale, passage couvert pour piétons*, p. 5.
143 "Insulated cesspools": Quoted in Guerrand, *Mémoires du Métro*, p. 30.
143 "What difference does it make": Garnier, *Avant projet d'un chemin de fer aérien*, p. 42.
143 "permanent subterranean humidity and cold": Tellier, *Le véritable Metropolitain*, p. 22.
143 "The subsoil of Paris": Hugo, *Les Misérables*, p. 140.
144 "They are streets": *Ibid.*, p. 139.
144 "in the ground a species": *Ibid.*, p. 158.
145 "is no less attractive": Verpraet, *Paris: capitale souterrain*, p. 82.
145 "baleful evacuations . . . leavening": Quoted in Verpraet, *op. cit.*, p. 217.
145 "The Opera costs": Chretien, *Chemin de fer electrique des boulevards a Paris*, p. 56.
146 "to create a movement of opinion": Verpraet, *Paris: capitale souterraine*, p. 217.
147 "The men were now all talking together": de Maupassant, *op. cit.*, p. 54.
147 "a mop of hair . . . Just like a schoolboy": Quoted in Guerrand, *op. cit.*, p. 23.
147 "Under the rain, under the burning sun": Quoted in Guerrand, *op. cit.*, pp. 32–33.
148 "When they appropriated the shanties": Robert, *Nôtre Metro*, p. 12.
148 "We cannot destroy all of Paris": *Ibid.*, p. 17.
150 "asphyxia by miasmas . . . sudden breaking in": Hugo, *op. cit.*, p. 161.
150 "In front of a group": Verpraet, *op. cit.*, p. 219.
151 "A pilot gallery is cut": Wrottesley, *Famous Underground Railways of the World*, p. 99.
151 Early Metro labor gangs: see Guerrand, *Le Métro*, p. 10.
152 "Justifiably, one heard everyone": Quoted in Guerrand, *op. cit.*, p. 60.
154 *Le Figaro* announcement" Robert, *op. cit.*, p. 27.

154   *"manifestations réalisées"*: Robert, *op. cit.*, p. 27.

157   "unnatural indifference ... face the door": Kafka, *Diaries 1914–1923*, p. 280.

157   "Only those condemned to death": Verpraet, *op. cit.*, p. 217.

157   " 'The Metro is a badly ventilated cellar' ": Quoted in Guerrand, *Mémoires du Métro*, p. 115.

159   "hardest hitting": Appelbaum, *French Satiric Drawings from "L'Assiette au Beurre*, p. v.

160   "The laborers will no longer see his shadow": Le François, *Paris Souterrain*, p. 96

160   "The work of an artist": Quoted in Guerrand, *Mémoires du Métro*, p. 48.

CHAPTER 6

169   "a good place to hide in ... a favorite place": McCabe, *New York by Sunlight & Gaslight*, pp. 277–278.

171   "clumsy, uncomfortable vehicles": *Ibid.*, p. 158.

171   "dirty, badly ventilated": *Ibid.*, p. 241.

171   "animated billiard ball, caroming": *Ibid.*, p. 143.

172   "with scanty brown backs": Dickens, *American Notes*, p. 88.

172   "as much as your life is worth": Greene, *A Glance at New York*, p. 10.

172   "as treacherous as an Atlantic voyage": McCullough, *The Great Bridge*, p. 44.

172   "to tunnel Broadway": *Scientific American*, November 3, 1849.

173   "modern martyrdom": October 2nd issue.

174   "New York has already": March 1867 issue.

174   "broken by carts and omnibuses ... filth and garbage": Quoted from an unidentified contemporary source in Lynch, *Boss Tweed*, p. 99.

177   "There would be no dust": Robinson, *A Statement of the Character and Cost of the Proposed Metropolitan Railway Co.*, p. 32.

178   "The field is open": *Ibid.*, p. 6.

180   "scarcely said to exist": Wilson, *History of New York*, p. 100.

180   "slimy and venomous": Quoted in O'Brien, *The Story of the Sun*, p. 150.

181   "only dissipation": *Scientific American* obituary, January 11, 1896.

182   "screeching whistles, smoke and cinders": Beach, *Pneumatic Dispatch*, p. 6.

182   "scarcely a building": Quoted in *To the Friends of Rapid City Transit*, p. 3.

184   "as swift as Aeolus, as silent as Somnus": Beach, *op. cit.*, p. 6.

185   "The mechanism is of the simplest": *Ibid.*, p. 5.

185   "rival the telegraph": *Ibid.*, p. 4.

186   "which in shape resembled": New York *Herald*, February 27, 1870.

188   "It is free from that health destroying": *Scientific American*, February 19, 1870.

189   "hum like that of a cotton mill": New York *Mercury*, February 27, 1870.

189   "Aladdin's Cave": New York *Herald*, February 27, 1870.

189   Tribune reporter disguised as workman: see *Scientific American*, February 24, 1912 (article by Waldemar Kaempffert, "New York's First Subway").

190   "It will not be long now": *Science Record*, 1872, p. 254.

190   "dwarf into insignificance": Quoted in *Science Record*, 1874, p. 341.
190   "without endangering the foundations": Letter to Beach, March 22, 1871.
192   "the largest and most pious bank": Josephson, *The Robber Barons*, p. 170.
192   "All the money can be had": *Science Record*, 1874, p. 343.

CHAPTER 7

197   "Every year the legislature": Church, *The Great Need. A City Railroad As A City Work*, p. 2.
198   "to attach and detach the car": *Journal of the Franklin Institute*, 1867, p. 6.
200   "The market opened in Pandemonium": Josephson, *op. cit.*, p. 146.
200   "flung open the market . . . within fifteen minutes": *Ibid.*, p. 146.
200   "There was a reminiscence of a spider": Quoted in Lynch, *op. cit.*, p. 370.
203   "anatomy and engineering analogous": Quoted in *Appleton's Journal*, 1878, "Rapid Transit in New York," p. 6.
206   "South Fifth Avenue now presents": *Scientific American*, March 23, 1878.
207   "Even Asmodeus riding his two sticks": Quoted in the New York *World Telegram*, January 29, 1948, "When the Iron Horse Took to the Air."
208   "exhaustion brought on by chronic": New York *Times* obituary, July 11, 1885.
208   "this country is completely cut up": Quoted in Josephson, *op. cit.*, p. 42.
208   "mortgaged to the railroads": Quoted in *Ibid.*, p. 74.
208   "buying and selling, building and tearing down": *Ibid.*, p. 212.
210   "terrify and appall even": Bradford, *Great York*, p. 5.

CHAPTER 8

213   "in a taut energetic manner": New York *World*, October 30, 1904.
213   "Foreigners who penetrate into Hunan": Quoted in Parsons, *An American Engineer in China*, p. 49.
214   "No good to talk to": *World's Work*, Vol. 6, May, 1903, p. 3468.
214   "pushing ahead with indomitable will": *Ibid.*, p. 3469.
214   "I was the first foreigner": Parsons, *op. cit.*, p. 50.
214   "We had shown no fear": *Ibid.*, p. 50.
215   "future trains bearing": *Ibid.*, p. 51.
215   "Perhaps the cause": Parsons, *Engineers and Engineering in the Renaissance*, p. 2.
217   "The first and least in influence": Gardiner, *Speech to the Real Estate Owners in New York City and Westchester County*, p. 3.
217   "All we have are highly": "Argument of Parsons at Governor's Hearing on Arcade Railway Bill, Albany, 23rd April, 1886."
217   "It is not enough": *Ibid.*
219   "pityingly . . . wasting my life": Quoted in Walker, *Fifty Years of Rapid Transit*, p. 188.
220   "familiarized himself with": *World's Work*, Vol. 6, p. 3468.
220   "No attempt was made": Parsons, *Report to the Board of Rapid Transit Rail-*

road Commissioners in and for the City of New York on Rapid Transit in Foreign Cities, p. 50.

221   "It is not generally understood": *Ibid.*, p. 59.

221   "There is a widespread popular idea": *Ibid.*, p. 61.

227   "In thousands of New York homes": New York *World*, March 25, 1900.

227   "instead of throwing it out boldly": New York *Herald Tribune*, March 24, 1900.

227   "If your laborers shirk work": *Ibid.*

227   "No Roman citizen": Quoted in *Ibid.*

227   "For New York there is no such thing": *Scribner's*, May 1900, p. 554.

228   "The great cities of the Old World": Quoted in the New York *World*, October 30, 1904.

228   "Policemen had to work like football rushers": New York *World*, March 27, 1900.

228   "check stone weighting . . . tended bar": Longstreet, *City on Two Rivers*, p. 197.

230   "When it came to decide": *Scribner's*, May 1900, p. 547.

232   "The whole place was a great chasm": New York *Evening Sun*, October 27, 1904.

232   "infinite capacity for taking pains": *World's Work*, Vol. 6, p. 3467.

232   "all believed in him thoroughly": *Ibid.*, p. 3470.

232   "nothing to say . . . work was being done": New York *World*, October 2, 1904.

257   "Foul air is a factor": *Ibid.*

258   "might minister to the happiness": Quoted in the New York *Press*, October 28, 1904.

258   "When the dirt is off your shovel": New York *Evening Sun*, October 24, 1904.

258   "Do you know that this subway": New York *American*, October 28, 1904.

259   "not poisoned . . . same air": *Subway Air Pure As In Your Own Home*, p. 3.

260   "novelty of the whirlwind rush": New York *World*, October 27, 1904.

260   "Original sponsors of a subway": October 27, 1904 issue.

260   "quite unlike the ordinarily accepted": *Scribner's*, May 1900, p. 550.

260   "Underground railways have always been": *Ibid.*, p. 554.

261   "descending passengers from wind and": Silver, *Lost New York*, p. 159.

262   "cool little vaulted city": New York *World*, October 27, 1904.

262   "The beauty of the interior will never": New York *Commercial*, October 27, 1904.

262   "We congratulate Mr. August Belmont": October 28, 1904 issue.

264   "for a tour of the tunnels or a festive run": Tauranac, "Art and the IRT," p. 6.

264   "Having shoveled and blasted . . . There is not a street": Quoted in the New York *World*, October 2, 1904.

264   "I think we have made a beginning": Quoted in the New York *Herald*, October 27, 1904.

265   "given a few steel rails": *Fighting Engineer*, May 1919.

266 "every act we commit": Parsons, *Manifestation of Natural Laws in Human Nature*.

267 "became confused, then frightened": New York *Times*, August 30, 1959 article by Meyer Berger, "Shuttle Labyrinth Guide Lines Come Straight from Minotaur Legend."

266 "unexplained Maya ruins of Yucatan": Parsons, *Engineering and Economics*, p. 2.

268 "roaring cave": Fitzgerald, *The Beautiful and Damned*, p. 413.

268 "crowded horror . . . echo of hell": *Ibid.*, p. 231.

269 Open letter: *Subways or Children*. A Letter to the Board of Estimate and Apportionment, January 12, 1927.

CHAPTER 9

271 "criticism . . . shock brigadiers": Kaganovich, "The Construction of the Subway and Plan for the City of Moscow," p. 1.

271 "You, comrades, know, of course": *Ibid.*, p. 10.

272 "deteriorated into a form of red marl": Wrottesley, *Famous Underground Railways of the World*, p. 119.

272 "crumple twenty-inch thick timbers . . . which cut the route": Black, *The Story of Tunnels*, p. 14.

272 "overburdening the streets": Kaganovich, *op. cit.*, p. 55.

273 Every method of tunelling known: see *Christian Science Monitor*, 1/24/35.

273 "in some cases they rendered the soil": Black, *op. cit.*, p. 14.

273 "The metallurgical plants": Troitskaya, *The L. M. Kaganovich Metropolitan Railway of Moscow's Metro*, p. 1.

274 "check, criticize . . . on all specific": Quoted in Crankshaw, *Khrushchev, a Career*, p. 86.

274 "self-seekers": *Ibid.*, 87.

274 "We knew, of course": *Ibid.*, p. 88.

275 "What's the matter with you": *Ibid.*, p. 89.

275 " 'The shield approached the silt' ": Quoted in Pistrak, *The Grand Tactician: Khrushchev's Rise to Power*, p. 94.

276 " 'The main task' ": *Ibid.*, p. 92.

276 " 'The time schedule' ": *Ibid.*, p. 91.

276 "We must detect the unconscientious": *op. cit.*, p. 28.

276 "whose past experience": Pistrak, *op. cit.*, p. 96.

277 "it was a difficult time": *Ibid.*, p. 96.

277 " 'My men descended' ": Quoted in Crankshaw, *op. cit.*, p. 91.

277 "lack of modern machinery": Gonzalez, *Listen, Comrades: Life and Death in the Soviet Union*, pp. 80–81.

278 "Almost 90 percent": *Ibid.*, p. 80.

278 "It sometimes happened": *Ibid.*, p. 81–82.

279 "The alternative was Siberia": *Ibid.*, p. 80.

279 "When a forest is cut down": Quoted in Conquest, *The Great Terror*, p. 100.

281 "like the hue of sunrise": Troitskaya, *op. cit.*, p. 4.

CHAPTER 10

283 "A world of scientific specialists": Parsons, *Manifestation of Natural Laws in Human Nature*, p. 2.

283 "oldest art there is": Parsons, *The Architect and the Engineer*, p. 1.

284 "when canals, harbors, lighthouses": Parsons, *The American Engineers in France*, p. 4.

284 "application of steam as a source of power": *Ibid.*, p. 4.

284 "Railroads and roads, their construction": *Ibid.*, p. 5.

286 "broke through the pavement": Harrison, *London Beneath the Pavement*, p. 168.

287 "The elevated, half a block away": Fitzgerald, *op. cit.*, p. 27.

306 "in the stuffy, dark-paneled bars": New York *Times*, April 20, 1975.

308 "with a grin . . . If I see any old stones": New York *Times*, January 23, 1971.

308 "in accordance with Mao's policy": New York *Times*, May 9, 1971.

309 "Robed oriental clerics": *Asia Magazine*, January 20, 1980.

309 "torture pit": September 23, 1980 issue.

309 "lung cancer and emphysema": January 30, 1981 issue.

309 "with a black blast of iron": Burroughs, *Naked Lunch*, p. 202.

310 "once every morning and": New York *Times*, April 15, 1976.

310 "You're standing there in the station": Quoted in Mailer, *The Faith of Graffiti*, p. 6.

313 "selective and deeply patriotic": Strong, *London Transport Posters*, p. 1.

314 "glow in a dazzling . . . soaring structural forms": *Aviation Week and Space Technology*, p. 2.

315 "seismic movement through the ages": New York *Times*, April 2, 1974.

316 "demonstrated a taste for wiring": *Wall Street Journal*, November 11, 1972.

316 "barrelled on, lurched severely": San Francisco *Post*, November 23, 1972.

316 "To Washingtonians the New York Subway": Chicago *Sun Times*, 1975.

317 "cross-bearing priests": Washington *Post*, April 3, 1976.

318 "Dr. Robert M. Salter, senior scientist": February 14 issue.

319 "Montrealers say they can shop": Los Angeles *Times*, August 10, 1972.

319 "As above, so below . . . you can get": New York *Times*, March 1970.

320 "is so dense and so complicated": Cooper-Hewitt Museum, *Subways*. A collection of articles which accompanied an exhibit at the museum, p. 30. (article by Peter Gluck, "Inner Space").

320 "had come into being": New York *Times*, February 11, 1967.

320 "Living underground like this, people lose": New York *Times*, February 11, 1967.

321 "It is much easier for commuters": New York *Times*, February 11, 1967.

321 "In a single day": *Newsweek*, February 2, 1961.

321 "The physical exercise involved": Quoted in *Ibid*.

321 "Travel in Japan has always been": Cooper-Hewitt Museum, *op. cit.*, p. 30.

325 "The Victorian Industrialist, exposing": Mumford, *The City in History*, p. 481.

BIBLIOGRAPHY

GENERAL REFERENCES

Brockhaus Lexikon, Encyclopedia Americana, Encyclopedia of American Biography, Encyclopedia Brittanica, Encyclopedia Larousse, National Cyclopedia of American Biography.

NEWSPAPERS AND PERIODICALS (c. 1830–1904)

Appleton's Journal, L'Assiette au Beurre, Boston *Globe, Engineering News, Le Figaro, Frank Leslie's Illustrated Newspaper, Harper's Weekly, London Illustrated News, Mechanic's Magazine,* New York *Commercial Advertiser,* New York *Evening Mail,* New York *Evening Post,* New York *Evening Telegram,* New York *Sun,* New York *Times,* New York *Tribune, Railroad Gazette, Scientific American.*

NEWSPAPERS AND PERIODICALS (c. 1905–present)

Baltimore *Sun,* Chicago *Daily News,* Chicago *Tribune, L'Express, Far Eastern Review, Engineering Record, Everybody's Magazine, Le Figaro, Fortune, Journal of Hygiene, Life,* London *Financial Times,* Los Angeles *Times,* New York *Daily News,* New York *Evening Telegram,* New York *Herald Tribune,* New York *Post,* New York *Times,* New York *World, Le Nouvel Observateur, Le Point, Pravda,* San Francisco *Chronicle,* San Francisco *Examiner, Smithsonian, Der Spiegel,* Toronto *Star,* Washington *Post,* Washington *Star-News.*

FURTHER READINGS

Abakumov, Yegor Trofimovich. *The Moscow Subway.* Moscow: Foreign Languages Publishing House, 1957.

Adams, Charles F., Jr., and Adams, Henry. *Chapters of Erie and Other Essays.* New York: H. Holt and Co., 1886.

Adams, Henry. *Mont Saint-Michel and Chartres.* New York: New American Library, Mentor Books, 1961.

Agricola, Georgius. *De Re Metallica.* 1556. Translated by H. C. Hoover and L. H. Hoover, 1912.

American Society of Civil Engineers. *Rapid Transit and Freight.* New York, 1874.

Angéley, A. *Chemin de fer à voie suspendue.* Paris: Chaix, 1884.

Appelbaum. Stanley. *French Satirical Drawings from "L'Assiette au Beurre."* New York: Dover, 1978.

Barker, T. C., and Robbins, Michael. *A History of London Transport*. Vol. 1: *The Nineteenth Century*. London: Allen & Unwin, 1962.

Beach, Alfred E. *The Pneumatic Dispatch*. New York: The American News Co., 1868.

The Beach Pneumatic Transit Company. New York, 1873.

Beamish, Richard. *Memoir of Brunel*. London: Longman, Green, Longman & Roberts, 1862.

Belleni, Amerigo. *Metropolitana di Milano*. Milan: C. Tamburini, 1954.

Benevolo, Leonardo. *The Origins of Modern Town Planning*. Cambridge, Mass.: M.I.T. Press, 1971.

Berger, Rudolf. *Untergrundbahnen und ihre Einsatzgrenzen*. Berlin: W. Ernst & Son, 1957.

Berlier, J. B. *Paris, Tramways souterrain*. Paris: Cusset, 1887.

Biette, Louis. *Les Chemins de fer urbains parisiens*. Paris: J. B. Baillière et fils, 1928.

Bingham, Col. Sidney H. *New Ideas for Efficient Passenger Transportation*. New York: Transportation Authority, 1956.

Black, Archibald. *The Story of Tunnels*. New York: McGraw-Hill, 1937.

Blake, William. *Complete Writings*. London: Oxford University Press, 1966.

Boorse, J. W. *Rapid Transit in Canada*. Philadelphia: Almo Press, 1965.

Bradford, Edward Anthony. *Great York. An Inquiry into the Relation of Rapid Transit and Consolidation to Past and Present Poverty, Disease, Crime & Mortality and their Remedy*. Brooklyn: The Consolidation League, 1894.

Britton, John. *Autobiography*. 1850. London: Printed for the author, 1849–50.

Brunel, Sir Marc Isambard. *Diaries*.

———. *A Letter to the Proponents of the Thames Tunnel*. London, 1829.

———. *A Tunnel Under the Thames*. London, 1883.

Burney, Charles. *Music, Men and Manners in France and Italy, 1770*. London: Ernst Eulenburg, 1974.

Calfas, P. "Le Métropolitain de Paris, Traversée de la Seine par la ligne No. 4, Parties executée au bouclier et par congelation." *Genie Civil* 57 (Paris, 1910): 41–47.

Callow, Alexander B., Jr. *The Tweed Ring*. New York: Oxford University Press, 1966.

Chesebrough, R. A. *System of Gravity Locomotion*. New York, 1877.

Chicago City Council Committee on Local Transportation. *Report on the Transportation Subway Systems of Boston, New York, Philadelphia, Paris and London*. Chicago, 1909.

Choate, J. H. *Concise Argument on Rapid Transit*. New York, 1876.

Chrétien, Jean. *Chemin de fer électrique des boulevards à Paris*. Paris: Baudry, 1881.

———. *Tramway électrique aerien*. Paris: Capiomont et Renault, 1882.

Christinger, Raymond. "Le Myth du Labyrinth." *Archives Suisses d'Anthropologie Generale*. 1961.

Church, Simeon E. *The Great Need. A City Railroad as a City Work*. New York: Rapid Transit Association, 1873.

Clarke, Thomas Curtis. *The Gilbert Elevated Railway*. New York, 1877.

Clarke, W. Harrey. "Tokyo's Subway System." *Far Eastern Review* 29 (Shanghai, 1933): 154–61.

Clements, Paul. *Marc Isambard Brunel*. London: Longman, 1956.

Coleman, MacAlister. *Men and Coal*. New York: Farrar & Rinehart, 1943.

Coler, Bird S. "Shall New York Own Its Subways?" *Outlook* 79 (New York, 1905): 934–38.

Comparetti, Domenico P. A. *Virgil in the Middle Ages*. Translated by E. F. M. Benecke. New York: Macmillan, 1895.

Cooper-Hewitt Museum. *Subways*. New York, 1977.

Coulanges, Fustel de. *The Ancient City*. New York: Doubleday, Anchor Books, 1950.

Crane, Hart. *Complete Poems*. Edited by Waldo Frank. New York: Doubleday, 1933.

Crankshaw, Edward. *Krushchev, a Career*. New York: Viking, 1966.

Cudahy, Brian J. *Change at Park Street Under: The Story of Boston's Subway*. Brattleboro, Vt.: Stephen Greene Press, 1972.

Daley, Robert. "Alfred Ely Beach and His Wonderful Pneumatic Underground Railway." *American Heritage* (June 1961).

———. *The World Beneath the City*. Philadelphia and New York: J. B. Lippincott, 1959.

Darymple, Hay. *The Waterloo and City Railway*. London: B. M. Jenkin, 1900.

Davenport, John Isaacs. *Letter on Evils due to Lack of Rapid Transit*. New York, 1871.

Day, John R. *The Story of London's Underground*. London: London Transport, 1963.

Dean, Frederick E. *Tunnels and Tunnelling*. London: F. Muller, 1962.

Derry, John J. *Rapid Transit for the City of Philadelphia*. 1890.

Dickens, Charles. *American Notes*. London: Chapman and Hall, 1842.

———. *Hard Times*. Middlesex: Penguin, 1969.

———. *Little Dorritt*. New York: New American Library, Signet Books, 1980.

———. *Sketches by Boz*. London: Chapman and Hall, 1850.

Doré, Gustave, and Jerrold, Blanchard. *London: A Pilgrimage*. London: Grant & Co., 1872.

Douglas, Hugh. *The Underground Story*. London: Robert Hale, 1963.

Dumas, Alexandre. *Discussion sur le chemin de fer métropolitain de Paris*. Paris: Chaix, 1887.

East-Side Association. *To the Friends of Rapid City Transit*. New York, 1871.

The 1866 Guide to New York City. New York: Schocken, 1975.

Elevated Railways. The People Opposed. New York, 1887.

Ellis, Hamilton. *British Railway History*. 2 vols. London: Allen & Unwin, 1954, 1959.

Engineers' Report on the New York City Central Underground Railway Co. New York: John W. Amerman, 1869.

Evans, Arthur. *The Palace of Minos*. 7 vols. London, 1964.

Exposé of the Facts concerning the Proposed Elevated Patent Railway. New York, 1866.

Février, H. C. *Du Métropolitain: Question grave!* Paris: F. Levé, 1890.

Fitzgerald, F. Scott. *The Beautiful and Damned*. New York: Charles Scribner's Sons, 1961.

Forbes, J. Graham. "Atmosphere of Underground Railways." *Journal of Hygiene* 22 (London, 1923): 123–55.

Fraser, Sir James. *The Golden Bough*. New York: S. G. Phillips, 1959.

Furst, Artur. "Tunnel unter der Spree." *Westermann's Monatshefte* (Berlin, 1916).

Fyfe, H. C. "The New York Rapid-Transit Subway." *Factory and Industrial Management* 27 (New York, 1904): 881–912.

Gardiner, Henry C. *Speech to Real Estate Owners in New York City and Westchester*

County. December 1870.

Garnett, Emmeline. *Master Engineers*. London: Hodder and Stoughton, 1954.

Garnier, Jules. *Avant-Projet d'un chemin de fer aérien*. Paris: Chaix, 1884.

———. *Projet Compare d'un chemin de fer aérien*. Paris: Capiomont et Renault, 1885.

Gies, Joseph. *Adventure Underground*. New York: Doubleday & Co., 1962.

Gonzalez, Valentín. *Listen, Comrades: Life and Death in the Soviet Union*. New York: Putnam, 1952.

Goodrich, Arthur. "William Barclay Parsons." *World's Work* 6 (May 1903): 3467–71.

Graham, F. Lanier. *Hector Guimard*. New York, 1970.

Greene, Asa. *A Glance At New York*. 1837.

Guerrand, Roger H. *Mémoires du Métro*. Paris: La table ronde, 1961.

———. *Le Métro*. Paris: Les Editions du Temps, 1962.

Günther, Robert William Theodore. *Pausilypon*. London: Oxford University Press, 1913.

Hadfield, Charles. *Atmospheric Railways*. Newton Abbott: David & Charles, 1967.

Harrison, Michael. *London Beneath the Pavement*. London: P. Davies, 1961.

Havers, Harold C. P. *Underground Railways of the World*. London: Temple Press, 1966.

Hector Guimard. Architectural Monographs Series, no. 2. New York: Rizzoli, 1978.

Hendrick, B. J. *The Age of Big Business*. New Haven: Yale University Press, 1919.

Herodotus. *Histories*. Translated by Aubrey de Sélincourt. Baltimore: Penguin Classics, 1954.

Hervieu, Jules. *Le Chemin de Fer Métropolitain Municipal de Paris*. Vols. 1 and 2. Paris: C. Béranger, 1903–1908.

Heuzé, Louis. *Paris, chemin de fer transversal à air libre*. Paris: Lapirot and Boullay, 1878–1882.

———. *Chemin de fer transversal à l'air libre dans une rue speciale, passage couvert pour pietons*. Paris: A. Lévy, 1878.

Hoffman, John T. *Unanswerable Objections to a Broadway Underground Railroad*. New York, 1871.

Howson, Henry H. *Rapid Transit Railways of the World*. London: Allen & Unwin, 1971.

Hugo, Victor. *Les Miserables*. Boston: Little, Brown & Co., 1907.

Huysmans, J. K. *A Rebours*. Paris: Bibliothèque Charpentier, 1921.

Illustrated Description of Broadway Pneumatic Railway. New York, 1870.

Istoria metro Moskvyi; Raskazy stroitelei metro. [*History of the Moscow Metro; Stories of the Building of the Metro*]. Moscow, 1935.

Jackson, Alan A., and Croome, Desmond. *Rails Through Clay: A History of London's Tube Railways*. London: Allen & Unwin, 1962.

Josephson, Matthew. *The Robber Barons*. New York: Harcourt Brace Jovanovich, 1962.

Kaempfert, W. *A Popular History of American Invention*. New York: Blue Ribbon, 1924.

Kafka, Franz. *Diaries, 1914–1923*. Edited by Max Brod. New York: Schocken, 1965.

Kaganovich, Lazar M. "The Construction of the Subway and Plan for the City of Moscow." Speech delivered in Moscow, July 16, 1934.

Klingender, F. D. *Art and the Industrial Revolution*. London: Adams & McKay, 1947.

Krieger, Heinz. "Die Fortsetzung der Berliner Untergrundbahn." *Westermann's Monatshefte* 102 (Braunschweig, 1907): 492–506.

Kouwenhoven, John A. *The Columbia Historical Portrait of New York*. Garden City, N.Y.: Doubleday, 1953.

Law, Henry. *A Memoir of the Thames Tunnel*. London: Weale, 1857.

Lee, Charles E. *The East London Line and the Thames Tunnel*. London: London Transport, 1976.

————. *The Metropolitan Line*. London: London Transport, 1976.

Lefrançois, Philippe. *Paris Souterrain*. Paris: Editions internationales, 1950.

Lehan, Richard. *Theodore Dreiser, His World and His Novels*. Carbondale and Edwardsville, Ill.: Southern Illinois University Press, 1969.

Leugny, Georges. "Le Métropolitain de Paris, Étude d'ensemble." *Révue Technique Annales* (Paris, 1898).

Levey, Michael F. *London Transport Posters*. Oxford: Phaedon, 1976.

Longstreet, Stephen. *City on Two Rivers*. New York: Hawthorne, 1975.

Lynch, Denis Tilden. *Boss Tweed*.

Macaulay, Thomas Babington. *Works*. London: Longman, Brown, 1849–1861.

Mackay, J. *Life of Sir John Fowler*. London: John Murray, 1900.

Manhattan Railway Company. New York: J. Wiley, 1866.

Markham, Violet R. *Paxton and the Bachelor Duke*. London: Houghton & Stoughton, 1935.

Marlowe, Christopher. *Doctor Faustus*. New York: Hill and Wang, 1956.

Martin, John. *The Paradise Lost of Milton with Illustrations, designed and engraved by John Martin*. 2 vols. 1827.

Maupassant, Guy de. *Bel-Ami*. Translated by Douglas Parmée. New York: Penguin Books, 1975.

Maiuri, Almedeo. *The Phlegraean Fields*. Translated by V. Priestly. Rome: Libreria della Stato, 1947.

McAlpine, William Jarvis. *The New York Arcade Railway*. New York, 1884.

————. *The Opinion of Two Eminent Engineers on Rapid Transit*. New York, 1876.

McCabe, James D. *New York by Sunlight and Gaslight*. Philadelphia: Douglas Brothers, 1883.

Meigs Elevated Railway Company. New York, 1888.

Mercier, Sebastian. *Tableau de Paris*. 1782.

Miller, John Anderson. *Fares, Please*. New York: D. Appleton-Century Co., 1941.

Mines, John Flavel. *Rapid Transit and Its Effect upon Broadway Real Estate*. New York, 1884.

Morgan, R. P. *Report on a Gothic Arch Elevated City Railway*. New York, 1869.

Mott, Basil. "Underground Railways in Great Britain." *American Society of Civil Engineer Transactions* 54 (New York, 1905): 325–48, 367–76.

Mumford, Lewis, *The City in History*. New York: Harcourt Brace & World, 1961.

————. *Technics and Civilization*. New York: Harcourt Brace & World, 1934.

Museum of Modern Art. *Art Nouveau*. New York, 1959.

Musil, Franz. *Die Künftigen Wiener elektrischen Untergrund-Schnellbahnen*. Vienna: Akademische Verlag, 1910.

Myers, Gustavus. *A History of the Great American Fortunes*. 3 vols. New York: Charles H. Kerr & Co., 1910.

Nasmyth, James. *Autobiography*. Edited by Samuel Smiles. London: John Murray, 1883.

New York Arcade Railway Company. *Charter*. New York, 1886.

New York City Central Underground Railway Company. *Report, 1871*. New York: I. C. Titus, 1871.

New York City Rapid Transit Railroad Commissioners Board. *Report*. New York, 1891.

New York District Railway Company. *List of Officers & Description*. New York, 1886.

New York Parcel Dispatch Company. *The Broadway Underground Railway the Only True Solution*. New York, 1876.

———. *Illustrated Description*. New York, 1872.

———. *To the Friends of Rapid Transit*. Edited by Alfred Ely Beach. New York, 1872.

Noble, Celia Brunel. *The Brunels, Father and Son*. London: Cobden–Sanderson, 1938.

Nowlan, Samuel B. *Transit in New York City: The New York Arcade Railway*. New York, 1868.

O'Brien, F. *The New York Sun*.

Oral Statements by Parties Living on the Line of the New York Elevated. New York, 1879.

Panafieu, L., and Fabre, E. *Chemin de fer métropolitain de Paris: réseau aérien à rail unique*. Paris: Bernard, 1886.

Parsons, William Barclay, Jr. *Address Before the Washington Society of Engineers*. Washington, D.C., March 1, 1916.

———. *Address Delivered at the Annual Service Commemorating Washington's Birthday*. New York, Church of the Holy Communion, 1922.

———. *Address at the Seventh Annual Banquet of the Boston City Club*. Boston, February 8, 1916.

———. *An American Engineer in China*. New York: McClure, Phillips & Co., 1900.

———. *The American Engineers in France*. New York and London: D. Appleton & Co., 1920.

———. *The Architect and the Engineer*. An address delivered at the Architectural League. New York, February 8, 1911.

———. *Argument on the Arcade Railway Bill*. New York, 1886.

———. *Engineering and Economics*. An address delivered at the inaugural meeting of the Columbia University Chapter of the American Society of Civil Engineers. New York, November 3, 1927.

———. *Engineering as a Profession*. New York, 1902.

———. *Engineers and Engineering in the Renaissance*. Baltimore: Williams & Wilkins, 1939.

———. *Fighting Engineer*. 1919.

———. *Manifestation of Natural Laws in Human Nature*. A commencement address delivered at Trinity College, Hartford, June 21, 1921.

———. *Progress in Engineering*. An address delivered at Columbia University. New York, November 21, 1929.

———. *Relativity in Thought*. A commencement address delivered at Carnegie Institute of Technology. June 8, 1926.

———. *Report to the Board of Rapid Transit Railroad Commissioners in and for the City of New York on Rapid Transit in Foreign Cities*. New York, 1894.

————. "Rapid Transit in New York." (*Scribner's*) May 1900.

————. *Track; A Complete Manual of Maintenance of Way*. New York, 1885 [?].

————. *Turnouts: Exact Formulae for Their Determination, Together with Practical and Accurate Tables for Use in the Field*. New York: Engineering News Publishing Co., 1884.

Passingham, W. J. *The Romance of London's Underground*. London: Sampson Low, Martson & Co., 1868.

Pastore, Lorenzo Dagnino. "El Problemo de la construction de subterraneos en la ciudad de Buenos Aires." *Revista de economía Argentiña* Tomo 23, Año 12 (Buenos Aires, 1929): 197–209, 289–301.

Pearson, Charles. *An Address delivered at a Public Meeting on the 11th, 12th, and 18th of December, 1843*. London: Pelham Richardson, Royal Exchange, and John Ol livier, Pall Mall, 1844.

Petronius. *The Satyricon*. Translation attributed to Oscar Wilde. New York: Hogarth Press, n.d.

Pike, E. Royston. *Human Documents of the Industrial Revolution*. London: Allen & Unwin, 1966.

Pistrak, Lazar. *The Grand Tactician: Khrushchev's Rise to Power*. New York: Praeger, 1961.

Proceedings on the Presentation of a Gold Medal by the Chamber of Commerce of the State of New York to the Honorable Abram S. Hewitt, October 3, 1901. New York: Press of the Chamber of Commerce, 1901.

Rapid Transit Assured: A Feast of Thanksgiving. December 26, 1877.

Rapid Transit Meeting, Chickering Hall. June 5, 1877.

Rebecchini, Salvatore. "Il problema della metropolitana e quello delle communicazioni extra urbane di Roma." *Istituto di studi romani* (Rome, 1954).

Records of the Descendents of Nathaniel Ely. 1885.

Reeves, William F. *The First Elevated Railroads in Manhattan and the Bronx*. New York: New-York Historical Society, 1936.

Report of a Meeting held at Chickering Hall, June 21, 1871, to Protest the Destruction of Property by the Elevated. 1871.

Rice, Elmer. *The Subway: A Play*. New York: S. French, 1929.

Robert, Jean. *Notre Métro*. Paris: Musée des Transports Urbains, 1967.

Robinson, A. P. *Statement of the Character and Cost of the Proposed Metropolitan Railway Co*. New York: Clayton and Medule, 1865.

Rolt, L. T. C. *Great Engineers*. London: Bell, 1962.

————. *Isambard Kingdom Brunel*. New York: St. Martin's Press, 1959.

————. *Victorian Engineering*. Middlesex: Penguin Books, 1970.

Sandstrom, Gösta. *The History of Tunnelling*. London: Barrie & Rockliff, 1963.

Simonin, Louis Laurent. *Underground Life*. Translated, adapted, and edited by H. W. Bristow. New York, 1869.

Smiles, Samuel. *Industrial Biography*. London: John Murray, 1883.

Sommerfield, Vernon. *Underground Railways, Their Construction and Working*. London: T. Nelson and Sons, 1934.

Soper, George Albert. *The Air and Ventilation of Subways*. New York: J. Wiley & Sons, 1908.

Spargo, John Webster. *Virgil the Necromancer*. Cambridge, Mass.: Harvard University Press, 1934.

Speer, Alfred. *Treatise on City Travel*. New York, 1875.

Stephenson, Robert. *Report on the Atmospheric Railway System*. 1844.

Stevens, F. L. *Under London: A Chronicle of London's Underground Life-Lines and Relics*. London: J. M. Dent & Sons, 1939.

Strabo. *Geography*.

Stryker, H. C. *Historical Sketches*.

Subways or Children. A Letter to the Board of Estimate and Apportionment. New York: City Club, 1927.

Suetonius. *The Twelve Caesars*. Translated by Robert Graves. Middlesex: Penguin Books, 1957.

Tacitus. *The Annals of Imperial Rome*. Translated by Michael Grant. Baltimore: Penguin Books, 1956.

Tate, Allen. *Poems*. New York: Charles Scribner & Sons, 1948.

Taylor, Benjamin. "The Glasgow District Subway." *Cassier's Magazine* 14 (New York, 1898): 459–74.

Tellier, Charles. *Le véritable métropolitain*. Paris: Schlaeber, 1885.

Thames Tunnel Company. *Description of Proposed Work, with Proceedings on Laying the Foundation Stone of the Shaft*. London, 1825.

————. *Report on the State of the Works*. London, 1828.

Thompson, A. J. "Underground Railway Construction in Paris." *Cassier's Magazine* 35 (New York, 1909): 551–58.

To the Friends of Rapid City Transit. New York, March 1871.

Troitskaya, Z. *The L. M. Kaganovich Metropolitan Railway of Moscow's Metro*. English edition. Moscow, 1955.

————. The Metropolitan Railway of Moscow. English edition. Moscow: Foreign Languages Publishing House, 1935.

Underground District Railway Construction Co. New York: De Vinne, 1887.

Verpraet, Georges. *Paris: capitale souterrain*. Paris: Plon, 1964.

Virgil. *The Aeneid*. Translated by C. Day Lewis. New York: Doubleday, Anchor Books, 1952.

Vitruvius. *On Architecture*.

Vogel, Robert M. *Tunnelling*. Contributions from the Museum of History and Technology. Washington, D.C.: Smithsonian Institution, 1964.

Vrebus, J. *Travaux publics à relation avec la construction de métropolitains urbains*. Brussels: Offset Editest, 1969.

Walker, James Blaine. *Fifty Years of Rapid Transit*. New York: Law Printing Co., 1918.

White, Edward, and White, Muriel. *Famous Subways and Tunnels of the World*. New York: Random House, 1953.

Whitten, Robert H. "Comparison of New York's and Paris' Subway Systems." *Electrical Railway Journal* 34 (New York, 1909): 1178–84.

Williams, Frederick J. *Our Iron Roads*. London: Ingram, Cooke & Co., 1852.

Wilson, James Grant, ed. *History of New York*. New York: New-York Historical Co., 1892–1893.

Wittig, Paul. *Führung der Berliner Hoch und Untergrundbahnen durch bebaute Viertel*. Berlin: Architektur-Verlag, 1920.

Wrottesley, A. J. F. *Famous Underground Railways of the World*. London: Frederick Muller, 1956.

Young, Arthur. *Annals of Architecture and Other Useful Arts*. 1785.

PICTURE CREDITS

PORTFOLIO II—(pages 113–128) Portrait of Sir Charles Pearson (Keystone Photos); Iron-ribbed tunnel vaulting (Keystone Photos); Two views of the excavations (Keystone Photos).

PORTFOLIO III—(pages 161–168) Portrait of Fulgence Bienvenue (Keystone Photos); Typical cut-and-cover scene in Paris (Keystone Photos); Four varieties of Hector Guimard *édicules* (Keystone Photos); Curving electrical lines in a Métro station (Keystone Photos); A gathering of eminent citizens at the inauguration of the first Paris suburban subway line (Keystone Photos).

PORTFOLIO IV—(pages 233–256) Elevated pneumatic passenger railway designed by Beach (Museum of the City of New York); View of the pneumatic subway car in motion (Museum of the City of New York); Stereoscopic view (Museum of the City of New York); Rediscovery of the tunnel in 1912 (Museum of the City of New York); Groundbreaking ceremony at Bleecker and Greene streets (Museum of the City of New York); First formal subway inspection (Museum of the City of New York); Architectural drawing of once-standard kiosk (Museum of the City of New York).

PORTFOLIO V—(pages 289–304) Rhythmic archwork on a grand scale in a Moscow station (Mary Ann Joulwan); Official opening of the Moscow Metro (Keystone Photos); Mosaic panel in Kiev-Belt Station (Keystone Photos); One of Moscow's famous deep-level high-speed escalators (Mary Ann Joulwan); Walker-Schreiberplatz Station at rush-hour (German Information Office); Munich's new Marienplatz Station (German Information Office); A modern Mexican station reminiscent of Aztec architecture (Mexican Information Office); A ceiling fresco of swirling forms, in Station République in Paris (Keystone Photos); Black-and-white mural in Charing Cross Station (Keystone Photos); Wall Carvings in a Stockholm station (Sverker Hansson); Futuristic maze of corridors in a BART station (BART); Morning rush-hour in a Tokyo station (Ashai Shimbun).

INDEX